CHOOSING FAITH

DAILY

REAL LIFE DEMANDS REAL FAITH

BY

JANICE CONNER

ISBN: 978-1-965615-99-7

ACKNOWLEDGMENT

I must acknowledge my Lord Jesus Christ for saving my soul, giving me life, more abundantly, and real faith that prevails when real life demands it.

I also must thank my husband Henry Conner for being supportive of my writing and for cheerfully helping me take the time out of our busy lives to get this daily devotional book published.

Lastly, I give thanks to the many people, professionally and spiritually, who have sewn knowledge, hope, courage, love, forgiveness, and faith into the tapestry of my life.

DEDICATION

This book is lovingly dedicated to my family.

ABOUT THE AUTHOR

Janice Conner has taught adult Bible classes since the age of fourteen when her pastor handed her a Bible commentary and assigned her to teach the ADULT Bible CLASS in her home church. She was married to a youth pastor for twenty years who died of cancer in 1997. She worked as a paralegal and in non-profit agencies, serving clients for thirty years, ten of those years she served as Executive Director of a Child Abuse Council during which she battled Fibromyalgia. CHOOSING FAITH DAILY is her first published book but she has published numerous professional and religious articles and wrote a faith-based newspaper column for eight years. In 1999 God gave her a new husband and altogether they have four children, four bonus children, and eight grandchildren.

TABLE OF CONTENTS

January

For God so loved the world, that he gave his only begotten, Son, that whosoever believeth in Him should not perish but have everlasting life. John 3:16 KJV.

The thief cometh not, but for to steal, and to kill, and to destroy. I am come that they might have life, and that they might have it more abundantly. John 10:10 KJV.

There is no time like the beginning of a new year to make good choices and wise decisions. The greatest life decision anyone can make is to accept Jesus Christ as your personal Savior. When you accept Jesus into your heart, you become a new creation. Everything about you is brand new. You receive a fresh start. Social position is not important. Your educational level does not matter. Whether you are red, yellow, black, or white is meaningless.

Jesus is equally accessible to everyone. He has known you since you were formed in your mother's

womb. He knows all about you and he has been waiting for you to want to know him. Do not wait. Make the decision now to get to know Jesus personally. He is exactly who he says he is, ready to be closer to you than a brother.

Dear Lord, I thank you, that having you in my heart is what really matters. That is what determines real success in life. You are always there, day or night, whether a friend or a counsellor is needed. I pray that others will come to know you so that they too, can enjoy abundant life. Amen.

JANUARY 2
RECEIVING JESUS AS SAVIOR AND LORD

For all have sinned and come short of the glory of God. Romans 3:23 KJV.

For the wages of sin is death, but the gift of God is eternal life through Jesus Christ our Lord. Romans 6:23 KJV.

That if thou shalt confess with thy mouth the Lord Jesus, and shalt believe in thine heart that God has raised Him from the dead, thou shalt be saved. For with the heart, man believeth unto righteousness; and with the mouth, confession is made unto salvation. For whosoever shall call upon the name of the Lord shall be saved. Romans 10:9-10,13 KJV.

I asked Jesus Christ to forgive me of my sins at the tender age of eleven. I was with my cousins at my uncle's lake, wading in knee-deep water when I stepped into a drop off and could not come back up. I was so scared seeing all kinds of debris: tree limbs, roots, old rusty iron objects, and what appeared to be an ocean of muddy water. Some

early childhood Bible teachings came to mind, and I just knew in my heart that if I did not survive, I was a sinner and would be lost forever without God. I knew I would go to Hell. I was crying for the lord to please help me. Then everything went black.

The next thing I knew I was lying on the ground outside the lake. I had unbearable pain in my lungs, throat, and head. Water gushed out my nose and mouth. My cousin rescued me from drowning and performed C.P.R. I was fortunate to be alive.

That following week I asked my parents to please take me to church next Sunday. That following Sunday morning, I could hardly wait for Pastor Edward Davenport of the Ludville Church of God to finish his sermon on the Crucifixion and the Passion of Christ, (coincidental, I think not). His message was divinely inspired by the Holy Spirit. I knew I had to get to the altar as soon as possible so that I could thank God for sparing my life and ask Him to please save me. I knew He could do so much more with my young life than I could possibly do without Him.

After talking to God straight from my heart, I felt peace and joy like I had never felt before. It was better than a Christmas morning. I invite you to receive God's gift of salvation through His Son, Jesus Christ right now. Pray with me, please.

Dear Lord Jesus, I ask you to please save me and cleanse me from all my sins. I renounce my past life, living for the devil and I close the door to any of his devices. I know you died for me and that you are the Son of the living God, who raised you from the dead. I confess you, Lord Jesus, as my personal Savior. Thank you for saving my soul. Amen.

JANUARY 3
KNOW JESUS THROUGH PRAYER

Evening, and morning, and at noon, will I pray, and cry aloud: and he shall hear my voice. Psalm 55:17 KJV.

When trying to get acquainted with someone we like, we talk to them. We express our love, needs, and desires to Jesus through praying to him. Just as we get to know a person through our conversation with them, the same is true with Jesus. The more we get to know him, the more we love him, and our relationship grows.

Dear Lord Jesus, I am so thankful that I can talk to you just like I talk to a friend. You already know my needs and desires, but you want me to talk to you, come to you, and ask. What you really desire is to

spend time with me. Lord, please help me not to neglect spending time with you. I desire to develop a daily walk with you through prayer. I want to get to know you well. Amen.

So then faith cometh by hearing and hearing by the word of God. Romans 10:17 KJV.

When you meet someone, you want to get to know, you listen to what that person has to say. The same is true with Jesus. His word to us is the Holy Bible. There are many versions of the Holy Bible. Although I own a copy of almost every available version, I have chosen the King James Version for this devotional. There are more copies of the King James Version of the Bible sold internationally than any other version.

When you begin reading your Bible, I suggest you read the book of John first and then the book of Romans. These books will give you a greater understanding of Jesus Christ and salvation.

Lord, thank you for speaking to me through your holy word. It is a lamp unto my feet and a light on my path. I pray you give me great love for your word. Please help me to consistently read it so I can get to know you well. Amen.

GET ESTABLISHED IN WHOLE BIBLE-BELIEVING CHURCH

Not forsaking the assembling of ourselves together, as the manner of some is, but exhorting one another: and so much the more, as you see the day approaching. Hebrews10:25 KJV.

Let the word of Christ dwell in you richly in all wisdom, teaching, and admonishing one another in psalms, hymns, and spiritual songs. Singing with grace in your hearts to the Lord. Colossians 3:16 KJV.

It is important to get established in a whole Bible-believing church. You will hear and learn the complete word of God. You will have access to people of like faith, who will pray and believe with you when you have a need. Your faith will grow and flourish with their support, example, and encouragement. You will enjoy their fellowship and working together to help build the kingdom of heaven. You will discover and develop your talents and calling. You will have access to age-appropriate and fun activities. You may develop lifelong friendships and even find your spouse, like I did! No

wonder the Bible says in Psalm 122:1 I was glad when they said unto me, let us go to the house of the Lord.

Dear Lord Jesus, I thank you that you have established the church, the body of believers. There we can find people of like faith that can help us grow and become disciples of Christ. There we can find love, nourishment, Christian education, and a sense of belonging in the family of God. Please help me find my special place of worship. Amen.

JANUARY 6
THE ATTRIBUTES OF GOD

In the beginning, God created the heaven and the earth. Genesis 1:1 KJV.

I am Alpha and Omega, the beginning and the ending, saith the Lord, which is, and which was and which is to come, the Almighty. Revelation 1:8 KJV.

Behold, I am the Lord, the God of all flesh is there anything too hard for me? Jeremiah 32:27 KJV.

And we have known and believed the love that God hath to us. God is love and he that dwelleth in love dwelleth in God, and God in him. I John 4:16 KJV.

We serve a good, good father who is always interested in his children and their problems. Our hope truly is in God and our hearts rejoice because our trust is in him. With all the things that come against us in our current world, it would be easy to lose hope without prayer and God's holy word to encourage us. But he is faithful and has all we need.

We, as children of the highest God, have hope and joy because his compassion is renewed daily.

Dear God, our Father, thank you for loving me. You are so merciful and compassionate. Your provision and love for me daily make it so easy to trust and hope in you. I praise you. Amen.

JANUARY 7
KNOWING THE ALL-SUFFICIENCY OF JESUS

The Lord is my shepherd; I shall not want. He maketh me to lie down in green pastures; he leadeth me beside the still waters. He restoreth my soul; he leadeth me in the paths of righteousness for his name's sake. Yea, though I walk through the valley of the shadow of death, I will fear no evil: for thou art with me; thy rod and thy staff they comfort me. Thou preparest a table before me in the presence of my enemies; thou anointest my head with oil; my cup runneth over. Surely goodness and mercy shall follow me all the days of my life, and I will dwell in the house of the Lord forever. Psalm 23 KJV.

I can do all things through Christ, which strengtheneth me. Philippians 4:13 KJV.

Jesus is the Good Shepherd, and we are his sheep. He watches over us. He is our provider of lush green places to graze. He directs us to cool, still waters that take care of our thirst and restore our souls. He leads us on the right paths and keeps our enemies at bay. Though we may walk in unsafe

places, he will take care of us and protect us with his rod and staff. What a comfort to know. We can be confident because he gives us the needed strength to do all things through him.

Dear Lord Jesus, I am so thankful that you are my loving shepherd. You care for me when I am ill. You provide the food and drink needed for my physical and spiritual nourishment. You protect me from danger. You direct and show me the right path to take and keep me from wandering too far from the fold. Thank you so much for caring for me. Amen.

JANUARY 8
FOLLOWING JESUS IN WATER BAPTISM

Then Peter said unto them, Repent and be baptized for the remission of sins, and ye shall receive the gift of the holy ghost. Acts 2:38 KJV.

Buried with him in baptism, wherein also ye are risen with him through the faith of the operation of God, who hath raised him from the dead. Colossians 2:12 KJV.

Jesus was baptized by John in the Jordan River. Following Jesus in water baptism is being immersed in water. The beautiful part of being baptized is what it represents. It is symbolic of the cleansing you receive when you repent of your sins and are washed in the blood of Jesus. Water baptism also represents the death of the old you. When you are baptized. It represents the burial of the old sinful nature and then being raised to your new life in Christ.

I was baptized in Talking Rock Creek along with several other teenage converts. It does not matter

where you are baptized, if there is water and if your sins have been forgiven.

Dear Lord Jesus, I am excited about following you in water baptism. I love that its symbolic meaning represents my new life in Christ. I have died out to the old man and the new man is being raised in righteousness. Amen.

JANUARY 9
FOLLOWING JESUS IN HOLY COMMUNION

And in the evening he cometh with the twelve. Mark 14:17 KJV.

And as they did eat, Jesus took bread, and blessed, and brake it, and gave to them, and said, Take, eat: this is my body. And he took the cup and when he had given thanks, he gave it to them: and they all drank of it. And he said unto them, this is my blood of the new testament which is shed for many. Mark 14:22-24 KJV.

On the night that Jesus was betrayed and arrested was also the first day of unleavened bread, when they killed the Passover. Jesus secured the guest chamber of a home, a large upper room for him and his disciples to observe the Passover. When we take part in holy communion, we are doing it in remembrance of Jesus and what he suffered for us. It is a very solemn and holy time when we should search our hearts and know for certain that we have repented of all sins.

Dear Lord Jesus, thank you for how you suffered, bled, and died for me on the old rugged cross. I could never repay you for what you have done for me. I should have been the one on that cross. Please help me to be worthy of partaking in the holy sacraments that represent your body and your blood for the remission of my sins. Amen.

JANUARY 10
FOLLOWING JESUS IN WASHING FEET

He riseth from supper, laid aside his garments, took a towel, and girded himself. After that, he poureth water into a basin, and began to wash the disciples' feet, and to wipe them with the towel wherewith he was girded. John 13:4-5 KJV.

So, after he had washed their feet, and had taken his garments, and was set down again, he said unto them, know ye what I have done to you? Ye call me Master and Lord: and ye say well: for so I am. If then, your Lord and Master, have washed your feet ye also ought to wash one another's feet. For I have given an example, that, ye should do as I have done unto you. Verily, verily I say unto you, the servant is not greater than his lord; neither he that is sent greater than he that sent him. If ye know these things, happy are ye if ye do them. John 13:12-17 KJV.

In Bible days everyone wore sandals and often travelled for miles on foot. The roads were rough and dirty. When someone came to your home, it was customary to pour water in a basin and wash their

tired, dusty feet and dry them with a towel. As an act of Christian servanthood and humility, the washing of the saint's feet is often observed in churches today.

Dear Lord Jesus, what kindness was offered in Bible days to weary travelers. When I am given the opportunity to wash the saints' feet, please help me to be willing to humble myself and perform this act of serving others. It is an honor to follow you. Amen.

Now we have received, not the spirit of the world, but the spirit which is of God that we might know the things that are freely given to us of God. I Corinthians 2:12 KJV.

The Holy Trinity consists of God the Father, God the Son, and the Holy Spirit of God. They all work together but have different functions. The Holy Spirit helps us to discern and understand the spiritual things of. God that the world cannot understand; The Holy Spirit is comfort. He will bring things to our remembrance and give us the right words to say as needed. He will quicken our mortal bodies so we can rise, just as Jesus did from the tomb. He gives us the power to witness. When our enemies come in like a flood, he will raise a standard against them. The Holy Spirit gives life. There is liberty in the presence of the Holy Spirit.

I lost my father during a heart attack when he was forty-nine years old. He died two weeks before my wedding. Invitations had just gone out and my

wedding gown and veil hung in my bedroom. My dad, whom I adored planned to give me in marriage. I had never even lost a grandparent in death, and I was totally devastated. On the day of the funeral, I asked the Holy Spirit to please comfort me, as I needed to be strong for my mother and my sister. I felt the Holy Spirit's presence. He gave me strength, comfort, and peace like I had never experienced before. I can tell you he is real and does his job well.

Dear God, I praise you and thank you for the gift of the precious Holy Spirit. He is my comforter, teacher, counselor, help in times of need, and so much more. Amen.

But the fruit of the Spirit is love, joy, peace, long-suffering, gentleness, goodness, faith, meekness, and temperance; If we live in the Spirit, let us also walk in the Spirit. Galatians 5:22,25 KJV.

If you are a Christian, your life should be producing the fruit of the Spirit. This godly, positive, attractive, and pleasing lifestyle will start to manifest and become more profound as you grow spiritually.

Dear Lord, I pray that the fruit of the Spirit will flourish in the garden of my life. Please help me to prune out any bad fruit. Teach me to be a gardener, tilling the soil, planting healthy seeds, fertilizing, watering, and digging up weeds so that I may

produce and share pleasant and sweet fruit, all the days of my life. Amen.

LOVE IS OBEYING GOD'S TEN COMMANDMENTS

For this is the love of God, that we keep his commandments: and his commandments are not grievous. I John 5:3KJV.

Thou shalt love the Lord thy God with all thine heart, and with all thy soul, and with all thy mind, and with all thine strength: (Commandments 1-4: pertain to our love for God) Mark 12:30KJV.

Thou shalt love thy neighbor as thyself. (Commandments 5-10: pertain to our love for others and self) Matthew 22:39 KJV.

TEN COMMANDMENTS

1. **Thou shalt have no other God before me.**

2. **Thou shalt not make unto thee any graven images.**

3. **Thou shalt not take the name of Lord thy God in vain.**

4. Remember the Sabbath day to keep it holy.

5. Honor thy father and thy mother.

6. Thou shalt not kill.

7. Thou shalt not commit adultery.

8. Thou shalt not steal.

9. Thou shalt not bear false witness against thy neighbor.

10. Thou shalt not covet.

Dear God, I thank you for loving me. You are love. Please help me to keep your commandments. In doing so, I show my love for you, my love for my neighbor, and love for myself. Amen.

JANUARY 14
Joy

For this day is holy unto our Lord: neither be ye sorry; for the joy of the Lord is your strength. Nehemiah 8:10 KJV.

Joy is having gladness or delight. It is an emotion triggered by the expectation or acquisition of something pleasant. Joy is not only a response to God's current blessings, but it is also thinking about eternity, when we will enjoy the fullness of being in the presence of God, forevermore.

Dear God, I thank you for the joy I now possess in you and for what I am looking forward to hereafter. JOY is putting Jesus first, Others second and Yourself last. It is truly joyous to live outside yourself. I thank you so much for this personal realization. Amen.

JANUARY 15
PEACE

Thou shalt keep him in perfect peace, whose mind is stayed on thee: because he trusteth in thee. Isaiah 26:3 KJV.

Peace is solace, freedom from agitation or disturbance, calm, repose, and a state of quiet or tranquility. Those who trust in God are promised spiritual or inward peace. Christians, as children of the God of peace, are encouraged to be at peace with each other. The Gospel of Christ can be described as a message of peace from God to mankind.

Dear Lord Jesus, I cannot thank you enough for your gift of peace, that passes all understanding and keeps our hearts and minds through you. Amen.

JANUARY 16
LONG SUFFERING

Strengthened with all might, according to his glorious power, unto all patience and long-suffering with joyfulness. Colossians 1:11 KJV.

Long-suffering is having patience, while waiting, or bearing trouble, trials, evil, or wrong with fortitude, and without complaining. Patience implies self-possession and indicates a certain quietness and repose. The cultivation of a patient spirit aids one in avoiding a sinful action due to the petty annoyances and harassment we face.

Dear Lord Jesus, please grant us long-suffering to deal with trials and tribulations. Please teach us to be patient without complaining when we face injustices and harassment. Please give us grace not to resort to

sin as a response to the annoyances and harassment we face in life according to your glorious power that is within us. Amen.

And the servant of the Lord must not strive; but be gentle unto all men, apt to teach, patient. II Timothy 2:24 KJV.

Gentleness is being kind and soft in manner, ready to look reasonably and humanely at the circumstances of a situation. In the Bible, gentleness is looked upon as a beautiful virtue and believers are encouraged to cultivate it.

Dear lord Jesus, please help me to be a gentle and kind person in life. Please help me to cultivate meekness, without showing partiality and being hypocritical. Amen.

JANUARY 18
GOODNESS

Surely goodness and mercy shall follow me all the days of my life and I will dwell in the House of the Lord forever. Psalm 23:6 KJV.

Goodness is the quality of being good, pure, holy, virtuous, excellent, kind, generous, and benevolent. It is the best part or valuable element of anything.

Dear Lord Jesus, I pray that you would help me develop the quality of goodness in my life and that I may dwell in your house forever. Amen.

And Jesus answering, saith unto them have faith in God, for surely I say unto you, that whosoever shall say unto this mountain, be thou removed and be thou cast into the sea, and shall not doubt in his heart, but shall believe that those things which he saith shall come to pass: he shall have whatsoever he said. Mark 11:22-23 KJV.

Faith is being firm, reliable, and steadfast in what you believe. A person of faith holds on confidently, strengthened by his confidence in God. It is an act by which one avails himself of the gift of God, submits himself in obedience to God's commands, and abandons all thoughts of self, trusting only in God. It is a confident trust in the unseen power of God.

Dear Lord Jesus, I pray that you would help my faith in you to be strengthened. Help me to be submissive and obedient to you so that your gifts can be available to me. Amen.

JANUARY 20
MEEKNESS

The meek shall eat and be satisfied: they shall praise the Lord that seek him, and your heart shall live forever. Psalm 22:26 KJV.

But the meek shall inherit the earth; And shall delight themselves in the abundance of peace. Psalm 37:11 KJV.

For the Lord taketh pleasure in his people: he will beautify the meek with salvation. Psalm 149:4 KJV.

I lost a job once that I really enjoyed. Another entity came in and took over and had one of their employees that they wanted to put in my position. If that was not sad enough, to add insult to injury, I was required to train that person. I was hurt and really had to pray hard and trust God. Not only did he give me the grace to train my replacement but gave me a good attitude and helped me present probably the best training I have ever done. The trainee and I are good friends today and God blessed me with a higher paying position with better

benefits. That's my God! If we show meekness and obedience, he loves coming on the stage and blessing his children.

Dear Lord, I praise you. That even in hurtful times if we obey and are meek you will take the situation and turn it around for our good and your glory. Thank you for loving us and using what we consider bad times in our lives as teaching opportunities for you. Amen.

And every man that strives for the mastery is temperate in all things. I Colossians 9:25 KJV.

They shall not drink wine with a song; Strong drink shall be bitter to them that drink it. There is a crying for wine in the streets; All joy is darkened; the mirth of the land is gone. Isaiah 24:9,11 KJV.

Temperance is habitual moderation in the indulgence of appetites, patience, and moderation. Temperance involves mastery of oneself to such a degree that one can abstain from anything which might hinder effective service to God and to subject all physical impulses to the will of Christ. This is the condition of the heart that cannot be replaced simply by external abstinence.

Dear Lord Jesus, thank you that you give us temperance and help us to be strong in times when we are weak. Help us, Lord Jesus, to be moderate in everything that we do, especially the things that affect our service to you. Amen.

All scripture is given by inspiration of God, and is profitable for doctrine, for reproof, for correction, for instruction and righteousness, that the man of God may be perfect, thoroughly furnished unto all good works. II Timothy 3:16,17 KJV.

Human nature is the opposite of righteousness. We cannot attain righteousness on our own. Righteousness is not obtained by any works. We become righteous through faith in Christ. Studying God's word helps us grow in righteousness.

Dear Lord Jesus, I know I cannot become righteous on my own. Please help me to study and apply God's word to my life. Then my faith in you will grow and righteousness will manifest. Amen.

JANUARY 23
TRUTH

This thing is the message which we have heard of him, and declare unto you, that God is light, and in him is no darkness at all. If we say we have fellowship with him and walk in darkness, we lie and do not the truth: but if we walk in the light, as he is in the light, and we have fellowship one with another, and the blood of Jesus Christ his son cleanseth us from all sin. I John 1:5-7 KJV.

Truth is the state of being true, sincere, genuine, honest, correct, accurate, and certain. It corresponds with the fact of reality. Truth is more than thoughts or beliefs. It is something to be done. Acceptance of and dedication to this truth equips men for acceptance by God and fellowship with one another.

Dear heavenly father, your word is truth. Please help me to always keep it before me, read it, study it, and not deviate from what it says. Amen.

For God hath not given us the spirit of fear, but of power, and of love, and of a sound mind. II Timothy 1:7 KJV.

Many are concerned that they will fail in living the Christian life. But what they must understand is when they accept Jesus into their heart, He lives within them, and the life they now live in the flesh they live by the faith of the Son of God.

Dear Lord Jesus, I thank you that you are living in me and have given me the power to live for you. Thank you for your word. It reminds me the spirit of fear comes from the devil, and he was a liar from the beginning. I rebuke the devil in the name of Jesus. Amen.

JANUARY 25
WHEN I FAIL

Create in me a clean heart, O God; and renew a right spirit within me. Cast me not away from thy presence; and take not thy holy spirit from me. Restore to me the joy of my salvation; and uphold me with thy free spirit. Then will I teach transgressors thy ways; and sinners shall be converted unto thee. Psalm 51:10-13 KJV.

If you fail, please do not quit, give up, and go down in defeat. All of us have failed in some form. Go to the Lord immediately in prayer and repent. Jesus knows your heart and he knows if you truly are sorry. He is quick to forgive you. He will put his loving arms around you and give you the grace to carry on.

Dear Lord Jesus, I have failed you miserably. My heart is broken because I have hurt you most of all, I am so sorry. Please forgive me and give me the strength to carry on. Please give me back the joy of my salvation. Thank you for restoring me. Amen.

As newborn babes, desire the sincere milk of the word that ye may grow thereby. I Peter 2:2 KJV.

Have you ever seen a little child when it is just learning to walk? At first, it is afraid but then with constant encouragement from Mother and Daddy, it takes that first step. When it stumbles, Mother and Daddy are there to pick it up and encourage it to try once more. The child has learned to trust his parents. So, with a little more pulling up, taking another step, falling, and being set on its feet again, the child finally succeeds and begins to walk.

Growing in the Christian life is very much the same as growing from childhood to maturity. When we first receive the Lord into our lives, we are babes in Christ. We are beginning a whole new life, and we must grow and learn in the knowledge of the Lord. We must be fed milk until we grow mature enough to digest or understand the strong meat of the word of God.

Learning to walk in the steps of the master is very much the same as learning to walk as a baby. New converts need instruction and most of all, encouragement from those who have been Christians for a longer period. More mature Christians in the Lord need to pray for new converts and make it a point to be available when they need help. Just as a child learning to walk and trust its parents when it is taking those first steps, as more mature Christians we need to live the kind of life that new converts will trust and have confidence in us. Above all we need to show them love and let them know that we care. Then they will be encouraged to live and walk in the steps of the master.

Thank you, Dear Lord, for the encouragement your word gives and, through others. Help me never

to be too prideful that I fail to ask for help or refuse it when offered. I realize I have much to learn and that until we reach heaven, every day is a learning experience in the Christian life. Amen.

For we have not a high priest which cannot be touched with the feeling of our infirmities but was in all points tempted like as we are, yet without sin. Hebrews 4:15 KJV.

Temptation is to entice, to prove, or to taste. God does not entice us to sin but tests our faithfulness. Because Jesus suffered temptation, he can give assistance in times of need or stress to them that are tempted.

Dear Lord, you were tempted in all points as we are, and you understand how we feel and the stress we go through. Please give me the strength not to react in sin but to be strong and stand like you did when the devil tempted you in the wilderness.

But we are bound to give thanks always to God for you, brethren beloved of the Lord because God hath from the beginning chosen you to salvation through sanctification of the spirit and belief of the truth. II Thessalonians 2:13 KJV.

Sanctification is the process of being made or becoming holy. Holiness belongs properly to God as he is the only one who can impart holiness, and who can bring about sanctification in our lives. As seen in Jesus Christ, God desires to sanctify man to set him apart for life for his purposes The New Testament compels us to view sanctification in two aspects. It is not accomplished through the achievement of moral perfection but in the receiving of the gift of the Holy Spirit yet, the Saint, the one who has been sanctified must constantly seek to bring his sanctification through consecration to Christ which manifests itself in turning from worldliness to the service of righteousness and living a holy life.

Dear heavenly father, I thank you for the plan of salvation through your son, Jesus Christ. I praise you for choosing me to be saved and sanctified by your Holy Spirit and my belief in the word of God which is truth. I could never have done it on my own. Amen.

JANUARY 29
THE LORD'S PRAYER

And it came to pass as he was praying in a certain place; when he ceased, some of his disciples said unto him, Lord, teach us to pray, as John also taught his disciples. Luke 11:1 KJV.

The disciples recognized that Jesus was a man of prayer. They ask him to teach them to pray. Jesus taught them a simple model of communion with God that gives the criterion for acceptable prayer as not eloquent words or long length. It may be an expression of confession of sins and guilt and request for forgiveness, intercession on behalf of others, government officials, the sick, the church, our family or friends, our enemies, and request for our own needs. Things vital for meaningful prayer are the lack of hypocrisy, praying until you are satisfied as to the will of God, unquestioning faith in God's ability to perform that which is his will, and our spirit of submission to his divine purpose.

Our Father which art in heaven, hallowed be thy name thy kingdom come thy will be done in earth as it is in heaven. Give us this day our daily bread and forgive us our debts, as we forgive our debtors and lead us not into temptation but deliver us from evil: for thine is the kingdom, and the power, and the glory, forever. Amen.

Matthew 6: 9 -13 KJV.

JANUARY 30
DRESSING FOR SPIRITUAL SUCCESS

Put on the whole armor of God that you may be able to stand against the wiles of the devil. Stand therefore having your loins girt about with truth, and having on the breastplate of righteousness; And your feet shod with the preparation of the gospel of peace, above all, taking the shield of faith, wherewith you shall be able to quench all the fiery darts of the wicked. And take the helmet of salvation, and the sword of the spirit which is the word of God: praying always with all prayer and supplication in the spirit and watching thereunto with all perseverance and supplication for all saints. Ephesians 6: 11,14-18 KJV.

Much is said in the word of God about dressing for spiritual success. A conditional promise is given that if we put on the whole armor of God, we will be able to stand against the tactics of the devil. Those spiritual garments are truth, righteousness, peace, faith, salvation, the word of God, prayer, and being on guard.

Dear Lord Jesus, I thank you that dressing for spiritual success does not require an elaborate sense of style. It does not require an expensive wardrobe with elaborate clothing and accessories. It does require commitment and obedience to the word of God. I praise you that commitment and obedience to the word of God is available to every believer who desires and wills to be a successful warrior in the fight against the devil. Please help me, Lord, to stay equipped and fully dressed, in your army, in the battle against the devil. Amen.

JANUARY 31
BAPTISM OF HOLY SPIRIT

*I indeed baptize you with water unto repentance:
but he that cometh after me is mightier than I, whose
shoes I am not worthy to bear; he shall baptize you
with the Holy Ghost and with fire. Matthew 3:11 KJV.*

*An, behold, I send the promise of my father upon
you: but tarry ye in the city of Jerusalem until you be
endued with power from on high. Luke 24: 49 KJV.*

**The first occurrence of the baptism of the Holy
Ghost is recorded in Acts 2 of the Bible. The
outpouring of the spirit upon the disciples at
Pentecost was accompanied by tarrying in prayer
and praise, the physical manifestations of a sound
from heaven as of a rushing mighty wind, cloven
tongues like fire which sat upon each of them, and
speaking in tongues, as the Spirit gave them
utterance.**

**It did not stop there. It still happens today. At
the age of twelve years old, I received the baptism
of the Holy Ghost and fire, while praying and**

57

tarrying at the altar in the Ludville Church of God. Did I speak in other tongues? Yes! Do I speak in tongues today? Yes, as the Holy Spirit moves on me and gives the utterance.

Dear heavenly father, I praise you for sending us the baptism of the Holy Spirit and fire. It refreshes us, gives us comfort, qualifies us to witness to others, and equips us for other ministries. It is our teacher, counselor who gives us words to say and brings things to our remembrance, and one day, the power of the Holy Spirit will raise and quicken our mortal bodies, just as it did Jesus in the tomb. Thank you, Father, that as sanctified believers, we are candidates for this wonderful enduement of power from on high. Just as it fell in the upper room on the day of Pentecost in Acts chapter two, it falls today! I praise you for baptizing us with the Holy Ghost and fire! Amen.

FEBRUARY

That the God of our Lord Jesus Christ, the Father of glory, may give unto you the spirit of insight and unveiling in the knowledge of himself; the eyes of your understanding being enlightened that you may know what is the hope of his calling. Ephesians 1:17-18 KJV.

When I was in high school, I had a classmate to ask me in all honesty and sincerity, if God is the God of love that you say he is and he possesses all power, then why does he put up with so much evil and corruption, and allow so much suffering and pain? That was a question that I was just not prepared to answer. I had been a Christian since I was eleven years old and the Lord was very real to me and my friends knew it but that day, I realized that even though we live in a nation that claims Christianity, and even though almost every American knows the stories behind the manger or the cross, not everyone is acquainted with the Lord personally. They merely know about him. While few have voiced the question my friend asked me, others have silently pondered it within their hearts also.

I found myself asking why a few years later, when in the prime of his life, age forty-nine, my father unexpectedly passed away two weeks before my wedding. There are just some things that cannot be answered until we meet the savior face to face.

There is one thing for certain, if we will go to the Lord in prayer regularly and unhurriedly, our view of God and life itself changes. It is clarified and corrected.

We can learn some things about God through nature, some things about him by studying history, more about him through scripture, and even more through his self-revelation in his son Jesus Christ.

But until we have been converted, we have, heard about God instead of being introduced to him personally. Until we have been converted, we do not possess the spiritual nature or faculties to perceive spiritual understanding. That new nature still needs the supernatural illumination of the Holy Spirit. Without it the world remains a puzzle, the Bible just another book, and Jesus Christ a mere figure in history. It is there in the quiet time of prayer, when we can see God in the universe, down through history, and most importantly, in all the happenings of our lives.

Dear Lord Jesus, please give me spiritual insight and unveiling, so that I may understand and truly know you through your holy word I pray. Amen.

HOPE ANCHORS THE SOUL

Which hope we have as an anchor of the soul both sure and steadfast, and which entereth into that within the veil. Hebrews 6:19 KJV.

Last night my little nephew, Brent, asked me to listen to his book report on the Battleship Oklahoma, which he was to present in class today. He reported the ship was docked at Pearl Harbor and was one of the victims of the Japanese attack on December 7, 1941. The anchor of the Battleship Oklahoma is now a part of a monument in the civic center in downtown Oklahoma City. It commemorates the ship's gallant exploits as a part of the United States fleet. That anchor rode with the ship proudly as she plowed the high seas during an illustrious career. The Battleship Oklahoma no longer needs an anchor. It is only when a ship is afloat that it needs an anchor. An anchor is a symbol of life, of activity, of mobility, and the future, of hope. Its presence on the ship indicates that any stop is only temporary. The presence of an anchor indicates that the ship is not in the final resting place but when it reaches home that anchor can finally become a monument to where the ship has been rather than the hope of where it is going.

Often the three symbols the cross, the anchor, and the heart can be seen together representing faith, hope, and charity. To the Christian, the anchor symbolizes hope in Christ, the hope of eternal life in heaven. This life in which we now live is merely a stopping-off place. The Christian's destination will be when he reaches that home port in Glory, called Heaven.

Dear Lord Jesus, I thank you that the anchor holds no matter the severity of the storm I may be going through. The anchor symbolizes my hope in Christ and my hope of heaven eternal, my destination. Amen.

FEBRUARY 3
DECISIONS, DECISIONS, DECISIONS

Trust in the Lord with all thine heart and lean not unto thine own understanding. In all thy ways acknowledge him and he shall direct thy path.
Proverbs 3:5-6 KJV

The teenage years require more decision-making than any other time in life. Due to a lack of knowledge or experience, at that time in your life, you may be the least capable of making them. That is why it is so important that teens especially be guided by the Lord. Some of the decisions you make during your teenage years will affect and influence your life from here through eternity. The sure way to have the Lord's guidance is to not only follow him as your savior. But let him be the Lord of your life and have control. He has a special plan for you. You are a radiant possibility. By following his special plan for you, you will reach your greatest dreams and aspirations.

Dear Lord Jesus, please help me to learn to hide your word so deeply in my spirit that when I am tempted, I can rebuke the devil with it. He will flee and I will not sin against you. Amen.

But he answered and said it is written, Man shall not live by bread alone, but by every word that proceedeth out of the mouth of God. Matthew 4:4 KJV.

My former Pastor, R. Edward Davenport, once related the following story about a man on a safari hunt in South America who was startled by the alarming crisis of an exotic male bird hovering over a nest containing the mother and her babies. Suddenly he saw the reason for all the commotion.

Slithering up the trunk of the tree was one of the most dreaded venomous snakes of the jungle. Just as the man aimed his gun at the snake, the male bird flew off, darting from place to place as though looking for something. The man paused for a second, and in the flash, the male bird returned with a large green leaf, which he draped across the top of the nest. The man watched ready to fire as the snake started to strike. Suddenly the snake, for no apparent reason, recoiled and withered down the tree as fast as possible as if he had received a deadly blow. Then the male bird broke into a rapturous song.

The astonished hunters secured the leaf from the nest and took it to a native. Upon inquiring about it, they discovered that it was from a bush that was poisonous and at the very sight and odor caused snakes to flee. The little bird was aware of this and at a time of grave danger had plucked the leaf as a sure defense.

The story reminds me of another danger, in a defense familiar to Christians everywhere, the dragon is the devil, and the defense leaf is from the word of God. In Matthew 4 three times the devil stuck out his ugly fangs to tempt our Lord Jesus who came back at him with "it is finished, or it is written," verses 4, 7, 10, until the third approach. Then Jesus could say get thee behind me. The devil had to flee.

Dear Lord Jesus, please help me to learn and hide your words so deeply in my spirit that when I am tempted, I can rebuke the devil with it. He will flee and I will not sin against you Amen.

Delight thyself also in the Lord, and he shall give thee the desires of thine heart. Psalm 37:4 KJV.

As a child, I was gifted a storybook that contained the fable of King Midas. He had done some act of kindness to a Greek god and as a reward was told he could have one wish, any wish his heart desired. Too excited to think soberly, he foolishly asked that anything he touched be turned into gold. At first, it was fabulous. He touched a stone, and it turned into a gold piece. His throne became pure gold at the touch of his hand. But then the tide turned. His food and drink automatically turned gold before it reached his mouth. He kissed his little girl, and she became a golden statue. At his wit's end, he begged the Greek god to deliver him from the curse.

There is another king, our Lord Jesus, who in a more lovely, spiritual sense possesses a golden touch. Whatever his nail-scarred hand touches it blesses. It brings cleansing, forgiveness, restoration, and healing. It awakens love, faith, hope, peace, and joy. It dissolves fetters that bind and gives them the power to live happily and victoriously.

Dear Lord, please help me to be careful of what I ask and to ask if it be your will. You know what is best for me, for my good and your glory. Amen.

Behold the fowls of the air: for they sow not, neither do they reap, nor gather into barns, yet your heavenly Father feedeth them. Are you not much better than them? Matthew 6:26 KJV.

This morning as I was leaving for work, I stepped out the front door and locked it behind me. It was a cold brisk morning, calm and quiet, until I heard a rustling noise in the woods above our house. I turned around to see two little squirrels scampering back and forth in the leaves, gathering acorns to suffice them throughout the rest of the winter. As I stood there and watched for a minute, I thought of the weather report we had been hearing, calling for snow. God must have already told these little squirrels to prepare for more severe weather ahead. As I paused for a minute more, watching these little squirrels scampering up the tree to store their food, I remembered the passage of the scripture found in the Book of Matthew 6:26-34 that speaks of the fowls of the air and the lilies of the field and how our heavenly father takes care of them. If he loves the birds of the air and these little squirrels, then how much more does he care for you and me, whom he created in his very own image and likeness?

Dear Heavenly Father, I am amazed at your great love. You are Jehovah Jireh, my provider. I thank you so much for caring and providing for me and all your amazing creations. Amen.

And he said unto them, this is that which the Lord hath said, tomorrow is the last of the holy sabbaths unto the Lord: take that which ye will bake today, and seethe that you will seethe and that which remaineth over lay up for you to be kept until the morning, so the people rested on the seventh day. Exodus 16:23,30 KJV.

The day we set aside to worship the Lord, and as the day of rest is a day not only of assembling in his house, but a day also of withdrawing from the hurriedness of the world, searching our hearts, and strengthening the sinews of our spiritual life. At the hub of the Christian life where God is found is peace. When we draw close to him, away from the din, we find stillness, a hush, and an island of calm in a chaotic world racing to its destiny. The Lord's Day is a day not only of physical rest and relaxation for the Christian, but more importantly, a day of spiritual rejuvenation and revitalization, a refilling of joy and peace of mind.

Dear Lord Jesus, I praise you for loving us enough to see our need for the Sabbath, a day of sweet rest and worship of you, a time for us to bask in your love. Amen.

Let the words of my mouth, and the meditations of my heart, be acceptable in thy sight, O Lord, my strength, and my redeemer. Psalm 19:14 KJV.

When I was at Lee College, now Lee University, we prayed the above scripture at the closing of every chapel service. The Psalmist David prayed this scripture, also.

Not only on Valentine's Day but every day of the year, we should be concerned about the condition of our spiritual heart. People only see us as we are outside. But Jesus really knows us, for he sees inside the heart. How about our hearts? Are they right with God? That is the most important question we can ask ourselves.

Lord Jesus, I pray that my words, the thoughts I have, and what I meditate on daily be pleasing in your sight. Please show me, Lord, if there is anything in me unpleasing to you. Amen.

FEBRUARY 9
THE YIELDED HEART

And when he had removed him (Saul), he raised up unto them David to be their king, to whom also he gave testimony, and said, I have found David the son of Jesse, a man after my own heart, which shall fulfill all my will of this man's seed, hath God according to his promise raised unto Israel a Savior, Jesus. Acts 13:22-23 KJV.

In the story of Samuel's search for a king, God had sent him to anoint a son of Jesse to be king of Israel. Samuel was sure that Eliaf would be the one. After all, he was handsome, tall, and good-looking. But the Lord said, "Look not on this candidate, or on the height of his stature, because I have refused him, for the Lord seeeth not as man seeeth for man looketh on the outward appearance but the Lord looketh on the heart." Samuel 16:9 KJV. David was chosen because God could count on him to do his will. Could God say that about You?

Dear Lord Jesus, I really desire to be a person after your own heart. Please help me to reach that status. Amen

But the mercy of the Lord is from everlasting to everlasting upon them that fear him, and his righteousness unto children's children. Psalm 103:17 KJV.

There are some plants that exist today that are entirely too weak to stand alone. They must be supported by leaning on stronger plants, stakes driven in the ground, or wooden trellises. These leaners even put out special twining stems to attach themselves to their host. Often, we have much in common with just such plants. We search instinctively for support, and the Lord, who knows our frame, which is another way of saying our weakness, provides us, in his mercy, with the strength we so desperately need.

Dear heavenly father, you know my frame and just how weak I am. I thank you for your everlasting mercy. I respect you and your righteousness. Thank you for allowing me to lean on you when I am too weak to stand alone. Amen.

FEBRUARY 11
PURGED AS GOLD AND SILVER

He is like a refiner's fire, and like fullers sope, and he shall sit as a refiner and purifier of silver and purge them as gold and silver, that they may offer unto the Lord an offering in righteousness. Malachi 3: 2-3 KJV.

God is so patient with his children. He is willing to wait years for each of us to be molded and perfected. Oh, what love! How touching that he takes so much time with all the details. Every moment of every day the great refiner is waiting to add some new touch to our strength and beauty and to fit us for a higher place in his kingdom. So prone are incidents, mishaps, or personal injuries from personal hands, but after a while, we learned that it was no mere accident and that he was in control all the time. He was merely in the process of molding and making us a more beautiful and perfect image. If we could understand life as the heavenly father does, while we are being tried by fire, we would see nothing but his hand in every circumstance of every situation. Every unfriendly blow of the hammer would be warded off if we could have a shield of faith that could not be pierced. Out of every trial, we could proclaim as the Apostle Paul, "None of these things move me."

Dear Heavenly Father, please help me during the times of being refined and purged. These are times I do not like. Please help me to be patient because I genuinely want to be what you would have me be. Amen.

Let no man despise thy youth; But be thou an **example** *of the believers, in word, in conversation, in charity, in spirit, in faith, and purity. I Timothy 4:12 KJV.*

When I was in the fourth grade at Belwood Elementary School, we had a segment of time when we studied the life of Abraham Lincoln. Mrs. Amy Knight could absolutely make history come alive. I concluded from her teaching that Abraham Lincoln was one of the most renowned figures in all of history. He remains one of my favorite presidents. Mrs. Knight wrote a play that some of her students put on for the staff and student body. I was chosen to play the part of Sarah, his sister.

Abraham Lincoln was born on February 12, 1809, in a log cabin in Hardin, Kentucky. He and his sister, Sarah, attended a log schoolhouse when, they could be spared from the chores on the family farm. Altogether Lincoln's formal schooling totaled less than a year, but he possessed an unending desire to learn. Abe would walk for miles to borrow books from neighbors. The Bible was probably the only book his parents owned. He came to know it thoroughly and become a man of strong religious beliefs.

Lincoln has been noted for his most outstanding asset, insight, or knowledge, which he often contributed to prayer and the reading of God's word. It is recorded that he kept a Bible on his desk and turned to it often for comfort and guidance during his trying years as president. His second great asset was the ability to express his convictions so clearly that millions of people made them their own, as he did in his inaugural speeches, his letters to Congress, and in the Gettysburg Address. Because Lincoln was a man of deep religious convictions, biblical references, and quotations often enriched his writings and speeches. Some of them are regarded as great pieces of literature. Another great outlet of strength was his own will. It has been said that he often quoted Romans 8:31: "If God be for us who can be against us." During the Civil

War he never doubted that right would make might, his never ceasing faith in God and justice and liberty for all, tempered with persistence and dedication, helped win victory then as before, when it brought him from a log cabin to the White House.

Dear Lord Jesus thank you so much that we have you, namely, and other men and women of excellence, that we can learn from and pattern our lives. Amen.

And the prayer of faith shall save the sick, and the Lord shall raise him up and if he hath committed sins, they shall be forgiven him. James 5:14 KJV

I have a good friend who seriously stands in need of prayer for the healing of his body and the salvation of his soul. I believe both needs will be met.

I was diagnosed with fibromyalgia, an autoimmune muscle and joint disease, in the early 2000s, after the death of my first husband. I suffered intensely with it for 20 years, after going through all kinds of tests and trying numerous medications to almost no avail. That lying devil bombarded me with guilt and shame for constantly asking for prayer.

He told me I was unworthy because my faith was weak, or I would have already been healed. The pain was horrible, and at times, I could not even get out of bed. In 2019 I went to a College St. Church of

God Ladies Retreat. Our Pastor's wife, Pastor Melissa Smith, announced we were going up on the mountain to pray over burdens and needs and leave them there. When we got up there, she told us to find rocks and write our request on them, pray, and believe for them to be answered, and take them to a designated tree (representing the Cross of Calvary) and leave them there. That was in October 2019. I knew I had received my healing. I had no joint or muscle pain, and I went off my pain medication with no adverse reactions. On January 1 of the new year, knowing I was pain-free with no pain medication for over two months, I announced my healing publicly. I knew I had been miraculously healed because there was no known cure for fibromyalgia. Secondly, my doctor had told me that if I ever came off the pain medication, I had been on for so long, I would have to come off gradually to prevent serious side effects. I came off medication immediately and experienced no adverse side effects.

Dear Lord Jesus, I pray earnestly for my friend who desperately needs you to save his soul and heal his body. He is a good person, but only the blood of Jesus can make him white as snow. If he was to die, he would go to hell without you, Lord. I have prayed for him since I first witnessed to him in high school, but today, I believe beyond measure that he is going to be convicted of sin, repent, and invite you into his heart as his Lord and Savior and that all unbelief would have to flee. I declare that Salvation and physical healing both are coming to his household, and he is going to live many years to tell his family and others about it. I praise you, precious Jesus, for answering both requests; in your name, I pray!!! Amen and Amen.

FEBRUARY 14
EVERY DAY A DAY OF LOVE

If a man would give all the substance of his house for love, it would utterly be contemned. Song of Solomon 8:7 KJV.

Every day should be Valentine's Day, a day of love, a day set aside to especially show how much you care for that special person God has given you in love and marriage. There is simply nothing to compare when it is centered around God and based on his principles. I remember when I first met and fell in love with my husband. I thought this must surely be the very depth of love. I felt almost as if we had a monopoly on love. Like most young couples, we thought we had reached a height that no one else had ever reached. We were so incredibly happy then, but after over twenty years of marriage, I realized that I love him more every day that I live. We have shared so much, both joy and sadness. Because of our love, a precious gift from God, our joys have been doubled and our troubles divided. Teenagers and older singles may feel that they have

an edge on this thing called love. I know because I have been there, but now that I realize how true love has a way of becoming stronger and more precious with the aging of time, I simply cannot imagine what the joys of love will be like after fifty years of marriage. Every day is new and more exciting. I am so looking forward to the future!

Dear Lord, I praise you for my husband and the love you have given us. I am so thankful for the precious products of our love, our children. May we always center our marriage and our home around you. Amen.

Though I speak with the tongues of men and of angels and have not charity, I am become as sounding brass or a tinkling cymbal. And though I have the gift of prophecy, and understand all mysteries, and all knowledge; and though I have all faith so that I could remove all mountains, and have not charity, I am nothing. And though I bestow all my goods to feed the poor, and though I give my body to be burned, and have not charity it profiteth me nothing. Charity suffereth long, and is kind chariy envieth not; charity vaunteth not itself, and is not puffed up, doth not behave itself unseemly, seeketh, not her own is not easily provoked, thinketh no evil; rejoiceth not in iniquity but rejoiceth in the truth; beareth all things, believeth all things, hopeth all things, endureth all things, Charity never faileth: but whether there be prophecies, they shall fail ;whether there be tongues they shall cease whether there be knowledge, it shall vanish away. For we know in part and we prophesy in part. But when that which is perfect is come, then that which is done in part shall be done away. When I was a child, I thought as a *child:but when I became a man, I put away childish things. For now we see through a glass darkly; but then face to face:Now we know in part;but then shall I know even as.I am known. And now abiddeth faith, hope, charity, these three ;but the greatest of these is charity. 1 Corinthians 13 KJV.*

Did you know that courtship after marriage is as necessary and vital to a good relationship as when you were dating? Well, it is, if not more! One of the most important ingredients of a happy marriage is the continuance of expressing your love in little ways. In courtship, a couple will usually go out of their way to show appreciation and kindness to the person of their choice, only to later marry them and begin taking them for granted. How pathetic!

It usually is not intentional. Sometimes it just happens that way. You can get so caught up in the act of daily living and the pressures that accompany trying to make a living and providing the necessities that go along with it that before you know it, you cease to do the little things that show you care.

God does not intend for such to happen. The scriptural command as set forth is, "Husbands, love your wives, even as Christ also loved the church and gave himself for it." (Ephesians 5: 25 KJV.)

If a husband keeps this command, he will be all that a godly wife could desire, and if the wife fills in the same picture with, "she that is married cares how she may please her husband." Then she, too, will be right on track toward a happy and fulfilled marriage. Many unhappy marriages could probably be saved by a little wisdom, a little forgiveness, a little patience, and a whole lot of love. Love should be expressed in words and deeds and not ever withheld.

If, during courtship, it took all the special attention and sweet words to woo and win the person of your choice, then how can you expect to hold that person's affection and love after marriage unless you continue to show the same love, attention, interest, and gentleness as before. Yes, courtship after marriage is necessary.

94

An anonymous author once said: "If a happy marriage is yours to be, let every husband stay a lover true, and every wife remain a sweetheart, too!"

Lord Jesus, I praise you for my marriage and for the special partner that you have given me. Lord, I just pray that you would help both of us to show the same love, consideration and thoughtfulness as we did when dating. Please let us love each other every day and center our marriage around you. Amen.

For I am persuaded, that neither death, nor life, nor angels, nor principalities, nor powers, nor things present, nor things to come, nor height, nor depth, nor any other creature, shall be able to separate us from the love of God, which is in Christ Jesus our Lord. Romans 8:38-39 KJV.

One consolation we have as Christians is the fact that we are forever convinced that there is absolutely nothing the devil can produce that will ever change God's mind about us and separate us from his great love.

Dear God, I am so very thankful that you defeated the devil at Calvary when Jesus said it was finished. He died on the cross for my sins. Then went to hell and took the keys of death, hell, and the grave from the devil. I cannot praise you enough for the

*plan of salvation and the sweet love and the victory
we have in Jesus Christ Amen.*

FEBRUARY 17
PURE IN HEART

Blessed are the pure in heart: for they shall see God. Matthew 5: 5 KJV.

Every month is the month for hearts, but especially February. Can anyone ever say his own heart is pure? Yes! It is possible to have a pure heart, or Jesus would not have said it in Matthew 5:5 KJV. He never sets goals or standards that are impossible for us to attain.

The Christian must live so close to God that his thoughts and actions will be constantly guarded against evil.

Adam and Eve were pure and innocent in the Garden of Eden but the devil did not let that deter him from tempting them to sin. Before he succeeded, first, he had to plant doubt of God's word in Eve's heart. From that moment on he was in control of the situation.

Christians, especially young people, are constantly faced with subtle temptations to lower their standards, to throw off restraint, to experiment with what God says is sin. But if you have a real desire that your heart, be pure, you will accept God's word that sin is wrong and that if you commit willful sin, you must repent immediately. Unrepented sin brings forth death. Our Lord Jesus was tempted but he resisted the devil and remained pure. He gives us the power to do the same.

Dear Lord Jesus, please help me not to doubt the word of God. Help me to stand against the devil with the word when I am tempted, and to remain pure in heart so I can see you one day. Amen.

FEBRUARY 18
GOD WILLS PROSPERITY

Beloved, I wish above all things that thou mayest prosper and be in health, even as thy soul prospers. III John 2 KJV.

The above scripture is undoubtedly one of my favorites. It begins with beloved - to the one I love, desire above all things - what passion, emotion, and degree, that you prosper with excellence, financially, physically, mentally, emotionally, even as your soul prospers, and we know how much he desires us to prosper spiritually!

Dear God, I thank you that it is your desire that I prosper in all things, in all areas of my life. Please help me to always remember that it is you who is the source of all good things in this life, and in eternity to come. Amen.

Charge them that are rich in this world, that they are not high minded, nor trust in uncertain riches, but in the living God, who giveth us richly all things to enjoy, that they do good, that they are rich in good works, ready to distribute, willing to communicate, laying up in store for themselves a good foundation against the time to come, that they may lay hold on eternal life. 1Timothy 6:17-19KJV.

What a privilege being a Christian affords, but with added privileges, come added responsibilities. If we obey God's word and seek him then prosperity will be ours to enjoy in this life, plus treasures untold and incomprehensible by the world's standards, and our eternal life to come.

The true children of God that stand faithful and remain to the end will have the best of the here and now and in heaven to come. After all, what do you expect? Our heavenly father owns it all!

Dear Lord, I love you and I praise you for who you are and all you are. I pray that as you bless me and my blessings increase, you will help me to be who I should be. I pray you help me to meet my responsibilities and my obligations to you and to others. Please help me remain humble, be a good steward of all you bless me with, and forever give you honor, glory, and praise. Amen.

Wherefore do you spend money for that which is not bread? And you labor for that which satisfieth not? Hearken diligently unto me, eat that which is good, and let your soul delight itself in fatness. Isaiah 55:2 KJV.

God is not opposed to having possessions or property; however, he is opposed to the preoccupation or the undue stress of being so concerned with material matters that you have no time to take care of your relationship with God, your relationship with family, and your preparation to eventually live in heaven.

We live in a world longing for happiness and security but looking for it in all the wrong places. Never has there been a more materialistic society than ours; Yet never has there been a more dissatisfied world of human beings.

How tragic is it when material gains result in spiritual loss when temporal and worldly gains are traded for eternal treasures?

Dear Lord Jesus, please help me to be satisfied in life with things that will last eternally. Help me not to be so preoccupied with acquiring wealth that I fail to take care of what is important: my relationship with you, my family, and others Amen.

FEBRUARY 21
SUCCESS REQUIRES PATIENCE

O house of Israel cannot I do with you as the potter? Saith the Lord. Behold, as the clay is in the potter's hand, so are ye in my hand, O house of Israel. Jeremiah 18:6 KJV.

A few years ago, while vacationing in the Smoky Mountains, we had the privilege of stopping in an Indian village. There we watched and listened as a potter explained the steps in the age-old process of forming, fashioning, and reforming clay until a beautiful vessel was ready to be fired.

I was reminded again of that lesson today as I watched my four-year-old trying to print her name. I watched as she would print T, I, F, F, and then try to print an A, tear out the paper and start over again. I watched as she tore out three pages and then on the fourth try, finally wrote an A that she found acceptable. I thought how difficult this process of trying, failing, and trying again can be until success is finally reached. It takes a lot of patience, but oh, the satisfaction when success is finally reached. We can go on to greater challenges and more accomplishments.

It is all a part of God's plan for our lives in the natural and the spiritual. How patient God is, as he tries, proves, and establishes those who yield to his molding. It is often a slow unhurried process. He continues to work on each of us who are pliable in his hands.

Dear God, please make me pliable in your hands. I want to be soft and teachable so that you can mold me and make me into a vessel that you deem usable and worthy of being used in your service. Amen.

If my people which are called by my name, shall humble themselves, and pray, and seek my face, and turn from their wicked ways: then will I hear from heaven, and will forgive their sin, and will heal their land. II Chronicles 7:14 KJV.

Right after high school graduation, I had the privilege of taking a class trip to Virginia and Washington DC. We visited Monticello, the home of George Washington, the first president of the United States of America and the father of our country.

Although the tour was impressive and Monticello is beautiful, the thing about George Washington I remember most came from Mrs. Mary Greene, my third-grade teacher. She told us that George's father grew cherry trees and one of those trees won a prize. George went out and chopped it down and then confessed by saying," Father, I cannot tell a lie. I chopped down your prized cherry tree."

Such stories show that people believe he was an honest and upright young man. Later as his career progressed, people continued to believe in his honesty, integrity, and high caliber. One of Washington's officers, Henry Lee better known as Light Horse Harry, summed up the way Americans felt when he said: "First in war, first in peace, and first in the hearts of his countrymen."

There is certainly a lot of difference between the United States of Washington's time and that of today. Our country has certainly come a long way. But if it took a man of integrity and character to lead America to victory in Washington's day, think of the extent our nation could benefit from having leaders of such report in our political offices today.

Dear God, please bless our country and place leaders, of integrity, high caliber, wisdom, and strength who will stand for the right and not be afraid to fight to make this a nation under God-pleasing to you, for the good of all. Amen.

FEBRUARY 23
JEALOUS OF THE PROPEROUS

But as for me, my feet were almost gone; my steps had well-nigh slipped. For I was envious at the foolish when I saw the prosperity of the wicked. Psalm 73:2-3 KJV.

God's word never ceases to amaze me! No matter how long you have studied it, there are hidden gems to be discovered every time you open it. Today was such a day for me. I cannot remember ever learning about Asaph. Even though I have completely read the Bible seven times, I do not recall Asaph.

In Psalm 73 there was a man named Asaph. In the modern day, he would be known as a director of music. Asaph was a servant of God, but he got caught up in looking at other people and he saw that they were very wicked, yet very prosperous. He became jealous of them and his steps slipped and he found he had lost out with God. He went to the sanctuary and there he understood the end of the prosperous wicked. They may be prospering now but they shall perish and be destroyed. As for Asaph, he realized his foolishness when he said: thou shalt guide me with thy counsel and afterward receive me to glory. The lesson here is never to envy the wicked who are prospering because they may be prospering today but unless they repent and turn from their wicked ways, they will perish.

Dear Lord Jesus, please help me to never break your heart by envying the wicked. No matter how much they may prosper, they will perish unless they repent. Amen.

FEBRUARY 24
GREATNESS RANKS ABOVE ENVY

Envy slayeth the silly one. Job 5:2 KJV.

I recall a message once by Pastor Harold Jones about a 17th century famous architect Sir Christopher Wren in the 17th century. Sir Christopher was building a church edifice in London when he was severely criticized by a group of jealous architects. They told him his type of architecture would not support the massive roof he was putting on the building. After much debate, the officials ordered Sir Christopher to put in additional pillars. Sir Christopher still reluctantly insisting that they were not needed did as he was told. There was a genius in his field who was forced to go against his own conclusions because of the envy of his competitors. Funny, how jealousy can get into our system. Someone can do something just a little better than we can, someone gets recognized as being just a little more capable than we are,

112

someone rises above us, and we seek to pull them down.

They treated the man of Galilee that way too. He came with a new way, a better plan, clearer revelation of what the creator, was like, and his fellow counterparts sought a way to destroy him.

But life has a way of never letting anyone climb higher by pulling another down. Fifty years after Sir Christopher had finished the church, painters were doing repair work on the church. It was then discovered that the additional pillars that Sir Christopher placed in the building missed the top of the roof by two feet! Greatness cannot be destroyed by jealousy. Greatness always ranks higher than jealousy.

Dear Lord Jesus, please do not let me ever become jealous, envious, or full of strife. Please remind me that you created me as uniquely as a snowflake with talents and abilities of my own that you can bless and get credit for. Remind me, that I can admire but do not have the need to covet anyone else.

Jesus Christ the same yesterday, and today, and forever. Hebrews 13: 8 KJV.

We are living in an ever-changing world. Circumstances change daily that concern each of us. Changes take place due to prosperity and therefore produce a positive effect in our lives. New homes and businesses are springing up all around us, offering novel places to live and more jobs in our community. Positive changes are often brought about when we reach personal goals, such as completing our education. When goals such as these are checked our lives change favorably because new doors of opportunity are opened to us.

Regretfully, not all changes are favorable such as the loss of a job, the loss of a home to fire or tornado, or even the loss of a loved one to divorce or death. We can be in great health and suddenly be told we have cancer or diabetes. Things can happen such as the loss of a loved one that alters our life forever. Children grow up, leave home, and have children of their own.

Life is an ever-changing process. The only thing certain in life is the uncertainty. Even though our lives change, and our circumstances are altered we have the consolation that he is God, and he changes not. He will go with us to the very end and all things are working together for our good and his glory.

Dear Lord Jesus, I am so thankful that in an ever-changing world, you are my constant and nothing will ever cause you to change. Amen.

I am the door: by me, if any man enters in, he shall be saved and shall go in and out and find pasture. John 10:9 KJV.

Did you know that the devil's favorite pastime is going around and spreading the lie that if you live the Christian life, then you cannot enjoy living. Imagine that! And to top the cake, some people believe him. He tries to tell them that God is a killjoy and that if they give their heart and life to Jesus, they will forfeit good times. Nothing could be further from the truth. Jesus said in Matthew 11: 28-30 KJV Come unto me all ye that labor and are heavy laden and I will give you rest. Take my yoke upon you and learn of me for I am meek and lowly in heart and you shall find rest unto your souls: for my yoke is easy and my burden is light. Does that sound like he wants us to be all burdened down and unhappy? No indeed! He did not say that he came so we might endure life but that we could have an abundant life. He came not that we could just have eternal life in heaven, but also that the life we are now living on this earth, this day, this very moment, could be meaningful, blessed, and above all happy!

Dear Lord Jesus, I thank you for giving me a meaningful life of happiness and fulfillment. No one enjoys life more than the Christian who possesses peace, love, and joy. You sure knew how to plan it. Amen.

FEBRUARY 27
ALL THINGS WORK FOR OUR GOOD

And we know that all things work together for good to them that love God, to them who are the called according to his purpose. Romans 8: 28 KJV.

The other day I was invited to attend a Garden Club meeting with a friend. While there I learned that the tropical flower known as jasmine produces a much stronger fragrance while growing and blowing freely in the wind than after its blossoms have been cut and crushed for perfume.

The rose on the other hand is just the opposite. The rose's greatest fragrance potential is when its pedals have been pressed and bled. Most Christians can be classified as a spiritual jasmine or a rose. Some Christian lives are more fruitful while they are young in the Lord and still maturing. They seem to express more enthusiasm and zeal. With their newfound joy, they are excited and eager to witness and serve in whatever capacity is open unto them. Oh, that all of us would maintain that fire and passion of newfound joy. Other Christians are more like the rose. They have gone through adversity and pain in life and have been crushed and bled and their spiritual fragrance is at its best.

Whether your Christian life resembles the jasmine or the rose, the Lord loves you and knows what is best for you.

Dear Lord Jesus, I am so glad that you know our frame and you know how strong we are and just what we can stand. I pray that you will help us, whether we be a jasmine or a rose, that our perfume, our faith, would radiate like a sweet-smelling fragrance that is so precious to you and that others would be drawn to you through our aroma. Amen.

FEBRUARY 28
FAITH IS THE LINK THAT BINDS

If ye have faith as a grain of mustard seed, ye shall say unto this mountain, Remove hence to yonder place, and it shall remove, and nothing shall be impossible unto you. Matthew 17:20 KJV.

There is a healing force at work in the world when you and I have blundered about and come to the end of our resources. Great reservoirs of power open to us which we cannot begin to tap until we have despaired of our own ideas and means of working out the situation.

Faith is the link that binds our nothingness to God's almightiness. The answer to our question of how is one word: God! Faith in God enables us to do a thing in a way when no way seems possible. This is the greatest victory the world has ever known.

Dear Lord Jesus, I praise you for my faith, which may be the size of a grain of mustard seed now. But I know that my faith is growing daily. My faith muscles are strengthened and become stronger as I trust and believe in you. Amen.

DON'T WORRY, PRAY, GIVE THANKS

Be careful for nothing; but in everything by prayer and supplication with thanksgiving let your requests be made known unto God and the peace of God, which passeth all understanding shall keep your hearts and minds through Christ Jesus. Philippians 4:6-7 KJV.

It is understood that most of the things we worry about never take place. Usually, the things we worry about that do happen are beyond our control.

Every morning when my daddy would leave for work my momma would tell him to have a lovely day and be careful. Her words," Be careful, girls" were the last my sister and I heard as we left for school. Mother meant for us to be watchful and cautious so we would not get hurt.

The word care in the noun form means something to worry about or watch over and being full of care, therefore means full of worry or anxiety. As a child, I brought all my care home to my mother.

Whether it was a skinned knee or hurt feelings she always knew just what to do to make things well again. Her comfort and her advice were invaluable.

Our heavenly father can do so much more. He wants us to worry not about life's situations but to bring our requests to him in prayer and receive peace of mind and joy of heart. He has the power, and he possesses the ability to control the situation if we are only willing to hand over the controls.

Dear Lord Jesus, I thank you so much for your word that advises us on what to do when we worry or are full of the cares of life. Please help me to always bring my worries to you in prayer and supplication, and then to give thanks to you because I know you are taking care of me. Amen.

MARCH

MARCH 1
AT YOUR WIT'S END

I was brought low, and he helped me. Psalm 116:6 KJV.

Have you ever felt like you were at your wit's end? The other day, I turned in the book of Psalms, and there was a verse that said are at their wits' end. Psalm 107:27 KJV

How many times I have been there, but I never realized the Bible contained the phrase, wits' end, which is another way of saying at the end of your rope or at the point of desperation. The pressures of present-day business and domestic life often wear us down, both physically and spiritually. There are more neurotics and drug addicts today in this tense, complex, speed-made, competitive world of ours than ever before. Our ancestors lived by the calendar, but we live by the clock.

Worry, overwork, stress, bad health, frustration, competition, being misunderstood, shunned, and being taken advantage of are some of the things that bring us to our wits' end, and we feel a sense of helplessness and destitution. What if you are a Christian and you feel you have reached your wits' end? Our adversary, the devil, concentrates on the Christian. He zeros in and strives to drag the Christian to the point of desperation. He uses his strategy to try to smother our joy and silence our testimony. His motives sometimes backfire. For when our ever-overwhelmed hearts cast themselves on God, the enemy has defeated his own purpose. Sometimes, during all the pressures and struggles, we fail to take the time to pray and commune with God as we should. Satan will even use our failure as an excuse to make us feel guilty about calling on the Lord for help. But Jesus is a sympathetic Christ. He is no slave driver. We serve him by choice, not force. When we cast our cares upon him, we find sympathy, understanding, and sufficient grace for our needs.

Dear Lord, I am so thankful that you hear our prayers. When we have reached our wits' end, you know just how to calm. Amen.

MARCH 2
FAITH IN CRITICAL TIME

Many are the afflictions of the righteous: but the Lord delivereth them out of them all. Psalm 34:19 KJV.

It is great to be a Christian and enjoy the benefits when the sun is shining, and life is beautiful. It is even more wonderful to personally know God when life's problems become unbearable.

One evening, my little niece and nephew were hit by a car when collecting money for Easter Seals in their community. In times like these, it is so comforting to know that you can call on God on the scene. My husband and I arrived at the place of the accident before the ambulance got there. My little nephew was lying in the ditch. I went to him first, and he was unconscious but breathing. I then went to my little niece, who was covered in blood. She looked up at me and asked if she was going to die.

That was the longest night of my life. My nephew Brent was in intensive care with a concussion and a broken leg. Tina, my niece, underwent surgery on her leg that was broken in two places. Brent was moved into the same room as his sister. Both were in traction but more content. Everyone was so thankful, especially their parents, that it was not worse.

The children remained in Pediatrics at Floyd Medical Center for the summer. And had to be homeschooled for the first semester of the following school year.

It took time for broken bones to be healed and nerves to calm down, but our family was so very thankful that their lives were spared.

Dear Heavenly Father, I praise you for calling upon you in critical times. You always hear our prayers. You join us in our situations, bringing peace, calm, and healing. Amen.

MARCH 3
LET US BE GLAD

This is the day that the Lord hath made. Let us rejoice and be exceedingly glad. Psalm 118:24 KJV.

As I was awakened this morning at half past six by the clanging of an alarm clock, I thought: "Lord, why couldn't this be Saturday morning?" But it was Thursday instead, so I pulled myself out of bed and was off to take a shower.

On my way, I stopped to draw the drapes to see what the world looked like outside. Perched on a limb just outside the window was a little robin red breast. As it sat there singing softly in the quiet calm of the morning, I knew this was a brand-new day. It was going to be a good one!

Dear Lord, thank you for each brand new day you give us to live for you. I praise you. Amen.

But now are you light in the Lord: walk as children of light. Ephesians 5:8b KJV.

Every day of your life, you are either influencing someone for the better, or you are influencing those you encounter for the worse. It is true the life you live, the things you say, the places you go, and the deeds you do produce either a positive or a negative effect on the lives of those around you. Your attitude is contagious. It has been proven that you can walk into an office with a radiant and cheerful smile and produce the whole mood and atmosphere for the rest of the day. If a mere smile has the power to do that, then think of the overall effect and influence our lives are passing on to those around us.

There was a lady once who could always find something to complain about. She was a chronic fault finder. Not only could she find fault with people, but she found fault with life in general. If you mentioned the fact that it was a beautiful sunny day, she would say oh, how terrible the heat is. If you mentioned the wonderful increase in church attendance, she would make it a point to comment on how many hypocrites were in the church. Something was constantly the matter to hear her tell it. One day, someone said that instead of letting her light shine when she walked into a room, it was as if someone had turned off the lights. She had influence, but the wrong kind.

The Bible says ye are the light of the world. A city that is set on a hill cannot be hidden. Neither do men light a candle and put it under a bushel but on a candlestick, and it gives light unto all that are in the house. Let your light shine before men so that they may see your good works and glorify your father, who is in heaven. Matthew 5:14-16 KJV.

Once, while giving a devotion, I saw a girl take one single candle and light it. Then she took another candle sitting beside it and used the flame of the lit taper to light it. After giving light to the one beside It, the flame of the first candle increased. It burned larger and much brighter. The same thing happens in our Christian lives. If we let our light shine on someone in darkness, it illuminates their path. Our spiritual light increases and the flame of faith burning in our hearts grows greater and brighter.

Dear Lord, please let me always look for the good in life. Help me to be grateful and not complain. May I let my light shine instead of snuffing out someone else's. Amen.

And hope maketh not ashamed; because the love of God is shed abroad in our hearts by the Holy Ghost which is given unto us. Romans 5:5 KJV.

Hope is a small word with an extremely big meaning. It means going anyway when people tell you there is no need to go. It means batting after you have already struck out. It means finding a match on the table after all the candles have burned out.

Some people find the secret of living in this world. They are successful people. The ones that cannot be daunted cannot be deterred, cannot be dismayed. Hope has done many things for different people at diverse levels of society and in different periods of history. It made a light bulb for Edison, wings for the Wright brothers, a steamboat for Fulton, and a telephone for Bell.

What is hope? Hope is going against the odds. Hope is playing the games of life and risking your all

on what is good, pure, and just. Hope is giving life your best regardless of the past returns.

Who needs it? We do. You and I. What would life be without it? Why would we care if we woke up in the morning if we did not have it? No one is ever so rich that he has no need for hope. Everyone needs it.

Every time I turn on the news this week, I have heard a grim economist projecting how bad this year is going to be. It is true we have problems. Our nation has problems. We face problems individually. But if Jesus Christ had enough hope to carry him to Calvary and to see him through to victory over death, hell, sin, and the grave, then surely, we can face our future with enough hope to help us work out problems.

Without it, we cannot make it. With it, we can face another year with the confidence that it will be rich and full. Because he lives, we have hope. Let us profess it.

Dear Lord Jesus, if you can surely have hope after going through what you went through, then surely, I can have hope to face tomorrow. Because you live, I am professing it! Amen.

MARCH 6
SECRET TO STRENGTH

Rejoice in the Lord always, and again, I say rejoice. Philippians 4:4 KJV.

Mention joy to some people, and like a reflex, they produce a mass of reasons why they do not have any: I am not an emotional person, our church is not like that, I prefer keeping a level head, expect too much out of life, and you get disappointed.

While it is true that we all differ emotionally, scripture says the joy of the Lord is your strength. Nehemiah 8:10 KJV.

Paul realized the importance of joy as he was divinely inspired to include it in the list of the fruit of the spirit in Galatians 5:22 KJV. Why, then, do so many of us insist on explaining away a quality God wants us to have, a quality that would only make us happier people? Maybe the problem is that we do not understand what Christian joy is: the joy of winning, the successful completion of a challenging task, a wedding day, the birth of a new baby, and

being surrounded by those we love are all familiar to us. We feel elated because something important has happened in our lives. We also know the joy that comes over us as we think about our spouse, our children, our parents, close friends, and the relationships we share.

All these give us the clue to Christian joy. It has its beginning in a historical event, the death and resurrection of Christ. We experience it every time we pause and recall that Christ died for us, who God is, and what he has become to us. The key lies in Paul's instructions in Philippians. If we think joy is something that will descend on us, whether we want it or not, we will keep standing around waiting to be bowled over by it, and we will have a long wait. Paul asked us not to wait but to rejoice and do it now.

Dear Jesus, I praise you for the privilege of being joyful. Every time I choose to rejoice, I feel spiritually and emotionally strengthened. Amen.

Let the redeemed of the Lord say so, whom he hath redeemed from the hand of the enemy. Psalm 107:2 KJV.

The above verse was taken directly from David's own diary as he recalled what the Lord had done for him. It has been passed down through the ages, read by many, and will be read hopefully by generations to come. Just as David testified to the Lord hearing and answering his prayers, we should certainly keep in mind the outstanding answers to prayers and the deliverance God has brought to us. They should be like beautiful flowers in a memory garden so that we can be encouraged during present difficulties to bless the Lord at all times and to remember what God has done for us in the past; thereby, we can renew our faith and believe in him to see us through today's problems and troubles.

How much we miss because we fail to tell others what the Lord has done for us. If the Lord has redeemed us, let us say so. Suppose he has heard and answered or come on the scene in a mighty way in our life. Then, let us share it with those we encounter.

There is something miraculous about personal testimony to others. Not only does it encourage and bless the one you are sharing it with, but it strengthens your own faith and makes you more effective and a bolder witness for the Lord.

Dear Lord, please help me to become an effective witness for you. As I share with others what you have done in my life, may they be blessed and the embers of my hearth glow even brighter. Amen.

Whatsoever thy hand findeth to do, do it with thy might; Ecclesiastes 9:10 KJV.

Mrs. Lois B. West, my home economics teacher at Fairmount High School, had a profound impact on my life. Not only was she a wonderful, elegant, Christian lady, but she was one of the most positive role models I ever had. Not only did she teach cooking, sewing, and managing finances, but she also taught morals and principles to live by. One day in class, she told us that she had a change in curriculum for the day and wanted to share a poem with us that she would give us extra credit if we would commit to memory. The poem is basically about being the best that you can possibly be in every circumstance.

As the years have passed and the words of the poem have remained with me, I realize we were all richer for it. Today in life when an unpleasant task lies ahead, I am reminded of those words and encouraged to strive to do the absolute best I can in any situation. She quoted an unknown author that day as saying anything that one does, from cooking a meal to governing estate, becomes a work of art if motivated by the passion for excellence and done as well as it can be. A man who does his job in that spirit will be the one who gets the most satisfaction out of life.

Dear Lord, I praise you for having placed the desire in my life to do my absolute best at whatever task I may be doing. I also thank you for the satisfaction that comes with doing it with excellence. Amen.

MARCH 9
PATIENCE BRINGS DOWN WALLS

I waited patiently for the Lord, and he inclined unto me and heard my cry. Psalm 40:1 KJV.

In Joshua 6:1-16KJV we find that thirteen times, the children of Israel marched around Jericho in silence. As they quietly circled the great walls, they probably began to doubt and were tempted to complain, but instead, they said nothing.

Then, a sense of anticipation of what God was about to do began to sweep over them. So many times, we rush about fretting and worrying when we should leave the matter to the Lord. We should remain silent before him with confidence that he will come on the scene and manifest his great power,

The scripture says that in his own sweet way, if we but wait, the Lord will take our burdens and set crooked matters straight.

Dear Lord, I do not want to pray for patience because I dread trials, but could you please take the patience I have and enhance it? I genuinely want to obey you in all things. Amen.

MARCH 10
LET JESUS RULE

Then said Jesus unto his disciples, if any man will come after me, let him deny himself, and take up his cross, and follow me. Matthew 16:24 KJV.

Mrs. Gertrude Akins, childhood Sunday School teacher at the Ludville Church of God, taught a story once using a picture of Jesus and a mirror as props. I remember it well and have since taught it to my youngest grandchildren, Natalie and Hudson. All can benefit from her illustration.

There was a little girl once who had a picture of Jesus over the head of her bed. She came in one afternoon tired from playing and went to her room to rest. As she lay there on her bed, she happened to look into the mirror on the dresser across from the foot of the bed, and there she saw the reflection of a picture of Christ. When she sat up in bed, her own reflection was shown in the mirror. When she lay down, she again saw Jesus in the mirror. Just then, the little girl's mother came into the room and asked what was going on. The child replied Mother,

I can see Jesus until I put myself in the way. He vanishes. One of the hardest battles to fight in living the Christian life is denying self and making Jesus the Lord of our life. The Lord never asked the impossible of us. God did not actually require Abraham to sacrifice his son, Issac. He only wanted to see if Abraham was willing to give up that which meant the most to him. When God saw that Abraham was willing, no matter what, to do his will, then God provided a lamb in place of Isaac for the sacrifice. Some people are afraid to live the Christian life because of fear of being called for a task they do not feel capable of accomplishing. But if the Lord calls you to do a special work, then he will equip you for the job. The key is willingness. Willingness to deny self and to say yes to the will of God in our lives.

Dear Lord Jesus, I sincerely ask that you help me to do your will. I pray that you will help me to take myself out of the equation and let you truly rule and be the Lord of my life. Amen.

MARCH 11
RESPONSIBILITY OF PARENTING

Lo, children, are a heritage of the Lord; and the fruit of the womb is his reward. As arrows are in the hand of a mighty man; so are children of the youth. Psalm 127:3-4 KJV.

An arrow has the potential to go far, but that potential is locked inside the arrow until it gets into the hands of a mighty man of strength, who will put the arrow in place inside the bow and produce the required thrust it takes to then send it soaring through the clouds to reach its destination.

Our biological clock has been ticking for a few months now. My husband and I barely realize the responsibility of bringing children into the world. They will be eternal beings that will make an impact on good or bad. We are youth pastors but have little clue as to the responsibility of being parents.

If you are a parent, teacher, or a Sunday school teacher, you may be training a future President of the United States right this very minute. The idea of teaching and training is such a formidable responsibility. The concepts you are striving for, the material, the morals, the standards you teach, and the character you are molding in that child will soon be unveiled. Children learn so quickly and they often imitate those who mean the most to them. It teaches them the sense of responsibility that lies on the shoulders of their parents. As adults, may God help us to be the teachers we should be and to gain the respect and admiration of our children so that they will be influenced to live upright and outstanding lives. Our world tomorrow will be largely determined by what we do today in our homes, our schools, and our churches.

Dear Lord, you know the desires of our hearts to have a child. As my husband and I sincerely pray and ponder over this life-changing decision, please speak your will to both of us clearly. Amen.

MARCH 12
HECTIC DAY

Deep calleth unto deep at the noise of thy waterspouts: all the waves and thy billows are gone over me. Psalm 42:7 KJV.

Yesterday, undoubtedly, was one of the most hectic days of my life. I was slowly but surely making my way through the heap of work piled high on my desk at the office when the phone rang. I answered it to find my husband on the other end of the line calmly, but as a matter of fact, he said, "Honey, you might want to come home. Drop everything you are doing. The kitchen is ankle-deep in water, and the downstairs bath is flooding onto the carpet in the den."

"What?" I screamed. "Yes," he said. "I got to it in time. And turned the water off, but evidently, we have some frozen, bursted water pipes.

After mopping up what must have been gallons of water, we both sat down on the stairs for a while. Tired in body, yes, but mostly tired in spirit.

"It could have been a whole lot worse," my husband said softly after we had been sitting there silently for a few minutes. I knew that if he had not been there to turn the water off when he did, our carpet, furniture, and the whole downstairs area could have been ruined.

Then, I was made to remember the man of Calvary. All the waves and billows of suffering, indignation, and wrath broke over him as he bore the cross in our stead. Every individual anguish and every humanistic trial, tribulation, or even minor irritation finds an answering call in the depth of his loving sympathy.

With that in mind, I found the strength and the courage to go back to work and face the papers piled high on my desk once again.

Dear Lord, I thank you that nothing I go through catches you off guard. When I think of all you have gone through, I realize I should be undaunted. Please help me to be patient in life's situations. Amen.

MARCH 13
GOD IS ALWAYS THERE

*For David speaketh concerning him, I foresaw
the Lord always before my face, for He is on my right
hand that I should not be moved: Acts 2: 25 KJV.*

It is almost the anniversary of my dad's passing
and like most daughters. I thought the sun rose and
set in my daddy.

This time of year, is usually a sad time for me
because of the loss of my father, and last
Wednesday night was no different. I was feeling
blue as I got ready for church. While sitting in that
service listening to a program being presented by
the young marriage class, Ricky Allen spoke about
always being able to talk to our Heavenly Father.

As I sat and listened with tears in my eyes, she
talked about losing her father at the age of two and
about only knowing him through seeing the pictures
and hearing what her mother had to say about him.
Ricky went on to say that after she married and left
home, she would call her mother every night until

she moved to Calhoun from Cartersville. Now, she did not have the chance to call her as often as she would like. Unlike her mother, she could call her Heavenly Father anytime, no matter how often or what the hour or the situation. He is always there, ready, willing, and able to hear the cries of his children. How true. With those thoughts in mind, I left that service feeling uplifted and with a new awareness of God's presence and his great love.

Dear Heavenly Father, I thank you for always being with me and never leaving me. Amen.

MARCH 14
NO PLACE LIKE HOME

Choose you this day whom ye will serve: but as for me and my house, we will serve the Lord. Joshua 24:15 KJV.

Last week my husband and I experienced problems with frozen water pipes and were left without water for a couple of days. During that time, we had to temporarily move in with my mother, until the plumber could take care of this situation.

No matter how much you love your parents or how much you enjoy going back for a visit, once you have moved out and made a home of your own, there is no place on earth that can replace your home. No matter how elaborate it may be, or no matter how humble, there is no place like home. It is the place you want to go when you are sick. Home is the place you head when you are tired, hungry, or when you have been hurt or disappointed. There is just no place that can take its place. Home. It has been described as the most precious place on this side of heaven. The Bible does not say very much about homes. It says a great deal about the things that make them. It speaks of life, love, joy, peace, and rest. If we get a house and put these in it, then we shall have made a home.

Dear Lord Jesus, I praise you for my home. I thank you for being the center of it. Amen.

MARCH 15
FEAR NOT, STAND STILL

Fear ye not, stand still, and see the salvation of the Lord, which he will show to you today. Exodus 14:13 KJV.

Have you ever been in a drastic situation? In Exodus 14:23-31. At your convenience, read the whole passage and see how God came on the scene for the Israelites when they needed it the most.

Most of us faced situations in life when it seemed like walls and ceilings were falling on us, and there seemed to be no way of escape. No doubt, the Israelites felt such when Pharaoh's army came barreling down upon them. But what a great victory! God took control at the point where obedience had done it all. When we have done all to stand, let us stand and see what the Lord will do. Cast all your care on God. He is the anchor that will hold.

Dear Lord Jesus, I praise you that you indeed are my holding anchor when I do not fear and stand still in obedience. Amen.

MARCH 16
PRESENT MOST IMPORTANT

His compassions fail not. They are new every morning. Lamentations 3:22-23 KJV.

Have you ever stopped to think of how much time we spend thinking about the past or wondering about the future? If we could only realize it is what we make of the present that is so especially important.

Often, we waste precious moments looking back at our past. Worrying about what has already happened, we waste time thinking about what could have been if we had taken a different direction in life, perhaps if we had chosen a different career, or perhaps if we had taken advantage of an opportunity passed up long ago. And so goes the list on and on and on.

We waste time feeling guilty about past failures and about times when we did not exactly put our best foot forward. What time do we not look back in regret? We waste hanging, longing for the good old

161

days, and wishing certain situations or circumstances could again be as they were long ago. On the other hand, we often waste time wondering about the future. We are either wishing it was already here, or we are looking forward to it with fear and dread about what it may bring forth, when all the while, we should be living in the now and living it to the very fullest. Even though we cannot change the past, we can learn from our mistakes and hold the pleasant memories of days gone by in our heads as a precious keepsake.

But unlike the past, our future can be affected. The outcome of our future, to an extent, can be determined by what we do with our present. By living this day, this hour, and this very moment to the fullest, we can pave the way for a brighter future and a better tomorrow.

Dear Lord, please help me to live in the present, learn from the past, and commit the future to you. Amen

MARCH 17
CAST ASIDE WEIGHTS

Let us lay aside every weight, and the sin which doth so easily beset us, and let us run with patience the race that is set before us, looking unto Jesus, the author and finisher of our faith; Hebrews 12:1 KJV.

I was watching a TV program the other night where a wagon train was attempting to cross a swollen river. The weight of the wagons was too great, and they began to sink. At the wagon master's orders, the people began discarding the cargo of each wagon. And finally, with much care and skill, they made it safe.

Soon after we begin our walk in the Christian life, we often realize that there are things in our lives that must be discarded if we are to make it to heaven.

Not only should we discard sinful acts and unpleasant habits, but we should discard the weights and the cares of our lives that seem to bog us down and discourage us from reaching our destination. The Lord's will for each of us is to cast our cares upon him because He cares so much for us. He instructs us to give him every problem and every care. What a wonderful consolation to know Christ.

Dear Lord, thank you so much for the gift of the Holy Spirit that speaks to my heart and advises me to lay aside sins, weights, and cares of life that weigh me down in running the Christian race. Amen.

MARCH 18
OUR PATH A SHINING LIGHT

But the path of the just is as the shining light, that shineth more and more unto the perfect day. Proverbs 4:18 KJV.

Yesterday undoubtedly was one of the most beautiful days God has given. The day from dawn until dusk was no less than perfect. It seems that the winter was so long. How anxiously I have awaited springtime. Right now, it is raining, and the day is dismal and dreary, but my heart is still singing, my spirit is soaring, and I am still drawing inspiration from yesterday's rays of sunshine.

Did you know the Bible also contains rays of sunshine? Just as the sun is vital for our good health and happiness, rays from God's Word are also necessary for our spiritual well-being. Some scriptures, rays from God's Word, specifically contain verses of love, light, and life. These reveal the bright, breezy, and happy side of the Bible. If read and applied in our lives, the Bible of sunshine, laughter, and good cheer will be just what the words imply. If you choose a ray for each day from the gospel of sunshine, it will brighten your life and reveal the pillar of life, Jesus Christ, in your darkest and most dismal times.

Come unto me, He says, who is the Son of righteousness, the light of the world. As we look at Him, shadows flee away, the light of life falls upon our way, and all is peace.

Thy sun shall no more go down, neither shall thy moon withdraw itself. For the Lord shall be thine everlasting light, and the days of thy mourning shall be ended. Isaiah 60:19-20 KJV.

Dear Lord Jesus, thank You for being the light of my life and the light of the world. Amen

Thou wilt keep him in perfect peace whose mind is stayed on thee: because he trusteth in thee. Trust in the Lord forever; for in the Lord Jehovah is everlasting strength. Isaiah 26:3-4 KJV.

The other day, I walked into a Christian bookstore, and a little plaque hanging on a rack immediately caught my eye. The inscription read: "I'm so used to being tense that when I'm calm, I get nervous."

As comical as it seems, everyday pressures of life can overwhelm us if we continue to worry and dwell on the negative. If we take our problems, our doubts, and our fears to the Lord in prayer, commit them to Him, and read his word, then we can possess his perfect peace.

Dear Lord Jesus, please help me not to worry and fret but to read your word, believe your word, live your word, and go forth in peace. Amen.

MARCH 20

BEAUTIFUL RAINBOW

And the bow shall be in the cloud; and I will look upon it, that I may remember the everlasting covenant between God and every living creature of all flesh that is upon the earth. Genesis 9:16 KJV.

The other day, after a much-needed afternoon spring shower, I stepped onto the lawn just in time to see a beautiful rainbow make its debut across the sky.

I was reminded of the Bible, where God made his covenant with man and every living creature upon the earth. After the great flood, He promised He would never destroy the earth again with water. The picturesque phenomenon of nature, known as the rainbow, is the symbol of that covenant. God's symbol is that behind a frowning providence, He has a smiling face. Often, life's darkest episodes are overruled to give our richest blessings.

In science class, I learned that the rainbow is formed by sun shafts falling on raindrops, which break up the rays into seven colors and paint an arch, a sevenfold hue, on the opposite sky. The cloud only needs the sun to shine on it and, lo, the rainbow.

There is a spiritual rainbow in every cloud, permitted to overhand God's people. Those ominous clouds that frighten or dismay you, if faced bravely and discerningly, will disclose heavenly goodness.

I can imagine Noah's concern after the deluge when dark clouds again came rumbling through the sky. Would there be further destruction? No, the showers flung a lovely archway sign across the expanse. God was in the cloud as well as the sunshine. His bow was the symbol.

Dear Lord, when clouds are hanging low in my life, please remind me that the same God who sends sunshine and rain uses both to send the beautiful rainbow after the storm. Amen.

MARCH 21
STAINED-GLASS MOSAIC OF LIFE

My meditation of him shall be sweet: I will be glad in the Lord. Psalm 104:34 KJV.

I have never sat through a morning worship service at the College Street Church of God without being completely overwhelmed by the breathtaking beauty of the stained-glass windows. As the sunlight billows through, each of the plates, in its colorful uniqueness, seems to stand out. Separately and individually. Each red, green, gold, and blue stands apart, yet beautifully united and arranged to form a mosaic of perfection.

Everyone's life is a mosaic of the pieces that others have put into it. If you take a few minutes for nostalgia, look back over the years of your life, and you will recall the various people who have placed tiles in the mosaic of your life. There are childhood memories of parents, grandparents, and other favorite uncles and aunts. schoolteachers, coaches, music teachers, band directors, Sunday school officials, church pastors, and many other close friends and co-workers are all people whom you have lived with, played with or worked with down through the ages. If you take time to trace the contributions made by the many people you have encountered. Each has enhanced your life; even those who have criticized, condemned, or blocked projects you have endeavored to launch served a useful purpose. The tiles added to the mosaic by these people may be shade of gray or even darker, but they seem to bring out the bright tiles by soft contrasts. This has taught you discipline, patience, and forgiveness. The total effect in the mosaic of your life brought about by those you have touched shoulders with is that of beauty.

Edwin Markham said: "There is a destiny that makes us brothers. None goes his way alone." All that we send into the lives of others comes back into our own.

Dear Lord Jesus, I praise you for all the people who have taught me so much. You have brought them into my life, and they have added to my mosaic, making it uniquely beautiful. Amen.

MARCH 22
DELAY NOT DENIAL

My little daughter lieth at the point of death: I pray thee, come, and lay thy hands on her, that she may be healed; and she shall live. Mark 5:23 KJV.

Jairus besought him greatly. Did Jesus turn away from that distraught Father? Did he ever turn away from deep need, sincere love, or true faith? It would not have been Jesus at all if he had.

Jesus never answered nay when a sinner sought his way. Jesus never turned away when a request to him was made. No. Each needy, weary one found a friend in God's dear Son.

In the 24th verse of Mark chapter 5, we find that Jesus went with him and them. In verse 42, we find that Jesus brought her forth, and she rose and walked. No pen could describe the joy of that Father. Let us be quick to learn that when Jesus seems to delay His answer to our urgent prayers or to delay His presence to our pressing needs, it is always because He has an even bigger or better thing for us in mind. Delay is never denial, but infinite love and wisdom, planning an answer bigger than our biggest asking.

Dear Lord, I love You, and I praise You for always knowing and desiring what is best for me. Please help me to always receive Your answers to my prayers graciously. Amen.

MARCH 23
HE IS IN COMMAND

Come unto me, all ye that labour and are heavy laden, and I will give you rest. Matthew 11:28 KJV.

I dashed in thirty minutes late with figures, loan balances, and drafts still swirling in my head. I had twenty minutes to get something in the oven before having to leave again for a 6:00 p.m. meeting.

"What's for supper?" My husband asked as I rushed past him to the refrigerator. Just then, the phone rang, followed by a knock on the door. A friend had called to tell me that our dog had just gotten sick on her front porch. Would I please get him? The knock on the door resulted in three neighborhood kids selling something for a school project. It is hard to imagine how much time could take in such a few minutes.

Finally, I was off to my meeting, where I ran into a cement block and scraped the paint on the car.

After returning home and putting the dishes in the dishwasher, I slowly climbed the stairs and collapsed exhausted into bed. But instead of falling asleep, I tossed and turned. I was so keyed up about tomorrow's schedule that it was impossible to rest. So many things to do and so many projects yet to be completed.

I slipped out of bed and went over to the window. In the cool, calm, quiet of the night, God seemed to speak to me. "You are my child. I am still in command of everything." He seemed to be saying. If you will only let me, be." "Yes, Lord, I had almost forgotten that" I whispered.

In a few minutes, I returned to bed and slept like a baby for the rest of the night.

Dear Lord, thank You for reminding me that You are always there and aware of how much I have on my plate. It is comforting to know You are in

command. Thank You for reminding me and sending sweet calm and rest. Amen.

MARCH 24
FAITH BEING TESTED

He faileth not. Zephaniah 3:5 KJV.

Beautiful flowers have been found blooming in rocky crevices. Scenic spots have charmed the traveler at surprising turns on the least promising of roads. Rainbow artistry has suddenly lit up the drabbest of skies. Priceless gems have often been found in the unlikeliest places. In the book of Zephaniah, in a context laden with rebukes to a perverse people, this expression of divine faithfulness shines like a solitary star on a dark night. "He faileth not."

What is the important thing in your life that you would have Him to do for you? Has faith begun to fail? Has the heart been looking at circumstances instead of God? Think again. If your answer seems unduly delayed, it is not through any collapse of His power. Perhaps faith is being evaluated for the sake of spiritual profit and progress.

Does faith begin to fail? Has hope departed?

Say not that the father has not heard your prayer.

That prayer shall be answered in time. Somewhere.

Dear Lord Jesus, it seems I have been waiting so long with no answer to my prayer. Please help my unbelief and renew my hope. You have answered so many prayers before. I think I shall praise You right now for all You have already answered! Amen.

Withhold not good from them to whom it is due,
when it is in the power of thine hand to do it.
Proverbs 3:27 KJV.

How quick we are to complain and criticize. And how prone we are to forget to show our gratitude and appreciation to those around us daily. Proverbs 25:11 KJV says a word fitly spoken is like apples of gold in pictures of silver.

Word fitly spoken might be a simple thank you, or I appreciate your thoughtfulness or a mere how nice you look. It only takes a few short seconds to voice your love or appreciation to those around you. That compliment you give just might be the very words that make someone's day a little brighter. This world would be a much better place in which to live if we took the time to voice our appreciation to those we encounter daily, whether in our jobs or in

our homes. It takes little time or effort to say something nice to others.

Dear Lord, please help me to remember that everyone is experiencing something in their lives about which they may not even talk. It costs nothing to be kind. Help me to be discerning. Give me the words to say that will bless and help someone along the way. Amen.

As I was with Moses, so I will be with you. I will not fail you or forsake you. Joshua 1:5 KJV.

Life is an uphill battle all the way. Just about the time you think that you have mastered it, something happens to disturb you. Your contentment disappears. What modern people need more than anything is something that will help them remain in the battle and not be defeated. To many, the Christian faith has been the answer because it is Christ who gives us the power to stand up to life. A person does not live long until he realizes one thing. Life is going to deal with hard blows. Life is a series of difficulties. It never runs on an even keel. It does not go our way all the time. We do not always get the things we want. Our God expects us to do the absolute best we can with what we get. For those who adopt this attitude in life, doors of opportunity will constantly be opened. If we are to stand up to life, we must be willing to make the best of what we have and remember that strength can be

ours for the asking. When things turn out wrong, you can feel sorry for yourself and cry that life has given you an unfair deal. Or you can take what comes your way, stand up to it, and make the best of it.

Remember, absolutely nothing in life can defeat you unless you are willing to let it. Philippians 4:13 says I can do all things through Christ, which strengtheneth me. Romans 8:31 says If God be for us. Who can be against us?

Our senior class motto at Fairmont High School was, when you get to the end of your rope, tie a knot and hang on. I will never forget the look on our senior sponsor's face when we told her what we had chosen for our motto. I do not exactly think she approved of the way we had worded it, but that class motto has come to me a lot of times since 12th grade, as I have been reminded to hang on because, after all, that was what the rope was there for anyway, to stand up to life.

Dear Lord, your word empowers me. When I read it, I feel like I can run through a troop and leap over a wall! Thank you for the empowering Word of God that strengthens me so that I can stand up to life. Amen.

MARCH 27
PATIENCE IN MORDERN WORLD

Thou, therefore, endure hardness as a good soldier of Jesus Christ. II Timothy 2:3 KJV.

Patience. A quality that all students, soldiers, athletes, farmers, and even Christians must possess if they are to be successful.

Our present-day lifestyle certainly devalues patience by emphasizing the quick and easy. For example, we are living in the day of instant potatoes, instant coffee, and even complete-course meals. You simply pop it into the microwave and heat and eat. And how about the all-American idea of buying now and paying later for items that we all must have immediately? It used to be a new color TV, but today it is a big screen TV or a new car.

It would be to our advantage to learn early in life that we cannot get everything when we want it.

When my husband was a Senior at Shorter College. it felt like he had been a Senior forever. He was the student, but I was the impatient one. But

187

just as with every worthwhile purpose in life, it takes time to get a degree and to do well while working toward it. Just as a soldier must patiently serve and endure his term of enlistment, an athlete must train and persevere. The same holds true for a farmer. He must plant his crops, tend them, and wait patiently for the harvest.

We too, as Christians, must patiently live our lives through every trouble and through every triumph because, just as Paul assured Timothy, the rewards and the joys of living eternally in heaven will be well worth waiting for.

Dear Lord, please help my impatience. So many times, I want something, and I want it now. Please help me to realize that the best things in life take time. Amen.

HOPE, AN ETERNAL REALITY

For the hope which is laid up for you in heaven...
Colossians 1:5 KJV.

The goal of this hope referred to in the above verse is yet to come. Lying ahead in the future and far away in heaven; however, hope itself is a present reality, something we can now possess and experience.

There is an old saying, "While there is life, there's hope." But is it not equally true to say while there is hope, there is life? Both hopefulness and the opposite, hopelessness, affect the mind greatly. Find a person hopeful about his future, and you will find a heart that is vivacious and buoyant. Find a person who feels hopeless about the future, and you will find a picture of present misery. Above all, our Christian hope is the loveliest and loftiest, and it should have a corresponding effect on us. With such hope of high destiny, our spirit should soar.

The Apostle John said: "When He (speaking of Christ} shall appear, we shall be like him, for we shall see him as he is, and every man that hath this hope set upon him purifies himself even as he (Christ) is pure." John 3: 2-3 KJV. If we are going to be like Him, then surely, we must strive to be like Him now in character.

Our hope should be a fountain of joyous effort as we toil to win our loved ones to Christ. Can you imagine what joy we will surely encounter when we see those in heaven we have introduced to the Savior?

This hope should keep us continuously laboring without present reward. The verse says the hope, which is laid up for you in heaven, laid up, stored securely away, where no one can break in and steal it. To hear the Savior say, well done, my child, enter the presence and the joy of the Lord, will be a more than sufficient reward for all our earthly toils.

Dear Lord, I praise You for making provision for your children to have hope in the present and forever in eternity to come. Amen.

MARCH 29
PRESS ON

Our heart is not turned back, neither have our steps declined from thy way. Psalm 44:18 KJV.

Have you ever set out to accomplish a task, and it seemed utterly impossible? Have you ever wanted to give up, admit defeat, and plain call it quits? The other day, I was in that mood.

I decided to take a break from my frustration and go to the post office. I soon realized what a sense of humor God has. I walked into the post office and took my place in line. There was a sign on the wall that said: "Consider the postage stamp, my child. It secures success through its ability to stick to one thing till it gets there.

After a good chuckle, I purchased my stamps, went for an ice cream, drove home, and completed my unpleasant task.

Dear Lord, I realized today that You do not always choose to speak to us through scripture. You are God, and you can get your message across to your children any way you choose, even through a comical statement. You did not chastise but You made me laugh while teaching me a lesson on the importance of stickability until the task is finished. Amen.

MARCH 30
GO FORWARD

Speak unto the children of Israel that they go forward. Exodus 14:15 KJV.

And when Pharoah drew nigh, the children of Israel lifted their eyes, and behold, the Egyptians marched after them. The children of Israel cried out unto the Lord, and they said unto Moses, because there were no graves in Egypt. "Hast, thou taken us away to die in the wilderness? Wherefore hast thou dealt thus with us to carry us forth out of Egypt? Is not this the word that we did tell thee in Egypt, saying, let us alone, that we may serve the Egyptians? Or it had been better for us to serve the Egyptians than that we should die in the wilderness."

And Moses said unto the people, "Fear ye not, stand still, and see the salvation of the Lord, which he will show to you this day. For the Egyptians whom ye have seen today, ye shall see them no more. Forever, the Lord shall fight for you, and you shall hold your peace." Exodus 14:10-14 KJV.

Often in our lives, obedience to God means marching on, whether we feel like it or not. Moses told the people to stand still and see the salvation of The Lord, that is, to watch passively while the Lord did the work. But the Lord cancelled such an order. He told them there was something that they must do. Go forward! Often, it is our own assertiveness in His name that brings deliverance and real victory.

Dear Lord, you have all power. You are Omnipotent. You can do all things. But often, you desire that I have a part in my own miracle. When that time comes, may I be obedient to your command. Amen.

MARCH 31
CONSIDER JOB

And there was a man in the land of Uz, whose name was Job; and that man was perfect and upright, and one that feared God, and eschewed evil. Job 1:1 KJV.

And the Lord said unto Satan, from whence comest thou? And Satan answered the Lord, and said, from going to and fro in the earth, and from walking up and down in it. And the Lord said unto Satan, Hast thou considered my servant Job, that there is none like him in the earth, a perfect and an upright man one that feareth God, and esheweth evil? And still, he holdeth fast His integrity, although thou movest me against him, to destroy him without cause. Job 2:2-3 KJV.

God loved and recognized Job because of his integrity. Job, being upright, honorable, honest, single-minded, wholesome, conscientious, and virtuous, recognized God as his only necessity in life. People today say no man can live as Job, but how much greater would the blessings of God and

the impact of our lives on the world be if we had such integrity?

Dear Lord, please mold me and make me a woman of integrity, upright, honorable, honest, single-minded, wholesome, conscientious, and virtuous. Amen.

APRIL

April 1
Marriage Is An Isosceles Triangle

The Lord our God will we serve, and his voice will we obey. Joshua 24:24 KJV.

Doctor Charles W Conn, President of Lee College, now Lee University in Cleveland, TN, gave an illustration once in a chapel service. I will always remember Doctor Conn speaking about choosing a marriage partner and the importance of seeking the Lord's will for the right one. Then, once you find that special person together, establish and maintain a Christian home.

Doctor Conn compared the marriage union to an isosceles triangle, with the couple forming the base and God at the top. He said as the couple each moved up and got closer to God, they became closer and closer together until the two, along with God, became one. I will never forget Doctor Conn and his illustration, which is so simple yet so beautifully presented. He will never know what an impression he had on the young lives present that night.

When you talk about love, everyone listens because it is a subject that interests us all. Did you know God is the author, creator, and initiator of this whole idea called love? That is right. We find in I John 4:7-8 KJV that everyone that loveth is born of God, for God is love. It just makes a lot of sense to put God first in your marriage and in your home because He Is the authority on the subject. With God in a home, elaborate or common, whichever the furnishings may be, it is transformed into a place of beauty, sweetness, splendor, and grace. The happiness and the blessings of a Christian home could never be numbered. A happy family is but an earlier heaven.

Dear Lord Jesus, I can never praise you enough for the Christian home and spouse that You have

blessed me with. May we always serve, obey, and make You the center of our home. Amen.

April 2
Two Shal Become One

For this cause shall a man leave his father and mother, and shall be joined unto his wife, and they two shall be one flesh. Ephesians 5:31 KJV.

Marriage is one of the greatest steps in life that two people can ever take. It should not be taken lightly.

Just what does the Bible say about marriage? As the biblical story of creation unfolds, we read in Genesis 1:27,31 that God created man in his own image. In the image of God, he created them, male and female. God saw all that he had made, and behold, it was incredibly good. Chapter two of Genesis tells us that God wanted to provide proper companionship for man, so God created woman. God saw that this creation was good. God planned marriage. In chapter two of John, we read of the wedding feast in Cana of Galilee. Jesus performed his first miracle there when helping the host in an embarrassing situation. His presence and helpfulness placed his stamp of approval on

marriage. This further demonstrates God's blessing upon marriage. The New Testament is filled with teachings pertaining to the honor of marriage. One of them is found in Hebrews 13:4, which states very plainly Marriage is honorable in all and the bed undefiled, but whoremongers and adulterers God will judge.

Since marriage is holy and blessed by God, what should your attitude be? Should the vows be taken lightly? Do you really love each other? Do your marriage plans include forever thoughts? Why not pray together as a couple about your wedding plans? Believe me, if marriage was God's idea, and it was, then He certainly is concerned. God himself spoke the nuptial asked to Adam and Eve in the Garden of Eden, while heavenly hosts witnessed the beautiful scene of the first wedding ever to take place. Jesus honored its celebration by His presence at the wedding of Cana of Galilee. He chose its beautiful relations as the model for the union between himself and his church.

The Apostle Paul declared it to be honorable in all and tells the husband to love his wife even as Christ loved the church and gave himself for it, and the wife to be faithful to her husband even as the Church is obedient to Christ, so it is ordered that a man shall leave his father and mother and cleave unto his wife, and the two shall become one, one in flesh, one in thought and intent, and one in hope in all the concerns of this earthly life.

Dear Heavenly Father, you certainly have a wonderful plan for a man and a woman to enter holy matrimony and enjoy each other while serving you together. Please help us to always follow and obey you in our marriage. Amen.

APRIL 3
COUPLE FACING PARENTHOOD

This is my commandment, that ye love one another, as I have loved you. These things have I spoken unto you, that my joy might remain in you, and that your joy might be full. John 15:11-12 KJV.

As a young couple faces parenthood for the first time, there is something especially important that they should discuss and prepare in advance. It is their marriage and love life with children.

Marriage and parenthood individually are different enough, but together, if not planned out and prayed about, they can be overwhelming.

Always make it a point to plan to take loving care of each other as a couple. Remember to be kind, thoughtful, and understanding. Discuss things. Both of you are facing this new role. Remember, you are in this together, as husband and wife, mother and father. This is an incredibly special time. If you read the word of God, pray, and make special time for each other, you will build a strong marriage, become good parents, and get closer to God.

Dear Lord, becoming a new parent is a big responsibility. Balancing a thriving marriage with new parenting obligations is a formidable task. But with your help, we can do all these things. We ask your blessings, God, on our home, our marriage, and our new family. Amen.

But the wisdom that is from above is first pure, then peaceable, gentle, and easy to be entreated, full of mercy and good truths, without partiality and without hypocrisy. James 3:1 KJV.

I am so nervous, not about having a baby, but about becoming a mother. Not just a mother, but a good one. I know how to change diapers and burp a baby. But what about all the challenges I will face in the coming months and years? When the questions come, will I have the answers to properly care for and guide my little one? Where will this wisdom and discernment come from?

This child will come to us as a pure, empty vessel to be filled. Everything that is dropped into this child will become a part of its life for all eternity. What a responsibility.

Then, in the quiet of the night, I hear God whisper peace and calm assurance. You have a source. A source that is pure, full of quiet gentleness, peace, loving, courteous, full of mercy,

sincere, wholehearted, and direct. What better wisdom is there?

Dear Lord, thank you for the wisdom in your word. Thank you for being the source of that wisdom. I am no longer afraid. I am not alone. As I open the door of motherhood, I know that the gentle whisper of your divine and all-discerning wisdom is there for me to hear if I will but listen. Amen.

GOD KNOWS HOW WE FEEL

I sought the Lord, and he answered me and delivered me from all my fears. Psalm 34:4 KJV.

What is so very wonderful about God and His Word is that He knows exactly how we feel. Every human fear and emotion that we experience, He is aware. He gives just the right prescription to cure our fears and doubts. In His holy Word, I sought the Lord, and He answered me and delivered me from all my fears. They looked to Him and were lightened. And their faces were not ashamed. Psalm 34:4-5 KJV. We live within the shadow of the Almighty, sheltered by the God who is above all gods. This I declare that He alone is my refuge, my place of safety. He is my God, and I am trusting Him. He will shield you with his wings. They will deliver you. His faithful promises are your armor. Now, you do not need to be afraid of the dark anymore, nor fear of the dangers of the day, for He orders the angels to protect you. Wherever you go, they will steady you with their hands to keep you

from stumbling. Psalm 91:1-2,4-5,11-12 KJV. Fear not, for I am with you. Do not be dismayed; I am your God. I will strengthen you; I will help you; I will uphold you with my victorious right hand. I am holding you with your right hand. I am the Lord your God, And I say to you, do not be afraid. I am here to help you. Psalm 41:10,13 KJV. For God hath not given us the spirit of fear, but of power and of love, and of a sound mind. II Timothy 1:7 KJV.

Lord, as I approach my time of natural childbirth, I have fears and apprehensions of the unknown that lie ahead of me. I have prepared myself for this moment the best I can, but I ask you to take complete control where my human weakness ends, and your strength and courage begin. May I feel the tenderness of your love as its warmth surrounds me in my hour of need. Amen.

APRIL 6
THE JOY OF BIRTH

*A woman when she is in travail hath sorrow,
because her hour is come; but as soon as she is
delivered of the child, she remembereth no more the
anguish, for joy that a man is born into the world.
John 16:21 KJV.*

I woke up to a beautiful, sunshiny day feeling wonderful and full of joy, although I had awakened in the middle of the night, having back pain and contractions. Just when I went to wake my husband to go to the hospital, the contractions stopped. I was so mentally ready to have this baby. I went downstairs and mopped the kitchen to see if the contractions would begin again. But there were no contractions, so I went back to bed and snuggled close to my husband until the alarm went off. The alarm sounded at 6:30 AM. My husband and I had oatmeal and fruit that morning for breakfast and he went to work, and I showered and headed to Dalton for an OBGYN appointment. There Doctor Roger Eidson told me that I was dilating and could possibly have this baby this weekend. I came home and rested for a while, then began getting ready for our usual Friday night date.

Just as my husband came home, I got up to greet him and my water broke. So, we headed to Hamilton Memorial Hospital and Tiffany LaRanda made her debut at 12:04 AM. It was an easy delivery, and my husband and I were thrilled beyond measure for this bundle of joy that God had blessed us with.

Dear Lord, thank you so much for blessing us with this precious baby girl. We could never praise you enough. She is going to be such a bundle of joy, a beautiful product of our love. You are so good to us. Amen.

WELCOME TO GOD'S WORLD

The just man walketh in his integrity. His children are blessed after him. Proverbs 20:7 KJV.

Hey Buddy,

You have been an integral part of your mommy now for almost nine months. Not so much with me, but I have heard your heartbeat in the doctor's office and felt your strong kick against her belly, under her breast. I cannot wait to toss a football with you. And judging by the strength of your jabs against her side, we may just have ourselves a kicker. And then there will be ball practices and Braves baseball games to attend together with Granddaddy and me, camping trips and so much more. I cannot wait to go on fishing trips. You will experience the beauty of God's creation for the first time. What a treat your first trip to the ocean will be as you play and splash in the water. Experiencing new sights and sounds of the mountains and ocean for the first time will be impressive.

God's beautiful world awaits you, and I am looking forward to being your guide and to explore and learn together. I already love you so much and I am looking forward to having another male in our home. Boys rule! All of God's creation awaits you, a journey of discovery in a brand-new world. A world that can be beautiful, exciting, and full of adventure. So, my little one, as your mommy and I love and parent you, we will be looking to our Heavenly Father to guide our steps in this journey. Then, you will reach your destiny in life, bringing glory to Him and joy to us and all humanity. Love, Daddy

Dear Heavenly Father, as you have chosen us to be the parents of this precious boy, we realize the grave responsibility you have placed on us to love, nurture, and train this little one to achieve his divine purpose in you. We sincerely ask for your love,

guidance, strength, wisdom, and patience as we endeavor this serious but joyous task. Amen.

THE PRESENCE OF GOD

Did not I fill heaven and earth? Saith the Lord.
Jeremiah 23:24 KJV.

I saw God today in the sun rise's golden hue as a new day dawned.

I saw God today as a little squirrel sat undisturbed in the cool, quiet calm of early morning.

I saw God today reflected in the shiny leaves of dew-covered shrubs.

I saw God today in the sweet, melodious courtship of two cardinals as they played in the gazebo.

I saw God today in the babel of a creek twisting and turning through a sunny pasture.

I heard God today in the giggles and the laughter of my child as she played and ran barefoot in the backyard.

I heard God today in the voice of the almighty thunder across the sky.

I felt God today as I touched the velvety petals of a pink rose.

I felt God today as a springtime breeze blew against my face.

I felt God today in the warm handclasp of my husband as we said grace before a meal.

I felt God today as I ran my fingers through the blond tousled curls of my two-year-old son.

Vividly, God can be seen, heard, and felt in the simple everyday things of life. How rich and meaningful our lives can be when we develop an ever-increasing sensitivity to the presence of God. So why wait until Sunday morning to be reminded of God's omnipresence? God is everywhere to those who are aware.

Dear God, you are everywhere. You know everything your children go through. There is nothing that touches us that ever catches you off guard. Please help us to be aware of your presence all around us and to commune with you as we go through our daily lives. Amen.

THE JOY OF MOTHERHOOD

Her children arise up and call her blessed; Her husband also, and he praiseth her. Proverbs 31:28 KJV.

An unknown author once said God knew He could not be everywhere, so he made mothers. We all know God is omnipresent, but what a tribute to moms. God has a purpose for every child that was born into this world. Each individual little one is a radiant possibility.

What a responsibility God has placed on the shoulders of each mother. But on the other hand, what an opportunity. God would not have given you that little bundle from heaven to mother and to care for if he did not think you were capable of being his heavenly link.

What a privilege being a mother is. Proverbs 22:6 KJV instructs to train up a child in the way he should go, and when he is old, he will not depart from it. We should have more Christian mothers today who would instruct their children about God and take the time to train them and bring them up in the fear and the admonition of the Lord. Not only would our homes, our churches, and our schools prosper from it, but our country would reap the benefits. So yes, being a mother is certainly a formidable responsibility, but oh, what a calling.

Dear Lord, I truly feel that being a mother is one of the greatest callings a woman can receive. Therefore, I pray you will help me to treat it with due respect, responsibility, and effort. Amen.

A MOTHER'S LOVE

She openeth her mouth with wisdom; and in her tongue is the law of kindness. Proverbs 21:26 KJV.

It has been said that a mother's love is second only to the love of God, so it just makes sense that God would choose a mother as the vessel he uses to give each of us the gift of life. Here is my version of Mother as seen from the eyes of a teenage daughter. Written and dedicated especially to my mom, Mrs. Jewell Watson, and every other mother who has a daughter.

A mother is the one who spends hours on end hoping, dreaming, and making plans for you even before you are born.

A mother is the one who teaches you to say, Dada, first so Daddy's feelings will not be hurt.

A mother is the one who dresses her daughter in lace and frills and goes all out to show you off, especially on Sunday morning.

A mother is the first person in life that a daughter tries to imitate. First, she tries to play mommy with her dolls and then she pretends she is cooking like her mother. It is not long until she finds her way into Mommy's closet and puts on her dresses and high-heel shoes. She can often be seen dragging a much too large pocketbook across the floor with blush and powder smeared from one cheek to the other. All because she wants to be just like Mommy.

A mother is the one who spends endless hours answering the questions of her inquisitive preschooler.

A mother is the one who introduces you to the ABCs 123s and your first day of school.

A mother is the one who gets up every hour of the night to check your temperature and give you Creamulsion cough syrup for children.

A mother is the one who nurses you through skinned knees, chicken pox, measles, and broken hearts.

222

A mother is the one who stretches dollars and sacrifices often so that her daughter can have nicer clothes and other opportunities in life that she did not have.

A mother is the one you can always count on to come through when you need a new outfit, a special costume for school play, or a new prom dress.

A mother's talents are unlimited, especially in the kitchen when there is a birthday, holiday, or other special occasion.

A mother is the one who teaches her daughter important things, such as how to make biscuits or cut out and sew a new dress.

A mother is the one who tells her daughter the facts of life and teaches her the importance of keeping herself pure so that she will not only have the respect of others but, most importantly, self-respect.

A mother is the one who comforts, protects, and tries to shield her daughter from all harm and hurt in life and, in the process, teaches and prepares her for life's responsibilities.

A mother is the one who softens up your father, so he will reconsider when you ask permission to go someplace.

A mother is the one you miss the most when you are away at college, your date is downstairs waiting, and your button pops off.

A mother is the one who cries when you graduate, cries when you go off to college, and who really cries when you announce your engagement.

A mother is the one who, even though she loves him dearly, tells her son-in-law-to-be, you better love her dearly and take good care of her because she will always be my baby!

Dear Heavenly Father, I thank you so much for choosing my mother, especially for me. What a precious blessing she was. I miss her, but I know I will see her soon in Heaven, never to be separated again. Amen.

APRIL 11
SPECIAL QUALITY TIME

The Lord is the portion of mine inheritance and of my cup: Thou maintainest my lot. Psalm 16:5 KJV.

Our new alarm clock sounds off at precisely 2:00 AM. A hungry little howl grows louder and louder. I slide through the grogginess of a sound sleep, gradually becoming aware that I must exchange this heavenly warm bed for the cold, the fate of a middle-of-the-night feeding. I groan and shiver and grope for my slippers. It seems I can never find them in the dark. By the time I reach the nursery, I am wide awake and looking forward to a blessed time of quietness with my hungry little Bundle of Love. A time of deep thought and quiet devotion with just the Lord, my child, and me. With such full and busy days, my spirit yearns for the peace and the quiet of the small hours of the morning. It is a time of renewal with spiritual food for the strength I need to face the day. Just as my child is renewed physically by the warm nourishment she receives from my body, I am

reminded that not only mothers but everyone, in general, needs a special quiet time to get alone with the Lord and commune with Him for renewal for the day's tasks that lie ahead. He will fill you if you ask.

Dear Lord, thank you for this special time with you and my precious baby girl. I pray you will continue to bless her and help her to grow and develop healthy. She is such a precious blessing. I pray for your continued healing and strength in my body as well. Help me to be rejuvenated not only physically but mentally, emotionally, and spiritually. Amen.

APRIL 12
STORMS OF LIFE

Fear ye not, stand still, and see the salvation of the Lord, which he will shew to you today. Exodus 14:13 KJV.

Many times, in the life of a Christian, the going gets tough, but an unknown author once said that when the going gets tough, the tough get going. Often, a lot of distance is covered, and a lot of time is made when we only remain steadfast and stand still in the faith that He is God and He is in control. There are several things to remember when we face the storms of life. I am a child of God. God has all things under control. God brought me to this place. He will keep me in the storm. He will teach me the lesson He wants me to learn through this experience. He is praying for me in the storm that my faith fails not. He will bring me out in His own time and in His own way with renewed vigor and a

deeper knowledge of him. So, I shall stand still and be steadfast.

.Dear Lord, there are many storms that come into our lives. Please give me the wisdom and knowledge to not panic because you are in control. Help me to know you will keep me and help me learn what you want me to know if I will only stand strong. Amen.

APRIL 13
WORRY LESS AND LISTEN MORE

STo everything there is a season, and a time to every purpose under the heaven: Ecclesiastes 3:1 KJV.

Someone asked me recently, if I could relive my life, would I do anything differently? My answer to that was yes indeed!

If I could have a remake of my life. I would worry less and listen more.

I would live in the present and not think so much of the future.

I would order more ice cream and less yogurt.

I would take more walks and do less laundry.

I would drive with my car windows down on a beautiful day and care less about my wind-blown hair.

I would sit with my kids cross-legged on the grass and not worry about grass stains.

When my husband came home in an amorous mood, I would give him my full attention and get off the phone with my best friend.

I would use the good dishes and linens and burn the beautiful candles instead of saving them for a more special occasion.

I would invite guests over more often instead of worrying about the stains on the carpet.

When pregnant, instead of dreading the next nine months, I would enjoy almost every minute, realizing that might be my last chance to assist God in creating a miracle.

Dear Lord, we cannot go back and make a retake of our lives. From this day forward I sincerely ask that you help me to be mindful of making the most of my life. I pray for assistance in living in the present and less in the past and future. Amen.

For every beast of the forest is mine, and the cattle upon a thousand hills. Psalm 50:10 KJV.

Because the Bible tells us that it is easier, not impossible, for a camel to go through the eye of a needle than for a rich man to enter the gates of heaven, many people believe that it is impossible for the rich to go to heaven. They think it is impossible to be prosperous in this life and still be a dedicated Christian. But the truth is quite the contrary. God wills that we prosper.

III John 2 KJV says, "Beloved, I wish above all things that thou mayest prosper and be in health, even as thy soul prospereth." The verse literally tells us that not only does God want us to be blessed spiritually, but also financially, mentally, and physically. God promises many times over that he, wills for us to prosper and be in health even as our soul prospers. The verse clearly tells us that not only does God want us to be blessed spiritually, but also financially, mentally, and physically. God

promises many times over that he will prosper the Christian if he keeps and obeys the Word of God and if the Christian seeks the Lord through prayer and searching of the scriptures. Deuteronomy 29:9 KJV says, "To keep therefore the words of this covenant, and do them, that you may prosper in all that you do." Joshua 1:8 KJV states, "This book of the law shall not depart out of my mouth, but thou shalt meditate therein day and night, that thou mayest desire to do according to all that is written therein, for then thou shalt make thy way prosperous, and then thou shalt have good success." Psalm 123:33 KJV says, "His delight is in the law of the Lord, and in his law doth he meditate day and night, and he shall be like a tree planted by the rivers of water that bringeth forth his fruit in his season, his leaf also shall not wither, and whatsoever he doeth shall prosper." II Chronicles 28:5 KJV says, "If he sought the Lord, God made him to prosper." The comparison of a rich man entering the gates of heaven to a camel going through the eyes of a needle is better understood in the 6th chapter of the book of I Timothy. Here, the Bible tells us that the love of money, the love of it and not the money itself, is the root of all evil. I Timothy 6:1 KJV says, "Because often it causes a good moral man or even a dedicated Christian to fail and go astray. Often, people get dollar marks in their eyes and do anything to get more money, no matter how sinful or immoral." I Timothy 6:2 KJV warns against this. "While some coveted after they have erred from the faith and pierced themselves through with many sorrows." This chapter further instructs. "O man of God, flee these things and follow righteousness, godliness, faith, love, patience, and meekness." Verse 11 says, "To fight the good fight of faith, lay hold on eternal life, wherein to thou art also called, and has professed a good profession before many witnesses." Verses 12,17-19. The same chapter gives a special warning to the Christians whom God has prospered. With added privileges always come added responsibilities. Charge them that are rich in this world, that they are not high minded nor trust in uncertain riches, but in the living God. Who giveth us richly all things to enjoy. That they do good, that they are rich in good works ready to distribute. In other words, pay your tithes and offerings. Willing to communicate, laying up in store for themselves a good foundation against the time to come that they may lay hold on eternal life. What a privilege being a Christian affords. If we obey God's word and seek him, then prosperity will be ours to enjoy in this life, plus treasure untold, the incomprehensible by this world's standards. In our eternal life to come, the true children of God that stand faithful to the end have the best of both the here and now and in their eternal life to come. After all, what more can you expect? Our Heavenly Father owns it all.

Dear Lord Jesus, please help me to always appreciate my financial blessings and be a good steward of what you give me. Help me to give willingly of my tithes and offerings. It would be wonderful to be able to be a pipeline of blessings to others, helping in whatever capacity was needed. Amen.

For my yoke is easy, and my burden is light.
Matthew 11:30 KJV.

Pastor Edward Davenport delivered a message about a man who was attempting to carry a heavy-laden basket. His son offered to help him carry the load. The father, knowing that his son's willingness to help was much greater than his ability, cut a long stick and placed it through the handle of the basket so that the end toward himself was noticeably short while the end toward the small boy was three or four times as long. Each took hold of his end of the stick, and the basket was lifted and easily carried. The son, while feeling like he had helped his father greatly, was sharing the burden with the father but found his work bearably easy and light because his father assumed the heavy end of the stick.

This story reminds me of the Christian bearing the yoke with Christ. The Lord always sees to it that the burden laid on us is light while He carries the heavy part of the load. The Bible confirms it in Matthew 11:29 KJV where the Lord gave us the following invitation. "Come unto me, all ye that are labor, that labor, and are heavy laden, and I will give you rest. Take my yoke upon you, and learn of me, for I am meek and lowly in heart, and you shall find rest for your souls."

Dear Lord, I am so thankful I can come to you when I am tired and weary and find rest. I can come to you with all the cares of my world, and you will help me bear them. You are a kind, loving, wonderful Father. I love you so much! Amen.

APRIL 16
GIVE TIME TO OTHERS

Give, and it shall be given unto you good measure. Pressed down, and shaken together, and running over shall men give unto your bosom. For with the same measure that you meet withal, it shall be measured to you again. Luke 6:38 KJV.

I used to think that verses of scripture referred to giving your tithes and offerings and, in turn, being blessed by God financially and materially. But there is another form of giving, that of giving of ourselves, our time, and our love. While it is true that finances are necessary to carry on God's work, just as in any other type of business, what the world needs the most today is people who care enough to give of themselves. There are people everywhere who may be surrounded by crowds of people. Yet they are lonely. They are dying for love and attention. Loneliness can be one of the worst types of sickness because it stems from the heart. It causes depression and a feeling of unworthiness, which in turn produces fatigue and lethargy. It can develop into a physical ailment in children, especially. Even in some adults, you find that they complain of being sick because of lack of attention. It has been proven that if this feeling of unworthiness, loneliness, and lack of love goes on for a period, a physical element may develop with real symptoms being present. If we only realize the importance of showing our love and making ourselves available to those who really need our time and our love, not only would their world be brighter, but so would ours. When you give away love, the returns are unlimited. Not only are you loved by the one you gave to, but you developed self-respect and a sense of worthiness that you never realized before. Suddenly, your life takes on a new meaning.

A poem I committed to memory in grade school by Emily Dickinson says: "If I can stop one heart from breaking, I shall not live in vain. If I can ease one's life, the aching, or cool one pain, or help one feigning robin unto his nest again, I shall not have lived in vain."

Dear Lord, I pray that you will help me to give of myself to you and in turn, be a blessing to those whose path I may cross. There are a lot of hurt people in this world. I truly desire to be your hand extended. Amen.

THE CROSS, THE SUPREME EXPRESSION OF LOVE

Herein is love. He loved us and sent his son to be the propitiation for our sins. I John 4:10 KJV.

The strength of humans or demons could not have held him there against his will. He was the Son of God, and he possessed the power to call down legions of angels to destroy the world and set him free at his command. It was not iron spikes but love that held Jesus on the cross. One died for all. What love! The Bible talks about it but never defines it. All the writers in the world could not put together a composition that could clearly state the power and the effect of that love. One must experience it personally to know it in all its fullness. One died for all. I was one of them. He died for me. The sin penalty of all humanity was laid upon him on that cross, all the way back to the beginning of time in the Garden of Eden, up to the final sin to be committed before the end of time. My sin and all its immensity were anticipated on that cross. When I think of how my sins somehow helped to nail him to that cross, and when I think of how my sins somehow added weight to His suffering, I am melted and broken. He Loved me, He died for me. It is said that no matter how far away you are from the ocean, if you hold a seashell to your ear, you can hear the waves. So, on the cross we can hear the mighty depth of Divine Love, far bigger than man's biggest sins. Herein is love.

Dear Lord Jesus, I could never do enough to prove my love for you. So, I am going to live for you because you died for me. Amen.

APRIL 18
GOD'S PLAN AT CALVARY

When Jesus therefore had received the vinegar, he said, it is finished: and he bowed his head and gave up the ghost. John 19:30 KJV.

The Word of God is the only thing I know that can say it is finished in completeness. A fragmentary plan marks the work of all others. The author lays down his pen and crumples up the rough draft. The artist lays down his brush and palette. Many souls have expired, saying if only I had finished the task, I set out to accomplish. Our Lord's last cry from the cross- it is finished.

Just what did he mean by these three words? Some people think that he meant that God's plan of salvation for humanity was completed and finished on the cross of Calvary. Was there some additional deed that he had finished? Jesus's whole life from the manger to the cross had been an ordeal. He was God's Son, a deity, yet human. Christ was tempted in all things such as are common to you and me and so much more, yet He stood true.

243

How many of us would be man or woman enough to stand the tests that Christ went through? He was tempted, scourged, beaten. But when He was nailed to the cross, it was finished. The battle over self-had been won, and he was the victor. His battle over sin and Satan was finished. Also, Satan had tempted him to surrender the fight by promising to give him the entire world. But Jesus knew that it all belonged to the Heavenly Father anyway. And Satan was defeated when Christ began quoting him the scripture. When man physically taunted and abused Jesus he refused to retaliate but responded truly in love. Jesus also conquered death when he died on the cross and arose again on the third day. He proved to the world that he was truly the Son of God, the complete victor over self, sin, Satan, and even death. His life from the manger to the cross was a mission. And he fulfilled it to the greatest extent. But Jesus, without elaboration and in his own humble way, merely said it is finished.

Dear Lord Jesus, I praise you for being willing to give up your heavenly home to come to this wicked world and be treated worse than an animal. You could have called in warrior angels at any point, but you chose to complete horrific, deplorable tasks to finish the plan of salvation. We will forever be eternally grateful! Amen.

He is not here: for he is risen, as he said. Come see the place where the Lord lay. Matthew 28:6 KJV.

.He is risen. He lives. Thanks be to God. There is victory; there is power in the all-triumphant Savior. In the midst of a world predominantly blinded by Satan, tarnished by sin, and amid the crash of armies and the crash of wrecked hopes and dreams and plans, and in spite of man's failures within himself, there is hope because of the cross of Calvary, because of God's great love for fallen man, and because Jesus was willing to bear the shame and pay the price for you and me and in our stead, there is hope. Jesus bled, He died, he was buried, he arose, and he lives again. And because he lives, all fear has vanished. Because of that first Easter morning and the message behind it, I have hope. Hope for tomorrow. Courage to face each day with joy and victory in my life. Because he lives. If you feel hopeless facing the future or fearful of what another day may bring forth, why not invite Jesus to come into your heart right now? The all-triumphant Savior is waiting to give you a new life and new hope.

Dear Lord Jesus, I praise you for the hope that we now have because you died, you arose, and you live today. Victory is forever ours! Amen.

APRIL 20
GOD NEVER FAILS

The just Lord is in the midst thereof; he will not do iniquity: every morning doth he bring his judgment to light, he faileth not. Zephaniah 3:5KJV

How do I know? The Bible tells me so. If we adults could only hold on to that innocent child-like faith. How much simpler and more blessed our lives would be. A child's view of God is if he said it, I believe it, and that settles it. No wonder God used David, a mere sibling of a boy, to kill the giant. He knew he could depend on a child's faith to get the job done.

Pastor Edward Davenport told a story once, and as silly as it may seem, so many of us fall into the very same category when it comes to believing and grasping what God has for us. The story tells how a bitter wintry night a man known for his intelligence approached a house. Inside, all was bright and cheerful. A warm, cozy fire crackled invitingly in the fireplace. The man took the key out of the mailbox where he had been told it would be found. He looked

at the key, and he rubbed his fingers across it. This is a very strange shape for a key, he said to himself. How could this weird little piece of metal open that huge carved door and let me inside the house? He looked at the keyhole. This is hard to understand, he muttered. Many others said they had used this. But they were not as intelligent as I am. I must reason this out, so he said. I will not try to unlock that door with this key. I do not understand how this simple device could turn a complicated lock. Until I can fully understand how this mechanism works, I shall refuse to insult my intelligence by even trying to use it. And he turned back into the cold, dark night, only to perish. This man, with all his intelligence, turned out to be a fool.

The Bible says, "The natural man receiveth not the things of the Spirit of God, for they are foolishness unto him. I Corinthians 2:14 KJV. Jesus once said, if thou canst believe, all things are possible to him that believeth. No matter what age, all it takes is a simple child-like faith to receive the best God has to offer. What are the important things in your life that you would have Him do for you? Has faith begun to fail? Has the heart been looking at circumstances instead of God? Think again. If your answer seems unduly delayed, it is not through any collapse of His power. Perhaps faith is being evaluated for the sake of spiritual profit and progress. Zephaniah 3:5 says, "He faileth not. Now take him at his word."

Dear Lord Jesus, please help me to have the simple child-like faith to take you at your word, believe what it says, and not try to analyze it. Amen.

COURAGE DURING DIRE CIRCUMSTANCES

Have not I commanded thee? Be strong and of a good courage; be not afraid, neither be thou dismayed: for the Lord, thy God is with thee whithersoever thou goest. Joshua 1:9 KJV.

You do not have to remember any numbers. All you need to know is one letter, C. You can dial for courage when the doctor's report says the cancer is malignant, when your husband or wife leaves you, or when you lose a loved one in death. You can dial C for courage. C stands for Christ. All you need to do is call upon Him, and courage that overpowers and overwhelms will come to you if you commit the matter to Him. God is listening. And he always gets our message. He knows just how and what to send in time of need. God has given us a courageous spirit and a conquering spirit, the Spirit of the Lord. We can be confident even during dire circumstances and situations. The devil tries, at times, to paralyze us with fear. And when you are fearful you cannot have faith, but that is when real courage is needed, the courage it takes to put the devil in his place and take your rightful stand. As a child of God, once you take your position, then he has no choice but to flee. Proverbs 28:1 KJV. The wicked flee when no man pursueth, but the righteous are bold as a lion.

What is courage anyway? Courage is one of those terms that is easier to give an example of than to define in words. We can all understand what courage is when we see a soldier fighting for our freedom as he heads for the front line. We can understand courage when we see a firefighter battling flames and smoke to save a life. We can understand courage when we see a police officer racing after an alleged armed criminal.

But there are many, many other levels of courage than those mentioned above. There is the courage of caring and loving, the courage of forgiving, the courage of starting over again after a failure, and the courage of commitment.

We can face today with courage, real courage. The feeling of adequacy to meet any challenge in any problem. We can feel God's power running through us. Philippians 4:13 KJV says, "I can do all things through Christ who strengtheneth me. We face a lot of situations in life and many trying times, but we have the power in the name of the Lord to become victorious.

I attended a youth rally once where two-star football players from the University of Georgia were giving their testimonies. They were both dedicated Christians, and one of the young men made a statement that his success throughout the years was because of the Lord. He said, I just get up every morning, and I say, "well Lord, there is nothing this day that you and I together cannot tackle." Watch ye stand fast. Stand firm in faith. Be strong. Corinthians 16:13 KJV.

April 22
Putting Together The Puzzle

The steps of a good man are ordered by the Lord:
And he delighteth in his way. Psalm 37:23 KJV.

It was Friday evening, and all day, I had been looking forward to an evening of rest and relaxation. It had been a very hectic week, and I was exhausted. Various engagements and activities had taken up much of our time, and with illness in our family, we had made several trips back and forth to the hospital in another town.

My husband had gone out to get our dinner, so after putting a few dishes into the dishwasher, I was ready to fall in front of the TV and relax for the rest of the evening.

I could not relax. I had so many things on my mind. I was restless and simply could not unwind.

Also, I happened to be one of those people who have mixed feelings about the value of a TV set. I have a tough time watching TV without feeling guilty about wasting valuable time, especially with all the foolishness that bombards the sets today.

Since I was tired, I did not want to balance the checkbook or do anything creative that required much physical or mental strength. So, I lay there for a few minutes and remembered a five-hundred-piece jigsaw puzzle we had started putting together previously. I went to the closet and took down the puzzle, and as I opened the box, I felt overwhelmed by all the pieces. As I stared at them for a minute, the Lord began to speak to my heart.

You may ask, does God talk to people through everyday things such as a puzzle? Well, certainly, He does. God will speak to you in many ways if you listen.

Those pieces reminded me of the lives of so many people who do not know Christ, in his power to put the pieces back together again, and then the rest of us who do know Him still often try to fit the pieces of our lives together without his help or his direction. It simply makes no sense to carry around your problems, the problems of your family or friends, and the problems of the entire world on your shoulders, no matter how strong a Christian you are. You may be a pastor or a deacon, or you may be head of the whole denomination, but you are still not strong enough to carry it all by yourself.

Cares of life will get you down. You will become discouraged and depressed and get insomnia and then ulcers if you try to carry them within yourself. Jesus said, "Come unto me all ye that labor and are heavy laden, and I will give you rest. Take my yoke upon you and learn of me, for I am meek and lowly in heart that you may find rest unto your souls. For my yoke is easy, and my burden is light." Saint Matthew 11:28-30 KJV.

I was reminded that even a hydraulic system, big and strong, has an escape valve. If it did not, it would explode under pressure. So, with that thought in mind, I went upstairs and knelt beside my bed and committed everything, every problem, every care, every worry that I had been carrying around to him in prayer.

I went back downstairs, relieved, refreshed, and fell sound asleep on the carpet in the den. There is sweet rest in the Lord.

Dear Lord, please help me to commit all my cares to you in prayer. Your rest is so sweet when I come to you with my burdens and lay them at your feet. Amen.

APRIL 23
HOME SHOULD BE A CLASSROOM

And thou shalt love the Lord thy God with all thine heart, and with all thy soul, and with all thy might. And these words which I command thee this day shall be in thine heart: and thou shalt teach them diligently unto thy children and shall talk of them when thou sittest in thine house, and when thou walkest by the way, and when thou liest down, and when thou riseth up. And thou shalt bind them for a sign upon thine hand, and they shall be as frontlets between thine eyes, and thou shalt write them upon the posts of thy house, and on thy gates.
Deuteronomy 6:5-9 KJV.

Parents, do you realize your home is a classroom? You are the teachers, and your children are the students. This school is always in session. Your children are constantly observing, learning, and patterning after your life and attitudes. They learn from the reading material you provide, from the radio and TV programs you allow, and from your conversation. So be careful, parents. The children

God entrusted you with are depending upon you. Under parental supervision, children get their training in human relations, learn cooperation and respect for the rights of others, learn obedience, and receive punishment for wrongdoings in the home. Children learn to have a good relationship with others outside the home. If they do not learn these things, they will be handicapped forever.

The mother is the heart of the home. She sets prime examples of love and understanding and teaches her children the art of sharing and being considerate of others.

The father is the head of the household. What a solemn charge has been given to each man who is the head of a home. He is responsible not just for the food and clothes his family wears but also for their spiritual welfare. As a father, what kind of a spiritual example are you being before your family? One day, you will have to stand before God and give an answer. May it be a good one.

Dear Heavenly Father, as we come before you, we realize that we are molding and making these precious children you have given us into the adults they will be tomorrow. What wonderful gifts you have placed in our hands. We know that one day, we will have to give an account of how we have parented them. Father, may we always seek your guidance in this ultimate task you have chosen us to fulfill. Amen.

APRIL 24
GOD HAS GREAT NEED FOR THE ELDERLY

They shall still bring forth fruit in old age; They shall be fat and flourishing Psalm 92:14 KJV.

Last night after talking with a dear older lady on the phone for over thirty minutes, I realized just how lonely and how destitute some people feel. Our elderly, who in a lot of cases are living on fixed incomes and have been separated from loved ones either by death or maybe the growing up and moving away of adult children. But even though I stay remarkably busy, and I have family. I personally have experienced times of loneliness in my own life and times when I felt anxious or uneasy and allowed my worries to overtake my faith. I think we all experience times like these, but elderly people especially need our prayers, our consideration, and deeds of kindness. We, as younger people, need to let them know just how much we love and appreciate them. After all, they have paved the way for us. There is much to be learned from our elderly, and even though they may have the beautiful snow of many winters adorning their heads, they still have much to offer in our society. God still has a plan for their lives. Just because they may have retired from working publicly does not mean that God has retired them. So, as middle-aged adults, let us get busy and show them just how much they are needed and wanted in our lives.

Senior adults get busy, also. Take your rightful place in society. Do not sit around and worry and fret. But the purpose in your heart today is to trust God for your every need. You have a job to do and a mission to accomplish. Do not sit down on the job. If God were finished with you, he would have already taken you home. There is work to be done, volunteering, taking grandchildren on outings, teaching others life skills and just being a friend.

Dear Jesus, you have a plan and a purpose for us all until you call us home. I pray that you will help me to never overlook the elderly who may be lonely and feel they may have outlived their purpose. Help the elderly to know they are needed in society and have unique talents and abilities that can benefit others. Amen.

APRIL 25
HE DOES WHAT WE CANNOT

Ah Lord God! Behold, thou hast made the heaven and the earth by thy great power and stretched out arm, and there is nothing too hard for thee. Jeremiah 32:17 KJV

The teachings of Christ are all based on the fundamental idea that He can do for us that we cannot do for ourselves. He is our supreme sustenance to those who know Him in His fullest. He is their bread from heaven, the staff of life, and comfort when weary. Whatever the situation, his limitless resources meet our endless needs.

John 6:31-40 KJV says, "Our fathers did eat manna in the desert as it is written. He gave them bread from heaven to eat. Then Jesus said unto them, verily, verily. I say unto you, Moses gave you not that bread from heaven, but my Father giveth you the true bread from heaven. For the bread of God is he which cometh down from heaven, and giveth life unto the world." And Jesus said, "Unto them, I am the bread of life. He that cometh to me

shall never hunger, and he that believeth on me shall never thirst. But I said unto you, that ye also have seen me, and believe not all that the father giveth me, shall come to me, and him that cometh to me I will in no wise cast out. For I came down from heaven not to do my own will, but the will of Him that sent me. And this is the Father's will which hath sent me, that of all which He hath given me I should lose nothing but should raise it up again at the last day. And this is the will of him that sent me, that everyone which seeeth the Son and believeth on Him may have everlasting life, and I will raise him up at the last day."

Dear Jesus, I am so very thankful and appreciative of what you can do for me that I cannot do, so that all my needs are met. Amen.

APRIL 26
TAKE IT TO JESUS

Casting all your care upon him; for he careth for you. I Peter 5:7 KJV.

Prayer is communion with God. Prayer is the opening of the heart to God as to a friend in which you would confide. Prayer is an offering of our desires to God for the things agreeable to His will, with confession of our sins and thankful acknowledgement of His mercies. Prayer is a wish turned heavenward. Prayer is incense that gives the devil a headache. Only someone who has experienced the power of a prayer-filled life can appreciate its value.

Dear Jesus, I am so thankful that I have the privilege to bring every need, every care, every

burden, and every joy to you in prayer. I know you love me, and if something is important to me, it is of utmost importance to you. Amen.

LESSON FROM GOOD SAMARITAN

And the king shall answer and say unto them,
Verily I say unto you, in as much as ye have done it
unto one of the least of these my brethren, ye have
done it unto me. Matthew 25:40 KJV.

A lawyer in the Bible once asked Jesus the question, "Master, what shall I do to inherit eternal life?" Jesus referred to the Scriptures. "Thou shalt love the Lord thy God with all thy heart and with all thy soul. And with all thy strength, and with all thy might, and thy neighbor as thyself, which covers it all."

Later, in the same chapter, Luke 10:30-37, Jesus related the story of a certain traveler who was robbed, beaten, and stripped of his garments and left to die alone. A priest came along, saw him lying there, but passed on by. He was probably dressed in what we would today refer to as our Sunday best, on his way undoubtedly to some important religious affair, and simply could not take the time to be bothered with this man who was probably socially and religiously a nobody. Then along came a Levite, and when he looked upon this wretched soul lying in his own blood, he thought, how unfortunate, but I simply cannot afford to get involved. Then, a Samaritan came by and had compassion for the poor man. Well, it was about time. He bound up the poor man's wounds and carried him to an inn, where he paid for his lodging and told the innkeeper that if the bill was more than what he had given him upon his return, he would pay the balance on his way back into town. A Good Samaritan could have passed on by like the priest and the Levite, but instead, he took the time to help his neighbor who was in need. He not only showed true love for his fellow man but also for his God.

Dear Jesus, I pray that you will never allow me to feel I am too busy to help someone in need. Please allow me to be your hand extended to humanity. I desire to be a pipeline of blessing to the less fortunate. Amen.

Rejoice with me; for I have found my sheep which was lost. Luke 15:6b KJV.

We have a friend in Ranger, GA, who raises sheep. Our friend related the following story to me. He said that he had a huge enclosure with a lot of sheep in it, and to keep a tiny lamb from being trampled, he put it in a small enclosure up front. The huge enclosure contained many, many sheep whose bleating was deafening. Then the lamb uttered a fatal cry, and the mother sheep at the very other end of the enclosure took note of the cries and began making her way toward her baby lamb.

Do not ever think that your problems are beyond the reach or the help of the Good Shepherd. He sees you. He hears you. Your every real need, good desire, and secret longing is known to Him. He sees you as if you were the only other child in the universe. Luke 15:37 KJV says, "And he spake this parable unto them, saying, What man of you having one hundred sheep, if he loses one of them, does he

271

not leave the ninety and nine in the wilderness, and go after that which is lost, until he finds it, and when he hath found it, he loaded it on his shoulders, rejoicing. And when he cometh home, he calleth together his friends and neighbors, saying unto them, rejoice with me, for I have found my sheep which was lost. I say unto you that likewise joy shall be in heaven over one sinner that repenteth more than. Over ninety and nine just persons which need no repentance."

Dear Lord, I thank you that when I was that one little lost lamb, you left all the others, and you came looking for me. I am so thankful that you did not leave me all alone in my sin. Amen.

Study to shew thyself approved unto God, a workman that needeth not to be ashamed, rightly dividing the word of truth. II Timothy 2:15 KJV

As a small child, I remember saying the Lord's Prayer not only in Sunday School class but in Mrs. Overton's first grade at Belwood Elementary. We would all recite it repeatedly until it was committed to memory. Then, we merely said it by heart and felt proud of our accomplishment. As I have grown older and more mature spiritually, I have come to realize just what that prayer constitutes. Did you know that the Lord's Prayer found in Luke 11:2-4 includes everyday concerns as well as great matters? If you know the words, you can repeat them to yourself. If not, you may wish to look them up sometime. We have such an elaborate, exalted view of God that we feel it is wrong to bother him with trivial things. God is great, and I do not mean to take away from the fact but only to emphasize His greatness by saying that He is God. And because of that, He has all the time in the world to talk with you and me. He is never too busy. That is what makes Him God, so much higher than man. Do you know He cares about everything that is important to you? God is our loving Father, and nothing that concerns his children is too unimportant for him to care about. Phrases such as thy will be done as in heaven, so in earth in the Lord's Prayer led me to believe that God cares about every problem you have. He cares not only about world peace and national situations, but God is so great that he even cares about that little trivial situation that worries only you. He created you in his own likeness and image, and He made you totally complete by giving you those human emotions that you so often experience. If something is important enough to concern you, then it concerns God. Why not go to Him and tell Him all about it in prayer? You will find Him willing and waiting with open arms and hands outstretched to comfort and console, encourage, and make whole.

Dear Lord, I thank you for the Lord's Prayer and how you gave it to us to teach us to pray for every situation in life. I am so thankful that we have the privilege to come to you with anything that concerns us. Amen.

APRIL 30
IT TAKES DISCIPLINE TO SUCCEED

If ye endure chastening, God dealeth with you, as with sons. For what son is he whom the father chasteneth not? Hebrews 12:7 KJV.

It takes discipline to succeed. There is no going around it. It takes discipline to accomplish any task you set out to do. Few of us were born with silver spoons in our mouths. I have yet to see anyone in my life born with enough money or brains to place them at the top of the ladder of success. For most people, it takes climbing the steps one at a time, consistently and in order. Have you ever watched a child as he attempted to climb a flight of steps two or three at a time? Often, the child will stumble and fall and end up on ground level, only to pick himself up and start again. The same pertains to life. It takes discipline to succeed. One step at a time. Discipline is bringing something under control or subject to a trained condition of order and obedience. If any goal is to be reached, it takes discipline, taking the steps one at a time.

Consistently and in order. Ask an Olympic star, a college honor student, or an accomplished musician, and they will all tell you that discipline is a necessity for success. There is no going around it. But oh, how great the rewards are. I heard a story in Miss Frances Linn's history class about a young man who was preparing to leave for his first year in college. His father handed him a check and told him that if he spent the money wisely, it would be more than enough to finish his education. The young man knew that his father was wealthy, and he went out and spent the total sum the first year. That summer, he returned home and told his father that he would need more money to return to school in the fall. Much to his dismay, the father told him he had foolishly squandered the money, that there would be no more money coming from him, and that he either must get a job to remain in school or become a dropout. The choice was left to the son. The young man did return to school but lived in poverty. He had to work his way through college and stay up long hours into the night trying to achieve good grades in his studies. He did finish college and even graduated at the top of his class. He was afterwards elected governor of New York and became Secretary of State during the Civil War. Later, he was responsible for what was known as Seward's Folly.

Today, that folly is known as the state of Alaska, one of our richest natural resources. The young man's name was William Seward. To some people, his father was unfair and cruel, but he loved his son enough to save him from a lifetime of possible wastefulness. It took discipline and a sense of selflessness on the son's part to succeed. For both, discipline paid off.

Dear Lord, I know it takes discipline to succeed at anything. Please help me become disciplined and stick with the program that would be your will for me

even when it is difficult and when I would rather be doing something easier and more fun. No matter what age we are, we all need discipline. If we do not discipline ourselves, you will discipline us. Please help us to learn that lesson well, so we do not have to retake the class. Amen.

MAY

EVE CHOSE DISOBEDIENCE OVER FAITH

And the Lord God caused a deep sleep to fall upon Adam, and he slept, and he took one of his ribs, and closed up the flesh instead thereof, and the rib which the Lord. God had taken from man, made him a woman, and brought her unto the man. And Adam said, this is now bone of my bones, and flesh of my flesh: she shall be called woman, because she was taken out of man. Therefore, shall a man leave his father and his mother and shall cleave unto his wife: and they shall be one flesh. And they were both naked, and the man and his wife, and were not ashamed. Genesis 2:21-25 KJV.

Can you imagine? You and your spouse are placed in a beautiful garden with provisions to meet your every need and desire. The climate is perfect. Food is luscious in the privacy of your own paradise, with plenty of opportunity to enjoy yourself and each other. You may freely partake of every tree in the garden except for the tree of the knowledge of good and evil. The day that you eat, you shall surely die.

Can you believe it? She did not resist temptation, disobeyed God, and talked her husband into sinning. Their perfect life was shattered, their paradise lost. In sorrow, she would bring forth children, and he would make a living by the sweat of his brow.

Dear God, please help us to choose life over death, and obedience over yielding to temptation. Amen.

Through faith also, Sara hereby received strength to conceive seed and was delivered of a child when she was past age, because she judged Him faithful who had promised. Hebrews, 11:11 KJV.

Sarah is a prime example of a person being rewarded by God because of having faith in His promises. Years passed from the promise to the provision. Her husband Abram was seventy-five years old and without children when God first met with him and promised him children, posterity, and land to dwell in. When he was ninety-nine years old, God changed his name from Abram to Abraham, meaning father of many nations, and Sara's name was changed to Sarah as matriarch of Israel. This was the beginning of one Kingdom of God on earth, which is now comprised of all people everywhere who have been redeemed by Jesus Christ.

Dear Heavenly Father, you are the Lord, the God of all flesh. There is nothing too hard for you. If we who believe will put our complete trust in you, who can do all things, then your promises to us will happen. Amen.

MAY 3
DEBORAH, PROPHET, AND JUDGE

The Inhabitants of the villages ceased. They ceased in Israel until that I, Deborah arose, that I arose a mother in Israel. Judges 5:7 KJV.

The era of the Judges in the Bible spanned about four hundred years, from the time of Joshua's leadership until Samuel crowned Saul as King of Israel. The only judge named in the Book of Judges was Deborah, a Jewish woman prophet and a judge with a unique form of leadership. There was no central government during that time, and Israel was led by tribal leaders. Most of the tribes had failed to drive out the Canaanites, and village life had ceased in Israel. Deborah was a wise and godly leader during Israel's conflict with the Canaanites. Her strong character and wisdom were revealed when she courageously led Israel to victory. When the commander of the Jewish army, Barrack, refused to go into battle without her, she prophesied that he would not get the credit for killing the leader of the Canaanite people. Another woman would kill Sisera.

Dear Lord, thank you for using Deborah as a deliverer of the Israelites from the Canaanites and giving them forty years of peace. Your Word was precisely fulfilled through Deborah's unique, courageous willingness to lead. God help us, like Deborah. We trust you completely, even in difficult circumstances. God, you are not a man that you should lie. If you say it, you will perform it. Amen.

MAY 4
NAOMI, GRIEVED AND BLESSED

And he shall be unto thee restorer of thy life, and a nourisher of thine old age: for thy daughter-in-law, which loveth thee, which is better to thee than seven sons, hath born him. And Naomi took the child and laid it in her bosom and became nurse unto it. Ruth 4:15-16 KJV.

The divine tapestries of our lives are often woven through tragedy and triumph, but God's Providence works in the lives of His people.

There was a famine in the land of Israel due to the oppressive tactics of the Midianites. Naomi, her husband, and her two sons fled into Moab. Naomi's husband died, and then her two sons took Moabite wives. Then, eventually, both sons died. When Naomi heard the famine was over, she decided to go back to Israel. One daughter-in-law, Ruth, went with her. Naomi was grieved and on the verge of being bitter.

So that they could eat, she sent Ruth to glean on the outskirts of the wheat fields. Naomi instructed her daughter-in-law what to do in another country. God blessed Ruth with favor, and she married the rich owner of the wheatfield. God blessed them with a son who was in the lineage of David and Jesus.

Naomi was nourished and provided for in her old age, and her joy restored. She took the child, held it close to her heart, and became its nurse. Down through the ages, there have been few blessings as joyous as grandchildren!

Dear Heavenly Father, thank you for your everyday provision for your children. You are so incredibly good to us. Thank you for meeting our needs and even the desires of our hearts. I love you so much, Lord. Amen.

MAY 5
RUTH RECEIVES A SECOND CHANCE

And Ruth said, Intreat me not to leave thee, or to return from following after thee, for whither thou goest I will go, and whither thou lodgest I will lodge. Thy people shall be my people, and thy God my God. Ruth, 1:16 KJV.

Ruth was a devoted, steadfastly minded daughter-in-law who went with her mother-in-law, Naomi, back to Israel and stayed with her. Their husbands had died in Moab, and the famine was over in Israel. After settling into Bethlehem, Ruth decided to go out and glean a provision in the Mosaic law to help the poor. It was a matter of picking up wheat that was left in the field after the reapers had been harvested. It was no coincidence that she went to Boaz's field, a relative of her father-in-law. God's hand was already working in Ruth's life. Ruth was in a different land, and her mother-in-law instructed her. Ruth did as she was instructed and remained in Boaz's field. He showed favor to Ruth, and they were married and bore a

289

son. The people celebrated Ruth's devotion to Naomi, and Ruth, who had been barren in the previous marriage, was now blessed with motherhood and a loving and wealthy husband. Naomi, Ruth, Boaz, and the child, Obed, had all been lauded by the people and blessed by God. Obed became the grandfather of King David and, eventually, an ancestor of Jesus Christ.

Dear Heavenly Father, thank you so very much for your love, your compassion, your provision, and for being the God of second chances. Amen.

HANNAH'S FAITH AND DEVOTION TO GOD

For this child I prayed, and the Lord hath given me my petition, which I asked of him. Therefore, also I have lent him to the Lord, as long as he liveth, he shall be lent to the Lord, and he worshipped the Lord there. I Samuel 1:27-28 KJV.

Hannah was barren, and in her distress and anguish, she sought the Lord earnestly and made a sacred vow. The Lord God heard and responded to her sincere prayer. God not only blessed her with the son Samuel but gave her more children. God is so faithful. He hears our prayers and gives us the desires of our hearts. It is our responsibility to go to God in faith, believing He will hear our cries and answer our petition.

Dear Heavenly Father, I praise you that you not only hear and answer our cries, but you want us to

pour out our needs and desires to you. Thank you so much for answering the cries of our hearts. Amen.

ABIGAIL, INTERVENOR

Pride goeth before destruction. Proverbs 16:18 KJV.

There was a woman, Abigail, who was exceptionally beautiful and not only intelligent, but understanding and had a good heart. She was married to Nabal, who was very wealthy but evil and churlish. He owned one thousand goats and three hundred sheep, and he sheared them in Caramel. King David sent ten men to Caramel to speak to Nabal and greet him in the name of King David.

Nabal arrogantly said, "Who is David? There are many who break away from their masters. Shall I give my bread, my water, and my meat to someone who I know not? Not so."

Then one of them went back to David and relayed the message from Nabal and went to Abigail and told her what had happened. She immediately gathered an abundance of supplies. She was on her way to take it to David to prevent bloodshed. She met David, and his men fell at his feet and pleaded for him to accept her offering and not bring bloodshed to her household. David, moved by her humility, kindly accepted.

That night, Nabal came home, hosted a large feast, and got drunk. The next morning, Abigail told him what had happened. His heart died within him. Ten days later, he passed, and Abigail later became King David's wife.

Dear Heavenly Father, thank you for ordering the steps of good people. Nabal's evil and selfish actions could have caused his household to be wiped out by David and his army. Instead, you gave Abigail the wisdom and the knowledge to act swiftly and to find favor in David's sight. The cruel husband's heart failed him. Nabal died, and she then

became David's wife. Thank you for ordering our footsteps. Just as Abigail intervened for her household, you intervene for us. Amen.

MAY 8
MARY, MOTHER OF JESUS

And the Angel said unto her, Fear not, Mary, for thou hast found favor with God, and behold, thou shalt conceive in thy womb, and bring forth a son, and shall call his name Jesus. He shall be great, and shall be called the Son of the Highest, and the Lord God shall give unto him the throne of his Father, David. Luke 1:30-32 KJV.

The Angel Gabriel appeared to a young Jewish virgin named Mary. She was engaged to a man named Joseph. Gabriel told her God highly favored her. It meant she found grace with God and was chosen to bear His Son. The Angel told her she was blessed among women. He assured her not to be afraid, for she was chosen to be part of God's prophetic plan of redemption. And John told her she would give birth to a son and his name would be Jesus. Mary asked how this could be since she had never known a man. The angel explained that this would be fulfilled by a divine act of the Holy Spirit, who would overshadow her. The angel called the

child that holy one. Meaning he would be more than human. Mary responded humbly, submitting and calling herself a servant of the Lord.

Dear Heavenly Father, what a beautiful plan you had when you chose Mary to be the mother of your precious Son. I cannot imagine what must have gone through her mind. I cannot imagine how I would have responded. Please help me to be submissive and obedient to Your will for my life and respond humbly, "I am a servant of the Lord." Amen.

MAY 9
ELIZABETH, MOTHER OF JOHN THE BAPTIST

And thou, child, shall be called the prophet of the Highest, for thou shalt go before the face of the Lord to prepare His ways. Luke 1:76 KJV.

Elizabeth was a member of the priestly lineage, married to Zacharias. She was the mother of John the Baptist, and the cousin of Mary, mother of Jesus. Elizabeth had no children until later in life. After Mary had received her news, she went to the city of Judah in the Hill Country to visit her cousin Elizabeth. When she went into her home and greeted Elizabeth, the babe in Elizabeth's womb leaped for joy, and Elizabeth was filled with the Holy Spirit. She shouted with a loud voice and said," Blessed art thou among women, and blessed is the fruit of thy womb." Then Mary exclaimed a beautiful song of praise, known as The Magnificat, penned in the holy scriptures sung and recited in many churches today.

Mary stayed with Elizabeth for about three months and returned to her own home before

Elizabeth and Zechariah's son, John the Baptist, was born. John the Baptist was the forerunner for Jesus. He preached repentance and baptized his converts, preparing the way for Jesus Christ.

Dear Heavenly Father, you have such a wonderful way of coordinating our lives so that your will transpires. Thank you for so intricately putting together the pieces so that they perfectly fit to accomplish your purpose in all of us. Amen.

Thy sins are forgiven thee. Luke 8:48 KJV.

Before Mary Magdalene met Jesus, she had seven demons. The number seven is used in the Bible to describe completeness. Could it mean that she was completely consumed with heartache? What did her list contain? Depression? Loneliness? Shame? Fear? Abuse? Abandonment? Prostitution?

But then Jesus entered her life. She could smile again. All the anguish left her face. Jesus restored her joy. Jesus cleansed her and gave her a brand-new life.

Dear Heavenly Father, thank you for your cleansing power that changes our lives. The changes show in our attitudes and shine forth on our faces. I

am so thankful we can keep coming to you with all our afflictions, hurts, brokenness, and troubles. Amen.

*And Pharaoh charged all his people, saying,
"Every son that is born you shall cast into the river,
and every daughter you shall save alive." Exodus 1:72
KJV.*

A handsome Hebrew boy, strong and perfect in form, was born one day in Egypt. His mother hid him for three months. The Pharaoh of Egypt had ordered all Hebrew male babies born to be thrown into the river to decrease the number and strength of the Hebrew people. When he was three months old, and she could no longer hide him, his mother took an ark made of bull rushes and dabbed it with slime and pitch, put him in it, and placed it in the flags by the river's brink. When the Pharaoh's daughter came to the river to bathe, she saw the ark among the flags. She sent her servant to get it. When she opened it and saw the child, he began to cry. She had deep compassion for him.

His sister Miriam, who was standing close by watching to see what happened, ran out and said, "I know a Hebrew woman who could nurse the child for you." Pharaoh's daughter said, "Go!" She went and called the child's mother. Pharoah's daughter paid wages to his mother to nurse him.

The woman took the child and nursed him, and he grew. When he was weaned, she brought him to Pharaoh's daughter, and he became her son. She named him Moses because she drew him out of the water.

Dear Heavenly Father. It is so amazing how you cause things to happen in our lives for our good and to accomplish your eternal purpose. Thank you for designing every minute detail, even years in advance. Amen.

Then said his wife unto him, Dost thou still retain thine integrity? Curse God and die. Job 2:9 KJV.

The Book of Job is one of the most remarkable books of the Bible. Job, the hero of the story, was a man of integrity and wealth and possessed immense pleasure in his family and his life.

Satan came to God one day and said he had been going forth seeking whom he could tempt and devour. God asked if he had considered Job. Satan responded that God had a hedge of protection around Job, and if God removed it and Job was tried, he would surely fall. God said you can do whatever you desire to Job except take his life.

Job's oxen were taken away. And the attending servants were killed. Fire burned up his sheep and servants. The Chaldeans took his camels and killed his attending servants. His children were killed by high winds.

Job said, "Naked came I into the world, and naked I will go out. The Lord has given and the Lord hath taken away. Blessed be the name of the Lord."

Then Satan caused sores to cover Job's body from the soles of his feet to the crown of his head.

Job's wife asked, "Do you still retain your integrity through all this? Just curse God and die." Job answered, "You speak as one of the foolish women. Shall we receive good at the hand of God and not receive evil?" In all of this, Job did not sin.

Dear Heavenly Father, thank you for Job and his example. He truly was a man who led his wife and his children, a perfect example of what the priest of the home should be. Not so much his wife. As a God-pleasing mate, please help me to be the helpmate, encourager and prayer partner my husband needs when adversity strikes our home. Amen.

JOB'S FRIENDS

And it was so that after the Lord had spoken these words unto Job, the Lord said to Eliphaz the Temanite. My wrath is kindled against thee and thy two friends: for you have not spoken of me, the thing that is right, as my servant Job hath. Job 42:7 KJV.

After Job's friends, Eliphaz, Bildad, and Zophar, heard of what had happened to Job, they came to visit. They did not recognize Job in all his distress and anguish. They sat with him seven days and nights without saying a word.

Job alleged he did not understand why all this had happened to him. He maintained his integrity and that he had not sinned.

Eliphaz accused Job of arrogance, reminded Job of God's justice and power, and insinuated that God's wrath had fallen on Job because of sin.

God then spoke His displeasure to Eliphaz and his two friends and let them know they had misjudged Job. He had done what was right throughout this trial. God then told Eliphaz to take seven bullocks and seven rams and go to Job and offer up a burnt offering. Job will pray for you, and I will accept his prayers, lest I deal with you in your folly. So Eliphaz, Bildad, and Zophar did as God commanded, and Job prayed for his friends.

Dear Heavenly Father, please help us to always choose our friends wisely. May we always have integrity and maintain it in the presence of our friends. Please give us the right words to say to witness to our friends. Even when our friends do us wrong, please help us to always forgive them and have a willing heart to pray for them. Amen.

And the Lord turned the captivity of Job, when he prayed for his friends also, the Lord gave him twice as much as he had before. Job 42:10 KJV.

God allowed Job to be tried by Satan to prove to Satan that Job was a man of integrity and righteousness. Job would not bow or bend when God's hedge of protection was removed from him. And he was stripped of his bountiful blessings. We can learn much from Job's example when our lives are devastated by tragedy, death of loved ones, loss of possessions, when our support is lost, when close friends turn against us, when our character and reputation are questioned. When good health is gone, and when we do not understand why God is allowing us to go through heart-rending circumstances. Job kept his faith and remained true to his GOD. God gave him twice as much as he had before his horrendous trials.

His sisters, brothers, and acquaintances came to comfort him. They each gave him money and a gold earring. The Lord blessed the latter life of Job more than the beginning. He also had fourteen thousand sheep, six thousand camels, one thousand yoke of oxen, and one thousand female donkeys. He had seven sons and three daughters. There were no daughters found in all the land as beautiful as Jobs. He gave them inheritance along with their brothers.

Job lived to be one hundred forty years, and he enjoyed his children, grandchildren, great-grandchildren, and great-great-grandchildren, four generations. Job died being old and full of days

Dear Heavenly Father, may the life of Job be a lesson During life's trials and tribulations, we can make it. You will turn the tide, and we will come through more blessed than before. Amen.

SHIPRAH AND PUAH, HEBREW MIDWIVES

But the midwives feared God and did not, as the king of Egypt commanded them, but saved the men children alive. Exodus 1:12 KJV.

A new pharaoh came to power in Egypt. He noted that the children of Israel were fruitful, increased abundantly, multiplied in number, and were strong and mighty, and the land was filled with them. He told his people to deal harshly with them because if war broke out, the Hebrews could join with their enemies and overrun the Egyptians. He put taskmasters over them to afflict them. The Hebrews built treasured cities, Pathom and Raamses, for the Pharaoh. Their lives were miserable with hard labor in mortar, brick, and in all manner of services in their field.

The pharaoh spoke to the Hebrew midwives, Shiphrah and Puah, and told them to kill all male Hebrew babies at birth. Because of their faith in God, they did not obey and saved the Hebrew babies. The pharaoh called for the midwives, demanding why they had disobeyed him. They replied that the Hebrew women were much stronger than the Egyptian women, and when they went to assist the Hebrew women, they had already delivered their babies. God blessed the midwives, and the Hebrews multiplied. Because the midwives feared God, He blessed them and made homes for them to live in.

Dear Heavenly Father. Please give us the strength to always do the right thing in every situation, whether it be popular opinion or laws. May we always choose to obey You and Your word instead of man-made laws. Amen.

For the poor always ye have with you; but me ye have not always. John 12:8KJV

Then Jesus, six days before the Passover, came to Bethany, where Lazarus had died whom, Jesus raised from the dead. It was quite a cause for celebration. There, they made supper. Martha was busy serving their many guests. But Lazarus was one of them who sat at the table with Jesus, eagerly telling of His Master's miracle. Then Mary took a pound of very costly spikenard and anointed Jesus's feet and wiped them with her hair.

All three of the hosts' personalities exhibited here are needed in our modern churches. Lazarus was the one exuberant about the miracles of God and ready to proclaim them. Marthas are certainly needed to prepare and serve the dinners, care for the nursery babies, and head up fundraisers. Marys are needed to show others how to worship and adore the Lord Jesus.

Martha felt Mary should be helping her in the kitchen. Jesus said, "Martha, you are worried and upset about many things. Mary has chosen the best part, and it will never be taken away from her."

All three types of personal qualities are mandatory in building the Kingdom of God. Jesus put it in perspective.

Dear Lord Jesus. You made each of us with unique talents and different personalities. Please help us to learn what our gifts are and teach us to operate in them. But most of all, please help us to prioritize our worship of You. Amen.

For we have heard how the Lord dried up the water of the Red Sea for you when you came out of Egypt. And as soon as we heard these things, our hearts did melt. Neither did there remain any more courage in any man because of you, for the Lord your God, He is God in heaven above and in earth beneath. Joshua 2:10-11 KJV.

Rahab was a harlot in Jericho. She protected two spies sent by Joshua to spy out the land of Jericho when the king of Jericho pursued them. Rehab hid them under stalks of flax on her rooftop, later letting them down over the wall with a scarlet cord. For this act of kindness, she and her family were spared. When Israel overran Jericho, the scarlet cord was hung in a window as a sign that her house was not to be destroyed. Because of her faith Rahab is listed in the genealogy of Jesus.

Dear Lord Jesus, in trying situations, we pray that you would please help our faith overcome our fear. Lord, we love you, and we need you, especially when we are in dire circumstances. Because of Rahab's faith in action, she and her whole family's lives were saved. Amen.

REMEMBER LOT'S WIFE

Then the Lord rained upon Sodom and Gomorrah, brimstone and fire from the Lord out of heaven.
Genesis 19:24 KJV.

Lot was the nephew of Abraham. They migrated together to the land of Canaan. Lot grew so rich in flocks, herds, and servants that it became impossible for them to stay together. When Abraham offered him the choice of the land that lay before them, Lot chose the lush green land toward the Jordan River and pitched his tents towards Sodom. He was to live to regret his choice. Despite his weaknesses, Lot had numerous good qualities. The Bible says that God would have been willing to spare Sodom and Gomorrah from destruction if only a few more men of Lot's character lived there. Even though the cities were destroyed, Lot and his family were given ample warnings and were able to flee. In time they were told not to look back as they were

fleeing. Lot's wife looked back and was turned into a pillar of salt.

Dear Heavenly Father, please help us to always remember Lot's wife and the price she paid for disobedience. Give us a desire to always obey you for our good and your glory. Amen.

JOSHUA'S FAITH IN GOD'S PROMISES

The Lord your God hath given you rest, and hath given you this land. Joshua 1:13 KJV.

Joshua was a man of great valor and tremendous military courage. He was one of twelve spies sent into Canaan to survey the land and gauge the inhabitants' resistance abilities upon invasion. He and his partner, Caleb, came back with a positive report. They saw land flowing with milk and honey. Grape clusters grew so large. They required two men to carry them. They reported giants in the land, but none the Israelites could not handle.

The other ten spies said the Israelites were like grasshoppers in comparison to the giants. The ten opposing spies attempted to incite a riot to have Joshua and Caleb stoned because of their positive report. Joshua and Caleb, because of their faith in God's promises, were the only two Israelite adults, according to the first census, who were allowed entrance to the promised land.

Dear Heavenly Father. I am so thankful that when you make a promise, you keep it. Please help us, amid fear, to believe and act upon your promises. Help us to have faith that is greater than our fear and others' negativity. Amen.

But Noah found grace in the eyes of the Lord.
Genesis 6:5 KJV.

Noah was a righteous man who walked with God. He lived in a very tumultuous time. Violence and corruption ran rampant in the land.

God said enough is enough. I am going to destroy all flesh except you, Noah, your wife, your sons, and their wives. I want you to take seven pairs of each clean animals, male and female. Two pairs, male and female, of each unclean animal, and seven pairs of each fowl of the air to keep seed alive on the face of the earth. I want you to build an ark out of gopher wood with rooms inside. Cover it with pitch, inside and out. When it begins to rain, take your family, the animals, and the birds inside the ark and close the door.

Noah did as he was instructed. It rained forty days and forty nights. One day, the twenty-seventh day of the second month, God told him the earth was dry. Go forward and multiply!

Dear Heavenly Father, please help us to know that our righteous living and communicating with you always pays off. Even when everyone is doing wrong around us, we can still live righteously and be faithful to You. Amen.

MAY 21
JONAH AND THE BIG FISH

For the gifts and calling of God are without repentance. Romans 11:29 KJV.

Jonah, a prophet of God, was called to go to the city of Nineveh to deliver a message of repentance. Since Nineveh was already in the process of destroying the Jews, Jonah refused and boarded a ship bound for Tarshish. A great storm arose and when the sailors found out Jonah's circumstances, they threw him overboard. God had prepared a sea monster to swallow him. After being vomited up by the big fish, Jonah did as God had told him. Not only were residents of Nineveh saved, but the sailors were saved as well. God showed Jonah he was concerned for all nations besides Israel.

Dear Heavenly Father, please help us to obey You and do Your will. Your gifts and calling are

without repentance. Your ways and Your plans are so much greater than ours. So many detours and trouble could be avoided if we would only obey You. Amen.

The God of Israel grant thee thy petition thou hast asked of Him. I Samuel 1:17 KJV.

Hannah and Elkanah had been childless for many years. Hannah had sought the Lord and promised to give the child back to him in service. The Lord granted her wishes and gave her a son, whom they named Samuel. After being weaned, Samuel was placed under the care of the priest Eli of the central sanctuary in Shiloh. One night, Samuel heard his name called three times. He thought Eli had called him, but Eli had not. Eli perceived it was God who called Samuel. The Lord came and stood by him and called him. Other times, Samuel answered, "Speak for thy servant heareth." Samuel grew, and the Lord was with him. He listened and obeyed as God directed him. All Israel knew that Samuel was established to be a prophet of the Lord.

Dear Heavenly Father. Please help me to listen, obey and do as you have asked. I desire to be established in my faith and to hear you when you call. Amen.

SAMSON'S WEAKNESS AND STRENGTH

And the Spirit of the Lord came mightily upon him. Judges 15:14 KJV.

There was a man named Manoah, and his wife was barren. An angel of the Lord appeared to her and told her she was going to have a son. He told her she was not to drink wine or any strong drink or eat anything unclean. He also said that no razor was to come upon the child's head and that he would begin to deliver Israel out of the hands of the Philistines.

Sampson was a great champion of Israel. In Israel's conflicts with the Philistines, he was known for his superhuman strength and novel weakness with women. He loved a woman named Delilah, and the Philistines offered her one-thousand-one-hundred pieces of silver each to entice him and learn where his great strength lie. She did so, and he told her his secret after much enticement. She had a man shave his head, and the Philistines captured him, put out his eyes, and forced him to grind stones in prison. His faith began to grow as his hair began to grow back. There was a great feast in the land where the Philistines praised their god Dagon, for giving them Sampson. They brought Blind Sampson in to make fun of him. They then placed him against the pillars of the building where all the people had gathered. Sampson prayed and asked God to renew his strength so he could have vengeance for the loss of his eyes. God empowered him, and he pulled the pillars down, killing more of the enemy at his death than he had ever killed in all his life.

Dear Heavenly Father, there is a lesson to be learned here. Please help us to take the strength you have given us and couple it with godliness so that the outcome can be for our good and your glory. Amen.

The Lord recompense thy work and a full reward be given thee of the Lord God of Israel, under whose wings thou art come to trust. Ruth 2:12 KJV.

Boaz was a wealthy landowner. He was a cousin to Naomi's husband, Elimelech. There was a custom in Bible days that if a woman became a widower, the next male kinsman could purchase the land from the widower, marry her, and have children. If he did not desire to do this, the offer would go to the next kinsman to save the widower from poverty and continue the deceased person's bloodline.

It was the divine providence of God that led Ruth to glean in Boaz's field, Gleaning is gathering leftover grain in a field once the harvesters have already gone through.

Boaz was not the first kinsman. He had to locate the first kinsman who was not interested in purchasing the land and marrying Ruth because of his own inheritance. Boaz was interested, so he

brought ten witnesses to hear the matter. It was customary that the first kinsman then take off his shoe and throw it down as a means of showing his consent. Boaz purchased the land, married Ruth, and she conceived and bore a son named Obed, who is in the lineage of Jesus Christ.

Our Heavenly Father, thank You for divinely intervening in the lives of your children. You bring good things from bad situations. Thank You for working situations in our lives for our good and your glory. Amen.

And whoso falleth not down and worshippeth, shall the same hour be cast into the midst of a burning fiery furnace, Daniel 3:6 KJV.

During the time the Jews were in Babylonian captivity, King Nebuchadnezzar had made and set up a large image of gold. Then he sent notice to provinces, governors, captains, judges, treasurers, counselors, sheriffs, and all the rulers of the provinces to come to the dedication of the image. Then, a herald cried aloud to the people, nations, and languages that when they heard the musical instruments, they were to fall and worship the golden image that Nebuchadnezzar had set out. Whoso does not fall and worship the image shall be cast into the midst of a burning fiery furnace.

Some Chaldeans came forward and said that certain Jews, Shadrach, Meshach, and Abednego, whom the king had set over the affairs of the province of Babylon, do not serve your gods and the golden image. They do not honor your orders.

Nebuchadnezzar, in raging fury, ordered the furnace to be heated seven times hotter than normal. He had the three young Hebrew men brought before him and explained their fate: if they did not bow and worship the golden image at the sound of the music, they would be cast into the fire. They said, "We are not careful to answer you in this matter. Our God whom we serve can deliver us from the fiery furnace and out of your hand, but if he does not, we will not serve your gods or your golden image.

The king ordered his most mighty men to bind the three Hebrews and cast them into the burning fiery furnace. Because of the heat, the flames consumed the king's men, who threw them in. The king rose up and asked if they had not thrown in three men. "True, O King," his counselors answered. The king said, "I see four men loose walking around with no burns, and the fourth looks like the Son of God!" There was no smell of smoke on them. Then Nebuchadnezzar said," Blessed be the God of Shadrach, Meshach, and Abednego who hath sent his angel and delivered his servants that trusted in him." Therefore, the king decreed that everyone who spoke against the God of Shadrack, Meshach, and Bendigo be cut in pieces, and their homes made a dunghill because no other God can deliver like this. Then, the king promoted Shadrack, Meshach, and Abednego in the province of Babylon.

Dear Heavenly Father, may we realize from your word that it is so much better to obey you. You have Your children's best interests at heart, and You will provide and take care of those who have faith in You. Amen.

DAVID, GIANT-SLAYER

This day will the Lord deliver thee into mine hand, that all the earth may know that there is a God in Israel. Samuel 17:46 KJV.

Young David was a shepherd boy, the keeper of his father's flock. The older three brothers were in Israel's battle against the Philistines. His father told him to take an ephah of corn, 10 loaves of bread, and 10 hoops of cheese to the captain of the army and to check on his brothers while there. When he arrived and was conversing with his brothers, a champion of the Philistines standing over 9 feet tall came out. He challenged the undescended man to fight him. David spoke to King Saul and said he would fight Goliath, who defied the God of Israel. Saul told David to go fight Goliath and the God of Israel be with him. When Goliath saw David, he laughed at him and said he would feed David's flesh to the fowls of the air. David told Goliath he came with a sword and spear, but David came in the name of the Lord. They ran toward each other. David took a stone out of his bag and slung it, hitting Goliath on the forehead, and he fell to the ground. He ran and stood on top of Goliath, took Goliath's spear, and took off Goliath's head. He went to King Saul, and Saul put him over the Men of War. David and Jonathan, Saul's son, became best friends.

Dear Heavenly Father, please help us, like David, to strengthen our faith by facing our battles and challenges, not within ourselves but In the name of the Lord. Amen.

JONATHAN, DAVID'S BEST FRIEND

And there is a friend that sticketh closer than a brother. Proverbs 18:24 KJV.

From the time Jonathan, son of King Saul, first met David, they became close friends and eventually became closer than brothers. They loved each other, and nothing could come between their friendship. Saul soon became jealous of David when women in the Kingdom began singing, "Saul has killed his thousands, but David his ten-thousands. Saul set out immediately to kill David, and Jonathan thwarted his attempts. On several occasions, David had the opportunity to take Saul's life, but he did not. Even after Jonathan's death, David showed favor to Jonathan's son, Mephibosheth.

Dear Heavenly Father, thank you for the blessing of friendship. Friendship can be a powerful force, even thicker than blood. It saved David's life from the hand of Saul on many occasions and saved King Saul from being slain by David. Amen.

And David said unto him, Fear not for I will surely show thee kindness for Jonathan thy father's sake. II Samuel 9:7 KJV.

Mephibosheth was Jonathan's son and King Saul's grandson. He was five years old when his father and grandfather were killed by the hands of the Philistines at Gilboa. To protect the child, his nursemaid fled in haste with him in her arms when she heard the Israelites had been defeated. She dropped him, and he became crippled in both feet.

Years later, when King David decided to show appreciation for Jonathan, his close friend, by showing favor to some members of Saul's family, he learned of Mephibosheth through a man named Ziba. King David summoned Mephibosheth to the court and gave him possessions and land that had belonged to Saul. He appointed Ziba to act as overseer of the land on Mephibosheth's behalf. In addition, Mephibosheth was invited to be a daily guest at the King's table.

Dear Heavenly Father, friendship is such a precious blessing that it can continue for generations to come. We could never praise You enough for your wonderful gifts. Let us ever be mindful of your admonishment in your word to be worthy of friends: A man who hath friends must show himself friendly. Proverbs18:24 KJV. Amen.

DANIEL IN THE LION'S DEN

The righteous cry, and the Lord heareth, and delivereth them out of all their troubles. Psalm 34:17 KJV.

When Darius the Median took over the Kingdom, he was happy with Daniel's great reputation as the first president and glad that Daniel was serving directly under him.

Then jealousy entered the picture when the king thought to set him over the whole realm. The other presidents and princes sought to find an occasion against Daniel. They could find no fallacy in him for his leadership, so they decided to find it against him concerning the law of his God. They consulted together and wrote a royal statute that decreed that whosoever shall ask a petition of any God or man except for the king for 30 days he shall be cast into the lions' den. The king established the decree and signed it so that it could not be changed. Daniel knew it had been signed, but he went into his house, his windows opened toward Jerusalem and kneeled upon his knees three times a day and prayed and gave thanks before his God, as he had always done. These men assembled and found Daniel praying and making application before his God, and they told the king. Then the king commanded they cast Daniel into the den of lions. The king said to Daniel. Thy God, whom you serve continually, will deliver you. The next morning, the king had the stone rolled back and inquired if Daniel's God had indeed delivered him. Daniel answered that his God had sent an angel and shut the lions' mouths, and they had not hurt him. The king commanded that the men who had accused Daniel and their families be thrown into the lions' den, and the lions had mastery over them. Then the king decreed that the God of Daniel, who delivered, rescued, and worked signs and wonders for Daniel, be reverenced and feared. Daniel prospered in the reign of King Darius and in the reign of King Cyrus and the Persians thereafter.

Dear Heavenly Father. Thank you so much for honoring Daniel's faithfulness to you and for making believers and converts of these kings and all the residents of the kingdoms because of Daniel not being afraid or ashamed of his faith. Amen.

Lord Jesus, receive my spirit. And he kneeled down and cried with a loud voice, Lord, lay not this sin to their charge. And when he said this, he fell asleep. Acts 7:59-60 KJV.

Stephen was one of the seven men chosen to serve in the daily distribution of food and supplies in the newly formed Christian community that was started after the ascension of Jesus. Some of the Jews remained very hostile toward the Christians after Jesus' death and resurrection. They believed their government and religious power were now threatened by the Christians and their teachings. Some Jews began asking questions of Stephen and falsely accused him of blasphemy against the law and the temple. They had him arraigned before the council. In presenting his defense to the council, the Jews' tempers escalated, and they threw him out of the temple, gnashing him with their teeth and then stoning him. Saul, later known as Paul, was

present and was thought to have instigated the matter against Stephen.

Dear Heavenly Father, thank You so very much for being with Stephen as he was viciously attacked and murdered for his faith.

Thank You for giving him the words to defend Christianity. Thank You for giving him the strength and the desire to pray for his assailants. Thank You for allowing him to peacefully fall asleep in your precious arms and awake eternally with You in heaven. Amen.

PAUL'S CONVERSION

Saul, Saul, why persecutest thou me? Acts 9:4 KJV.

Saul, whose Hebrew name was changed to Paul in Greek, was converted from a life of persecuting and killing Christians to that of a Christian apostle, missionary, and writer. His influence on Christianity is thought by Christian scholars to be second only to Jesus Christ. Paul was from a wealthy family and was well-educated. He sat at the feet of Gamaliel, a great teacher. Jesus's denunciation of the Pharisees probably angered Paul.

But God had plans for the persecutor. He was to be a chosen vessel in the preaching of the gospel to the Jews. On his way to Damascus to conduct further plans for the persecution of Christians, he was overwhelmed by a blinding light and a voice that said, "Saul, Saul, why persecutest thou me?" When asked who are you, he was told it was the risen Jesus who spoke to him. He was told to go on to Damascus. After three days of fasting, a disciple

344

named Ananias counseled him and baptized him. That night his sight was restored, and he then began preparing for his ministry ahead.

Dear Heavenly Father, thank You for the incredible conversion of Paul and what his life has meant to the furtherance of Christianity. He truly received a new life with a total change of direction and purpose. He became a Christian with a great love for writing, teaching, preaching, converting others to Jesus Christ, and for encouraging and instructing those in the faith. Amen.

JUNE

346

JUNE 1
JOSEPH THE DREAMER

Now Israel loved Joseph more than all his children, because he was the son of his old age. Genesis 37:3 KJV.

Joseph was the seventeen-year-old shepherd boy of Israel and Rachel, whom Israel very much favored as a product of his old age. Israel made him a beautiful coat of many colors. Already a victim of his brother's jealousy, Joseph had a dream. In the dream, he and his brothers were binding sheaves in the field. His sheaf stood up, and theirs' bowed, making obeisance to him. "So, we are going to bow down to you?" They asked, hating him even more. They planned to kill him, but Ruben talked them into casting him in a pit, putting goat's blood on the coat, and returning it to their father.

A merchant's caravan came along on their way to Egypt, and they sold him for twenty pieces of silver to be sold into slavery. He was bought in Egypt by the Potiphar, an officer of Pharaoh and Captain of his guard, but the Lord was with Joseph.

He was made overseer of Potiphar's house. Then, Potiphar's wife lied about him. He went to prison but found favor with men by interpreting dreams. He finally became ruler over all the land of Egypt and was eventually reunited with his family.

Never underestimate the plan of God for your life. If God promises you something, continue living righteously. You can rest assured it will happen.

Dear Heavenly Father, when we are standing in faith in your promises, please give us spiritual fortitude to live righteously. So, we will see them fulfilled. Amen.

JUNE 2
ESTHER, QUEEN BRIDE

And who knoweth that thou art come to the kingdom for such a time as this? Esther 4:12 KJV.

Esther's parents died and she was a Jewish orphan, being raised by her cousin Mordecai. He had an office in the palace of King Ahasuerus. in the capital city of Shushan.

Esther had what most young ladies would consider the dream of a lifetime, pampered with beauty treatments and glamorous clothes, and an appointment to be interviewed by the King, who was looking for the fairest virgin in the land to become his new bride. When all the beautiful young ladies of the Kingdom were collected at Shushan, unaware of her race and parents, King Ahasuerus chose Esther.

Have you ever thought how we sometimes can imagine the splendor of it all, then realize God has an even greater purpose? Sometimes, He has a

349

divine plan for our lives, with great difficulty prior to enjoying the fullness of the blessing.

Soon thereafter, because of Mordecai's refusal to pay homage to Haman, who was above all princes in the Persian government, Haman convinced the King to issue and declare a decree to have all the Jews in the land exterminated.

Mordecai even at the risk of Esther's life asked her to intervene on the Jews' behalf. Esther asked all the Jews in Shushan and all her maidens to fast for three days and three nights for the outcome before she approached the King.

Esther found favor with her husband, King Ahasuerus and revealed the plot of Haman. He was hanged and Mordecai was promoted to a place of high honor. To celebrate the deliverance of the Jews, the Feast of Purim was initiated.

Dear Heavenly Father. I pray that you will help us grasp the fact that our lives are intended for your purpose and your plan and for such a time as this. We are not created to choose our own path and pursue our own desires. Your plans are so much higher than ours, and if we follow you, then our lives will accomplish what you had in mind when you created us, and we will be happier for it. Amen.

JUNE 3
PROVERBS 31 WOMAN

Many daughters have done virtuously, but thou excellest them all. Proverbs 31:19 KJV.

There have never been more opportunities for a woman than the time in which we live. A woman can be anything she chooses with so many opportunities for education and the availability of jobs.

In Proverbs 31, the question is asked: Who can find a virtuous woman? Her husband safely trusts her, and he lacks for nothing because of her. She does him good all the days of her life.

Whatsoever her hands find to do, she does it with all her might.

She shops and finds great deals.

She rises early and provides food for her household.

She is a businessperson and knows how to purchase a piece of property.

She plants a garden and a vineyard for food or enjoyment.

She is physically strong and takes care of herself and exercises.

She has confidence and knows what she creates is good.

She leaves her lamp burning even at night.

She is kind and reaches out to the poor and needy.

She knows her family is well taken care of in all areas.

She dresses stylishl.

Her husband is known in the community and sits among the elders of the land.

She profits from the use of her hands and helps her family and others.

She is strong emotionally and honorable.

When she is older, she will be proud of what she has accomplished.

She uses wisdom and kindness when she speaks.

She protects her household from the snares of the devil.

She stays busy and is not idle.

Her children and husband rise and call her blessed, and her husband praises her, and others in the gates praise her also.

Dear Heavenly Father, I praise you for setting out the qualities of a virtuous woman in your word. I thank you for the privilege of choosing to be married or remain single. I thank you for the opportunity to be a wife, a mother, a businessperson, a person who works with their hands in arts and crafts, and for being able to be in health, education, politics, and any other career we choose. Please divinely direct us in

our life choices so that we will be pleasing to you and make the best of our talents and abilities. Amen.

ELIJAH'S MIRACULOUS EXPERIENCE

Now by this I know that thou art a man of God, and that the word of the Lord in thy mouth is truth. I Kings 17:24 KJV.

King Ahab ruled over Israel in Samaria for twenty-two years, and Ahab did eviler in the sight of the Lord than all before him. Elijah, the prophet, warned him. There would be no dew or rain for many years if he did not repent.

Kings usually killed the prophets of the Lord when they prophesied something they did not like. God told Elijah to go to Cherith and hide by the brook. He was fed manna by ravens twice daily and drank water from the brook.

Later, God told him to go to Zarephath, and a widow would sustain him there. When he arrived, she had enough meal and oil to make a small cake, and she planned to cook it for her son and herself to eat and die. He told her to prepare it and give him some first, for the Lord God of Israel said the meal and oil would not run out until the Lord sent rain and lifted the famine. She did as he directed, and her household ate for many days.

Her son became ill and died. Elijah took him up to the room where he slept, laid him on the bed, and cried out to the Lord and the child was healed and breath reentered his body.

Dear Heavenly Father, I praise you for using people and doing miracles in our lives still today. Please help us to always obey as you direct. Amen.

JUNE 5
ELISHA, FINANCIAL MIRACLE

There is not a vessel more. And the oil stayed. II Kings 4:6 KJV.

The prophet Elijah did not die. He was transported to heaven and received by chariots and horses of fire. His mantle fell on Elisha, who had asked for a double portion of Elijah's power. There was a woman who was the wife of one of the sons of the prophets under Elijah. She cried out to Elisha that her husband was dead, and he had pleased the Lord.

The creditor had come to take her two sons to be bondspersons for the debt they owed. Elisha asked what she had of value in the house. She had nothing except a pot of oil. He told her to gather every vessel she owned and go to her neighbors and borrow many vessels. When she returned, he instructed her and her two sons to go inside, close the door, and pour the oil into the vessels.

When the last vessel was filled to the top, the oil remained. Elisha told her to go sell the oil, pay the debt, and you and your sons live on the rest.

Dear Heavenly Father, thank you that you did financial miracles then and still do them today in the lives of those who serve you. Amen.

ENOCH PLEASED GOD

By faith Enoch was translated that he should not see death. Hebrews 11:5 KJV.

Enoch, Methuselah's father, was a man who walked with God, literally. He never died, for he was taken by God. He is one of the select few biblical characters to escape death. He was not found because God had translated him. Before his translation, he had the testimony that he pleased God.

Dear Heavenly Father, what an incredible testimony Enoch had. While it is astounding that he literally was taken by you, the fact that he walked with you and pleased you daily is a goal I would certainly like to be able to achieve. Amen.

HEZEKIAH, FIFTEEN YEARS LIFE ADDED

Thus, saith the Lord, the God of David thy Father. I have heard thy prayers, I have seen thy tears: behold, I will add unto thy days fifteen years. Isaiah 38:5 KJV.

King Hezekiah was a man who pleased God. He was one of the best of Judah's Kings. His father, King Ahaz, had led Judah into idolatry, causing much discontent both spiritually and politically. Early in Hezekiah's reign, he cleansed the temple of Assyrian cult matter.

King Hezekiah became ill at the point of death. He poured out his heart to God reminding him of how he had been faithful and had led his people into following God Almighty. The Lord heard his prayers and saw his tears, and Hezekiah received fifteen more years added to his life.

Dear Heavenly Father, thank you for your Word that strengthens our faith. Also, I thank you that when we have been faithful, we can come to you believing that you will hear and answer our sincere prayers. Amen.

JOEL FORTELLS HOLY SPIRIT OUTPOURING

Sanctify ye a fast. Call a solemn assembly, gather the elders and all the inhabitants of the land into the house of the Lord, your God, and cry unto the Lord. Joel 1:14 KJV.

Joel, the minor prophet, was greatly vexed over the infestation of insects that had occurred in the land of Judah. What the palmerworm did not eat, the locust ate. What the locust left, the cankerworm ate, and what the cankerworm left, the caterpillar ate.

A nation had come and destroyed the vineyards, and there was no meat or drink offering to take to the Lord's house. All the crops have dried up. The oil languished. Their meat had been cut off, and along with it went their joy and gladness.

Joel called for a sanctified fast and for the people to go into the House of God and cry out in repentance. They did, indeed.

The Lord heard their cries and pitied his people and told them to fear not for he would remove the enemy armies coming against them. He also told them to eat plenty, be satisfied, and praise the name of the Lord their God, who had dealt wondrously with them. God also promised he would pour out his spirit upon all flesh. Their sons and daughters would prophecy, their old men would dream dreams, and their young men would see visions.

Dear Heavenly Father, thank you for loving your children and meeting our needs. When we cry out to you in fasting and in prayer, it touches your heart. You know our earnestness and sincerity. Amen.

JUNE 9
ISAIAH FORTELLS CHRIST'S BIRTH

Behold, a virgin shall conceive and bear a son and shall call his name Immanuel. Isaiah 7:14 KJV.

The prophet Isaiah began his ministry in 734 B.C. He foretold the coming of the Messiah seven hundred years before it happened. No matter how long it takes, when God speaks, it will happen.

For unto us a child is born, unto us a son is given, and the government shall be upon his shoulder: and his name shall be called Wonderful, Counselor, The Mighty God, The Everlasting Father, The Prince of Peace. Of the increase of his government and peace there shall be no end, upon the throne of David, and upon his Kingdom, to order it, and to establish it with judgment and with justice from henceforth even forever. The zeal of the Lord of hosts will perform this. Isaiah 9:6-7 KJV.

365

Dear Heavenly Father, thank you for sending Isaiah to foretell the birth of your son. His birth was seven hundred years in coming, but it gave your people hope during some terrible times. We do not know when, but we know that your son is coming back again, and according to the signs of the times, it will be soon. We also have that blessed hope. Amen.

JEREMIAH, THE WEEPING PROPHET

Before I formed thee in the belly, I knew thee and before thou comest forth out of the womb I sanctified thee, and I ordained thee a prophet unto the nations. Then said I , Ah, Lord God, behold I cannot speak for I am a child. But the Lord said unto me, say not I am a child for thou shalt go to all that I send thee and whatsoever I command thee thou shalt speak. Be not afraid of their faces for I am with thee to deliver thee, saith the Lord. Jeremiah 1:5-8 KJV.

Jeremiah was called by God at an incredibly youthful age. His career as a prophetic minister lasted over half a century. Jeremiah's condemnation of the sins of the people around him aroused much hostility towards him, both in his home and in Jerusalem. He spoke out fearlessly, bringing on himself the anger of the court when he predicted the capture and the destruction of Jerusalem. He was called the weeping prophet because his tears flowed publicly and more in private when trying to get the people to repent and beg God to have mercy

on them. At one point, God instructed him to cry out no more for them because of their hardened hearts. Not heeding Jeremiah's warning caused them to spend seventy years in Babylonian captivity. What a price to pay for disobeying God by disobeying His message through his servant.

Dear Heavenly Father, thank you for calling and using men like Jeremiah who have a heart of love for you and a heart of compassion for sinners. Please help us help others realize that if they just obeyed you, their lives would be so much better. You love us and have our best interests at heart. Amen.

JUNE 11
AMOS' MESSAGE TO THE AFFLUENT WICKED

*Prepare to meet thy God, O Israel. Amos 4:12
KJV.*

Amos was from Tehoa, a tiny village on the edge of the Judean wilderness. Amos was a herder and trimmed Sycamore trees for a living when God called him. He was not a professional prophet nor the son of a prophet. He was attending his herd when the Lord called him to go prophesy to Israel.

Although his life was currently austere and simple, he had apparently traveled and encountered commercial centers of Palestine, as he displayed considerable knowledge in his writings of the lifestyles and attitudes of those to whom his message is directed. At the beginning of Amos' prophetic ministry, about 850 B.C. Israel was enjoying prosperity under Jeroboam II and Samaria had become a great center of commerce. There was a rich merchant class because of robbery, violence, and no regard for human life. They were enjoying lavish, elegant homes as described in the book of

Amos. Their wives, referred to as "cows of Bashan," loved living in the lap of luxury.

Although there were plenty of shrines of God and well attended socially, they were full of immorality and abuse. Fornication and drunkenness were being practiced in the very presence of the altar. The worship was devoid of any spiritual content and had a perverted effect on those who attended. Amos preached a message that sin will not go unpunished, and God's righteousness will ultimately triumph.

Dear Heavenly Father, although we live in similar times as Amos, I am so thankful I have never had to witness such disrespect for God's house going on in my place of worship. Thank you for the message of Amos that certainly speaks to our business and commercial world today and lavish current lifestyles. Amen.

JUNE 12
HOSEA AND GOMER

*I will heal their backsliding; I will love them
freely; for mine anger is turned away from him.
Hosea 14:4 KJV.*

Hosea was a prophet around the time of the
Prophet Amos, 850 B.C. At the beginning of Hosea's
ministry, Israel was enjoying a prosperous time
under the reign of King Jeroboam II; however,
Hosea saw some disaster brewing as Israel was
depending on their own political moves instead of
relying on God. Her part in future problems was
attributed by Hosea to her persistent practice of
running after other gods.

Hosea's marriage problems with his wife,
Gomer, illustrate Israel's unfaithful actions toward
God. The people were offering sacrifices on heathen
altars to heathen gods. God's love for Israel was
illustrated in Hosea's willingness to take his wife
back, even paying to buy her back from harlotry.
Hosea describes Israel's problem as a "lack of
knowledge." He is not referring to intellectual

371

knowledge but to a relationship of the most intimate sort between an individual and spouse that can be compared to the ultimate intimacy that can be enjoyed between God and a believer.

Dear Heavenly Father, what a beautiful love story that could easily have ended in tragedy. Just as Gomer realized, Hosea, her husband, was the one who genuinely loved her, forgave her, took her back, and even paid the price for her return. Please help us to understand that is what you have done for us. Help us to understand that true intimacy with our partner is what makes a marriage satisfying and beautiful. Likewise, an intimate, loving relationship with You is what brings true joy and contentment in life. Amen

MALACHI'S PROPHECY ON FINANCIAL BLESSINGS

And all the nations shall call you blessed for ye shall be a delightful land, said the Lord of host. Malachi 3:12 KJV.

Malachi, a prophet of the post-exile era, probably began his prophetic ministry around 450 B.C. The Jews had returned from captivity in Babylon full of hope and zeal.

They failed to find things as good as they had expected and became slightly disillusioned. There was crop failure due to the drought. They soon found themselves in doubt, skepticism, and neglect of spiritual matters.

The heart of Malachi's message was that their imperfect sacrifices and lack of giving their tithe would keep them from enjoying prosperity. Bring me all of the tithes into the storehouse that there may be meat in my house and prove me now herewith, saith the Lord of host, if I will not open you the windows of heaven and pour you out a blessing that there shall not be room enough to receive. **Malachi 3:10 KJV.**

Dear Heavenly Father, I praise you for the privilege of giving tithes and offerings and for your word that explains the reason for giving. Our family has been blessed by tithing. There have been times when our bank account was running low. We paid our tithes first and you allowed us to have enough to pay our bills and still have food on the table. For this, I give you praise. Amen

JOHN THE BAPTIST, FORERUNNER OF CHRIST

I indeed baptize you with water unto repentance but he that cometh after me is mightier than I whose shoes I am not worthy to bear. He shall baptize you with the Holy Ghost and with fire. Matthew 3:11 KJV.

John the Baptist was the son of Zacharias and Elizabeth who was a cousin of Mary, Jesus' mother. He was six months older than Jesus, and John remained in seclusion until he came forth from the wilderness to begin his ministry. Dressed in camel skins, fastened by leather girdle like the ancient prophets, he ate locust and wild honey. John's rustic lifestyle, his appearance, and the character of his message drew large crowds. He soon had many disciples. Although he had a great following, with many repenting and being baptized, he always portrayed himself as the forerunner of Jesus and eulogized him as the greatest of those born of women.

Dear Heavenly Father, what an incredible man was John the Baptist. With his fast-growing popularity, he remained subservient to Jesus. He undoubtedly spent much time with you in prayer in the wilderness, preparing for a remarkably effective forerunner ministry of Jesus, evidenced by the number of repentant souls and baptisms he had. Amen.

JOSEPH, HUSBAND OF MARY, JESUS' MOTHER

Then Joseph her husband being a just man and not willing to make her a public example was minded to put her away privately. Matthew 1:19 KJV.

Joseph was engaged to Mary, a young virgin when the Angel Gabriel appeared to her and told her she was going to have a baby, the Son of God. She did not understand. She had not had sexual intercourse with any man. The Angel reassured her to fear not. The Holy Spirit had overshadowed her. She was blessed and highly favored among women.

When Mary told Joseph, he was confused. Being a just man and not wanting to embarrass her, he decided to break up with her privately Then an Angel appeared to him and told him not to be afraid to marry Mary. That which was conceived in her was of the Holy Ghost. Then Joseph did as the Angel had instructed and took Mary as his wife. Can you imagine the love this young man had to have for Mary? Can you imagine the faith he must have possessed? Surely, he must have been steeped in

scriptures. He had to know what the word said. The Angel reminded him that this was just as God had spoken by the Prophet Isaiah.

Dear Heavenly Father, thank you for sending your precious son to earth to be born of a woman and to die for our sins. He was totally human, yet totally God. Thank you for the example the young couple, Mary and Joseph, set for all of us. What love, what trust, and what obedience they both had to carry out your will to deliver your precious gift to the world. Amen.

SIMON'S PROPHECIES CONCERNING JESUS

For my eyes have seen thy salvation. Luke 2:30 KJV.

When Jesus was eight days old, Mary and Joseph brought him to Jerusalem to the temple to be presented to the Lord. There was a prophet named Simeon, just and devout and full of the Holy Ghost. He had been waiting for the consolation of Israel. God had revealed to him that he would not see death before he had seen Christ. The spirit led him to go to the temple. Here, the parents brought in the child, Jesus, to do according to the custom of the law. Simeon took Jesus in his arms, blessed God, and said, "Let me depart in peace. For my eyes have seen your salvation." Simeon blessed them and prophesied to Mary that this child, wrapped in a soft blanket today, is set for the falling and rising of many and for a sign to be spoken against. A sword will pierce through your own soul so that the thoughts of many hearts may be revealed.

Dear Heavenly Father, what a heart-crushing prophecy to Mary, the young mother of this precious baby. She knew her son was to be the Savior of the World, but had she any idea how he would suffer and what all he would go through? Often, we do not know what the future holds, but sometimes, you do give us a glimpse so that we can slightly prepare. Thank you, God, for this precious gift, our Salvation. Amen.

ANNA SEES REDEMPTION IN JERUSALEM

And he shall grow, and wax strong in spirit, filled with wisdom: and the grace of God was upon him. Luke 2:40 KJV.

Anna, a prophetess, had been married for only seven years when she became a widower. She then moved into the temple, where she served God with fasting and prayer, night and day. Anna was eighty-four years old when his parents presented Jesus for dedication in the temple at Jerusalem. When Anna saw Jesus, she gave thanks immediately unto the Lord. She then spoke of him to all of them who looked for redemption in Jerusalem.

Dear Heavenly Father, what an encounter it must have been when Jesus and Anna met for the

first time in the temple in Jerusalem! What a praise and worship service as she gave praise to her Lord and soon-to-be Savior of the World. Amen.

JESUS HEALS AND DELIVERS

And his fame went throughout all Syria: and they brought unto him all sick people that were taken with divers diseases and torments and those which were possessed with devils, and those which were lunatick, and those that had the palsy, and he healed them. Matthew 4:24 KJV.

Jesus began his ministry around the age of 30 years. He performed many miracles because of the power of God, a fact which even his enemies admitted. He was never one to gain a reputation but to meet a need in the recipient's life, causing the people to believe and repent. In the religious world today, some believe that miracles disappeared after the church was established, but this is untrue. Miracles still occur when people ask and believe. I have experienced miracles in my own life and know of others who have received miraculous healings and answers to prayers.

Dear Heavenly Father, I praise you and I thank you that you performed many miracles when Jesus was here in body, and You are still miraculously answering prayer today. When your children believe and ask in faith and do not doubt, it shall be done. Amen.

JUNE 19
JESUS CALMS TEMPEST

But the men marveled, saying, what manner of man is this, that even the winds and sea obey him! Matthew 8:27 KJV.

Jesus and his disciples entered the ship. They were tired from ministering. Jesus got comfortable and went to sleep. A great tempest arose in the sea. The ship was rocking and covered with waves. His disciples came to him and awoke him, saying, "Lord save us! We will perish." He said to them, "Why are you fearful? Are you of little faith?" Then he arose, rebuked the winds and the sea, and there was a great calm. The men were astonished.

Dear Heavenly Father, I thank you that there are no storms in our lives that you cannot calm. You

speak peace, and even the wind obeys. By your example you endeavor to teach us to speak peace to calm our own storms. We have the power, in the name of Jesus! Amen

JESUS FEEDS FIVE THOUSAND

And they that had eaten were about five thousand men, beside women and children. Matthew 14:21 KJV.

Jesus went to a place in the desert, and the multitude followed him on foot out of the city. He was moved with compassion toward them and healed their sickness.

When it was evening, the disciples came to him and said, "It is getting late. Why not send them away so they can go into the city and buy dinner?"

Jesus said, "They do not have to leave. Just feed them."

They said, "We have no food, but there is a little boy here whose mother packed him a bag with five loaves and two fishes."

Jesus said, "Bring them to me and tell the multitude to sit on the grass."

Jesus took the five loaves and the two fishes and, looking up to heaven, broke them and gave them to the disciples to pass out to the multitude.

Everyone there ate and was filled. The disciples gathered up what remained and there were twelve baskets full.

Dear Jesus, you can do all things. There is no limit to your magnificent power. Amen

JESUS HEALS VEXED BOY

If you have faith...nothing shall be impossible unto you. Howbeit this kind goeth not out but by prayer and fasting. Matthew 17:20-21 KJV.

When Jesus and his disciples came to the multitude, there was a man who knelt down to Jesus and said, "Lord, have mercy on my son, for he is a lunatic and sore vexed. Often, he falls into the fire and into the water." Jesus rebuked the devil, and he departed out of the boy. The child was healed from that very hour.

Dear Heavenly Father, thank you so much for having men, inspired by the Holy Spirit, to write down the miracles you performed with instructions on faith in your holy word for us today. Amen.

NICODEMUS COMES TO JESUS AT NIGHT

Rabbi, we know that thou art a teacher come from God: for no man can do these miracles that thou doest, except God be with him. John 3:2 KJV.

Nicodemus was a Pharisee and a ruler of the Jews. He was impressed by Jesus' teachings but was afraid to seek him in the day, so, he came to Jesus at night. He knew Jesus came from God because no man could perform the miracles Jesus did except God be with him. Jesus taught him the doctrine of the new birth. There is no record of him openly following Jesus, but he is believed to have by the way he defended Jesus in front of the Sanhedrin court and by bringing and assisting Joseph of Arimathea in Jesus's burial. He brought a one-hundred-pound mixture of myrrh and aloes to bind Jesus in linen clothes with the spices.

Dear Jesus, only you know if Nicodemus was a true convert. Please help me never to leave people questioning if I am a believer. Help me to always be willing to stand publicly for you because you publicly died for me. Amen.

IMPETUOUS PETER BECOMES THE ROCK

For these are not drunken, as you suppose, seeing it is but the third hour of the day. But this is that which was spoken by the prophet Joel; And it shall come to pass in the last days, saith God, I will pour out my spirit upon all flesh: and your sons and your daughters shall prophecy, and your young men shall see visions, and your old men shall dream dreams, and on my servants, and on my handmaidens, I will pour in those days of my spirit, and they shall prophecy: and it shall come to pass, that whosoever shall call on the name of the Lord shall be saved. Acts 2:15-18,21 KJV.

Peter and his brother Andrew were fishermen and were probably disciples of John the Baptist before meeting and being called by Jesus. Peter, who often took on a leadership role as an Apostle of Jesus, preached on the day of Pentecost. After the Holy Spirit had descended, Peter preached a message where three thousand souls received the Word of God and were baptized.

Dear Lord Jesus, often impetuously like Peter, I make quick decisions without praying and thinking things through. Peter made some decisions and regretted them, as most of us have. He grew and matured spiritually. Jesus later referred to him as "the rock." What a powerful sermon he preached at Pentecost! This just proves Jesus sees our potential before we reach it. Please help us to follow you daily and produce growth. Amen.

JUNE 24
CORNELIUS' AND PETER'S VISIONS

Thy prayers and thine alms are come up before a memorial before God. Acts 10:4 KJV.

Cornelius was a Roman Gentile centurion who commanded one hundred Roman soldiers. He was a just man who feared God and prayed always. He gave alms to the poor and had a good report with the Jews. Because of a desire for spiritual truth, in a vision, he was instructed to send for Peter. Peter also had a vision that the Christian religion made no distinction between Jews and Gentiles. Their meeting and great discussion of their visions prompted the apostle Peter to make the statement, "Of a truth I perceive God is no respecter of person: But in every nation, he that feareth him, and worketh righteousness is accepted with him. Acts 10:34-35 KJV.

Then the Holy Spirit fell on all of them, which heard the word and Peter baptized Cornelius and his household. This event set a precedent for the admission of Gentiles to full Christian fellowship.

394

Dear Heavenly Father, thank you so much that you created all of us and you are no respecter of persons. Amen.

And he gave her his hand and lifted her up, and when he had called the saints and widows, presented her alive. Acts 9:41 KJV.

There was a woman in Joppa named Tabitha, aka Dorcas, who did many good works and gave alms to the poor and those in the ministry. She became ill and died. They bathed her and laid her in an upper chamber.

Peter was nearby in Lydda and had just prayed for a man named Aeneas, who had been bedfast for eight years with the palsy. Peter told him that Jesus Christ maketh you whole. Take up your bed and walk. He arose immediately.

Dorcas resided close by in Joppa. Two men were sent to Peter, and he came to where she was. Peter went immediately to the room where she lay. Many widows stood around her weeping and holding the coats and clothing she had made for them. Peter knelt down prayed and, turning toward the body, said, "Tabitha, arise!" She opened her eyes, and when she saw Peter, she sat up. He presented her alive to all that was present. It was known throughout all Joppa and many believed in the Lord Jesus Christ.

Dear Lord Jesus, thank you so very much for sending miracles into all our lives. If we only believe, all things are possible! Amen.

JUNE 26
PHILLIP AND THE EUNUCH

And he went on his way rejoicing. Acts 8:39 KJV.

Phillip, an apostle of Jesus Christ, was obedient and close to the Master. He soon became an evangelist, witnessing wherever he went. One day the Holy Spirit instructed Phillip to go toward the south, down from Jerusalem into Gaza.

He came across an Ethiopian official of Queen Candace who had charge of all her treasures. He had come to Jerusalem to worship. On his way back home, he stopped and sat in his chariot, reading the book of Isaiah. Philip came near him and asked if he understood what he was reading. He invited Philip to come into the chariot and sit and talk with him. There, Philip preached Jesus unto him and explained the scriptures from Isaiah to him. The Eunuch believed and wanted to be baptized. There was water close by, and Philip baptized him.

Dear Heavenly Father, oh, to be like Phillip! He had a zeal to evangelize and an ability and confidence to explain the word of God, even to those of different cultures. Phillip was successful in leading the Ethiopian eunuch, as well as many others, to Christ. Amen.

ADULTEROUS WOMAN

Judge not, that ye be not judged. Matthew 7:1 KJV.

Jesus was in the temple teaching and the scribes, and the Pharisees brought to him a woman caught in the very act of adultery. They said, "Moses in the law commanded us that such should be stoned. What do you say?" This they said to him, trying to tempt him that they could trick him and bring an accusation against him. He stooped down and wrote on the ground as though he had heard them not.

So, when they continued asking him, he lifted himself and said unto them, "He that is without sin let him cast the first stone at her, and he stooped down and wrote on the ground.

They who heard it, being convicted by their own conscience, went out one by one beginning with the eldest down to the last. Jesus was left alone with the woman standing in the midst.

When Jesus had lifted up himself and no one remained but the woman, he said, " Woman where are your accusers? Hath no man condemned you?" She said, "No man, Lord." Jesus said unto her, "Neither do I condemn thee. Go and sin no more."

Dear Heavenly Father, please help me not to be quick to judge others. You are God, and You are the only one without sin. Amen.

THE PASSION OF CHRIST

Father, if thou be willing, remove this cup from me: nevertheless, not my will but thine be done and there appeared an angel from heaven strengthening him. And being in agony he prayed more earnestly: and his sweat was as if it were great drops of blood falling to the ground. Luke 22:42-44 KJV.

Immediately after Jesus prayed the above prayer, he was betrayed with a kiss by one he had chosen. He then healed the ear of one that was arresting him. He was denied three times by another chosen disciple. Then, he was mocked, hit, blindfolded, struck in the face, slapped, made fun of, blasphemously spoken against, went through an unlawful mock trial, questioned extensively, and accused falsely of causing an insurrection. Herod had said he had done nothing worthy of death. Pilate also said he found no fault in Jesus. Pilate suggested three times, chastising him and releasing him. But the angry mob preferred the release of a murderer. He was beaten, scourged, given vinegar

to drink, and his beard plucked before the nails were driven through his hands and feet into the huge beams on which he was nailed.

Jesus was crucified between two thieves. One said, "If thou be Christ, save thyself and us. But the other answering rebuked him, saying, "Do you not fear God? Seeing you are in the same condemnation, and we indeed justly receive the reward of our deeds, but this man has done nothing wrong." And he said unto Jesus, "Lord, remember me when you come into your Kingdom," and Jesus said unto him, "Verily I say unto thee, "Today shalt thou be with me in paradise. Luke 23:39-43 KJV.

What mercy and compassion our Savior had during all the personal, emotional, and physical agony he was feeling to take the time to spiritually save one of the thieves when he asked to be remembered.

Dear Lord Jesus, I could never ever repay you for the love, mercy, and compassion that you have so vividly shown me. I plan to spend the rest of my life loving you in return. I am convinced if the one thief on the cross who believed in you that day was the only person ever to be converted, you still would have died just for him. Amen.

MIRACLE OF JESUS' RESURRECTION

He is not here but is risen. Luke 24:6 KJV.

On the first day of the week, early in the morning, some of the women followers of Jesus came to the tomb with spices and ointments prepared for Jesus' body. They found the stone rolled away from the sepulcher. They entered and found nobody lying there. Two men in shining garments stood by them and said, "Remember when Jesus told you that he must be delivered into the hands of sinful men, and be crucified, and on the third day rise again?" They remembered his words, returned from the sepulcher, and told all these things unto the eleven and to others.

Dear Heavenly Father, I thank you so very much for Jesus dying on the cross for all of us. What is even more incredible is the almighty power of God that raised him from the dead on the third day, just as he said Amen.

MIRACLE OF JESUS' ASCENSION

This same Jesus which is taken up from you into heaven shall so come in like manner as you have seen him go into heaven. Acts1:11 KJV.

The disciples were talking about how Jesus had risen indeed because he had appeared to Simon Peter. Then Jesus himself stood amid them and said, "Peace be unto you."

They were terrified and thought they had seen a spirit. He asked why they were troubled and having wrong thoughts. He showed them his hands and his feet.

He asked them if they had any meat to eat. They gave him a piece of broiled fish and honeycomb, and he ate it.

Then he said the scripture: It behooved Christ to suffer and to rise from the dead on the third day. Repentance and remission of sin shall be preached in his name among all nations beginning at Jerusalem. You have witnessed these things. I send the promise of the father upon you. Tarry ye in the city of Jerusalem until you be endued with power from on high.

He led them out as far as Bethany and he lifted his hands, and he blessed them. While he blessed them, he was carried up into heaven, and a cloud received him out of their sight.

Dear Lord Jesus, it must have been an incredible event to see you after you arose from the dead and then to see you again and watch as you ascended to heaven. Wow! I am looking forward to seeing you and spending time with you in person! Amen.

July

JULY 1
NEWS THAT SHATTERS

The Lord is nigh unto them of a broken heart; and saveth such as be of a contrite spirit. Psalm 34:18 KJV.

Once in my life, I thought I could never be happier. My husband and I have both been Christians since we were adolescents. We had a strong, happy marriage built on love, faith, and hope. As products of our love, God had blessed us beautifully with a daughter and a son, the pride and joy of our lives. We had a beautiful home and jobs we enjoyed. He was an insurance agent for Farm Bureau, and I was executive director of the Commission on Children and Youth, Inc., a child abuse council. We were youth pastors at the College Street Church of God to a fun and spiritually thriving group of young people. Our family was active in volunteer outreach in our community, and I was an inspirational columnist for the Calhoun Times.

On a Friday afternoon during a doctor's appointment at Emory University Hospital, our lives changed forever. My husband, Randy Holbert, who was 42 years old at the time, was diagnosed with osteogenic sarcoma, a very aggressive cancer of the bone and blood.

Dear Heavenly Father, we are heartbroken and shattered. We are not turning loose of our faith in You. You and each other are all our family has at this point. Please shelter us safely in your arms until this storm passes. Amen.

JULY 2
PRAYERS TO BE SUSTAINED

Cast thy burden upon the Lord and he shall sustain thee. He shall never suffer the righteous to be moved. Psalms 55:22 KJV.

Outside the Emory University medical office complex, my husband put his arms around our children and me. As our tears flowed, we asked our heavenly father to please guide us in making treatment decisions and guide the hands of the surgeons and the oncologist, but most of all, please keep our faith strong as a family as we faced this ordeal.

My husband then went inside the gift shop to get us something to drink. He came back with bottled water, snacks, and, always being so thoughtful and loving, a tiny little wooden music box for me that played "You are the Wind Beneath My Wings."

Dear Heavenly Father, please give all of us the strength to face what is coming. Please keep us close to You and each other. Please strengthen our faith and do not let it fail. Amen.

JULY 3
FAITH BEGINS TO ARISE

I will praise thee for thou hast heard me and art become my salvation. Psalms 11:21 KJV.

On the way home, we made a mutual decision that we were going to believe the Word of God and not allow negative medical reports to infiltrate our hearts and minds with fear. We were all spiritual warriors, including our fourteen-year-old daughter and nine-year-old son.

When we got home, we called our pastor and had our church family begin praying for us. We told our extended families and friends and immediately felt their prayers and support. I began looking for scriptures on faith and healing and we decided to read them daily, commit to memory, and incorporate them in our prayers. Friends and family began sending cards and leaving messages of faith and encouragement on our voicemail. Our faith began to arise.

Dear Heavenly Father, thank you for the rays of light breaking through the darkness. Words of encouragement and hope that come from You through others and Your Word are so sustaining. Amen.

July 4
Important Traditions And Holidays

It is of the Lord's mercies that we are not consumed, because his compassion fails not. They are new every morning: great is thy faithfulnesss. Lamentations 3:22-23 KJV.

When illness or tragedy strikes your family, it is very important to continue celebrating holidays, traditions, and special occasions if at all possible. This is the time when stability, happiness, and as much laughter as possible are needed.

We are a very patriotic family. My husband had always been the grill master in the family, so we made plans as usual and invited a few family members and friends over for the July 4th celebration. I decorated and cooked his favorite sides and dessert, and that night, we went to watch the fireworks at the fairgrounds.

It took our minds somewhat off the cancer and put them on celebrating our faith, freedom, family, friends, food, and fun.

Dear Heavenly Father, I thank you for our faith, our freedom, our family, friends, good food, and fun. You are our God of hope. You fill us with the strength to continue doing what we always do, even when we do not feel like it. Amen.

JULY 5
NATURAL CANCER FIGHTERS

And out of the ground made the Lord God to grow every tree that is pleasant to the sight and good for food. Genesis 2:a KJV.

I began researching vitamins, minerals, supplements, and cancer-fighting foods, trying to find foods especially that my husband liked that were beneficial. This can be done for any illness or condition and is so easy, especially now with so much information on the Internet. I do not know if these fruits and vegetables, especially an immense amount of broccoli and blueberries, improved his condition. It sure made me feel better, knowing I was doing something to try to help.

Dear Heavenly Father, thank you for the immense variety of good fruits and vegetables you have created for us to enjoy. I pray your healing power through these foods will bless, nourish, and heal my husband. Amen.

July 6
Importance Of Laughter

A merry heart doeth good like a medicine.
Proverbs 17:22 KJV.

Then I commended mirth, because a man hath no better thing under the sun, than to eat and to drink, and to be merry: for that shall abide with him of his labor the days of his life, which God giveth him under the sun. Ecclesiastes 8:15 KJV.

In our journey through cancer, I read that laughter was the best medicine. My husband had always had a great sense of humor. During the time he felt well, we would try to keep the mood as light and happy as possible. We watched comedy movies, looked at old family photos, or discussed fun things we would like to do when he recovered. I encourage anyone going through a family illness to stay as positive as your circumstances will allow. Not only for the morale of the patient but also for children in the family whose lives need structure and to remain as normal as possible. Children are also having to deal with fear, anxiety, insecurity, and possibly

anger, so keep the mood as happy as you possibly can.

Dear Heavenly Father, I cannot identify the emotions I am feeling now dealing with my husband's illness. What our precious children must be going through. My daughter seems quieter and more anxious, while my son is acting out in anger. I cannot commence to know how to help. Please, God, please pour in your healing balm and ease the pain, especially for my precious babies. Amen.

O Taste and see that the Lord is good. Blessed is the man that trusteth in him. Psalm 34: 8 KJV.

My husband had always prided himself on designing and maintaining a beautifully landscaped yard. We had Lebanon fir trees, pear trees, shrubs, and a garden of beautiful blooming azaleas. His green thumb and eye for aesthetics and design in our lawn were unsurpassed until he became unable to maintain it.

One evening, I heard a mower in our yard and looked out to see Dave Johnson, Randy's boss and agency manager of Farm Bureau on a riding lawnmower. Agents Neil Barwick and Andy Denton were bringing in fresh pine straw and reworking the azalea garden. The next day, Joan Bentley, president of the child abuse council where I worked, called and said she and her husband, Dale, were having John Davis, landscaper, come and set out a beautiful Myrtle tree that could be seen inside our bedroom window. Our family was appreciative

and elated by the kindness and generosity of those we worked with. This was just the beginning of kindness shown by family and so many friends.

Dear Heavenly Father, thank you so very much for the loving kindness shown to our family by special friends. I never realized what that means to a family, until walking in such hopelessness. Amen.

July 8
MUSTARD SEED FAITH

And above all taking the shield of faith,
Therewith, ye shall be able to quench all the fiery
darts of the wicked. Ephesians 6:16 KJV.

One day my husband had a very important doctor's appointment to discuss the plan of treatment. The news was certainly not what we had hoped. A surgeon was brought in to discuss the amputation of my husband's right arm, where the cancer had originated. An occupational therapist came to visit and began talking about ways of coping as an amputee. Then, the chemotherapy would start immediately using the strongest available due to the aggressiveness of the cancer. In destroying the cancer cells, the chemotherapy would destroy the healthy cells as well, leaving my husband too weak to work until time for another round of treatment.

That news left us feeling the lowest of lows, but despite our hopelessness, the oncologist said that the most important thing our family had going for us was our tremendous faith and belief in God. That statement of encouragement was filled with just the amount of hope needed to keep our family going.

Dear Heavenly Father, we love you, and we trust you to see us through; however, we are depleted and need your strength more than ever before. We trust you, Lord, for healing and to meet all of our needs. Amen.

HELD UP BY PRAYER

But Moses hands were heavy and they took a stone and put it under him and he set threron; and Aaron and Ham stayed up his hands the one on the one side and the other on the other side and his hands were steady until the going down of the sun exodus 17:12 KJV.

On the day of an oncology appointment, my husband was so weak physically he was barely able to stand. The doctor called an ambulance and sent him directly to the hospital, where he was admitted. We had no extra clothes with us. My mom packed a bag, and Pastor Donald Lee, our new pastor at the College Street Church of God, brought it to us at Emory when he came to visit. My husband was released one week later, and Margie Lee, the pastor's wife, prepared a six-course meal and came to our home and served Randy, our children, and me a banquet-style candle-lit dinner. How very special for our family to be served in our own home a

delicious, prepared meal, and all of us enjoy sitting down together.

Dear Heavenly Father, we appreciate the efforts of our new pastor, his family, and our church for loving us and holding us up in prayer. We are growing weary, but we trust You for strength, for courage, and for determination. Amen.

July 10
COURAGE TO MAINTAIN

I had fainted unless I had believed to see the goodness of the Lord in the land of the living. Psalm 27:13 KJV.

So many times in the journey with my husband and cancer, I have felt like I cannot do this. I have prayed for strength and courage to continue believing and fighting for his very life. So many nights, I have cried myself to sleep praying for our precious children. They are scared, tired, and weary of having to be away from their parents and from home so much. How can they go to school and function with their lives so uncertain? How can I even hope to keep any assemblance of normalcy for them? I am praying for his healing, but it is not up to me. How can I stay on top of family responsibilities and do my job at the child abuse council?

Then God reminded me that I have an incredible mother, sister Barbara, niece Tina, and nephew Brent, who will do anything for my children.

I am reminded of how appreciative I am of Calhoun City Schools and how teachers have let me know the children are maintaining excellent attendance and making honor roll consistently during this crisis. My son Isaac still speaks today of his teacher, Marsha Brown McAllister. What a blessing she was during his fifth-grade year when he was bombarded with our crisis. I am reminded of the board of directors I worked for and how they so graciously allowed me to work from home and the hospital, writing grants outside my office to keep our programs funded. I am so appreciative of my staff and what a blessing they were to me personally during such a hard time.

Richard Lee, Jeremy Jackson, Erin Douglas Proctor, Pat and Butch Richards, Carol Vedrody, Dave, Jeannie, and Brad Johnson, George Southgate, Joan and Dale Bentley, Robert and Ellen Lee, Tammy Burger, DennisThibodeau, Cindy Edwards, and Dr. Katie Naymick, were all ministering angels to all our family during this traumatic time I could never pay them for all they did but I know God will if He has not already. After counting our blessings, I realized that God had us and would never leave us or forsake us because he was our heavenly father, and he loved his children.

Dear Heavenly Father, you are the ultimate in what a father should be. We could never, ever praise You enough for how You have taken care of Your children during this crisis. Amen.

JULY 11
GOD SUPPLIED YOUTH MINISTRY CONFERENCE NEEDS

But my God shall supply all your need according to his riches in glory by Christ Jesus. Philippians 4:19 KJV.

Being Youth Pastors at College Street Church of God to an incredible group of young people was one of the highlights of our lives. We always funded our own youth activities and attended Winterfest by selling Indian River fruit, chili cook-offs, or huge yard sales. The past two years have been difficult for us with chemotherapy sessions and hospital stays. It was late in the summer, and we had not raised any money for our youth conference at Winterfest in February of the following year. So, my husband, right arm-amputee planned a car wash and raised enough money in that one fundraiser to send all the teens and four chaperones to Winterfest Youth Conference in Gatlinburg the following February.

Dear Heavenly Father, thank you for giving my husband the energy to organize, oversee, and carry out this car wash. Thank you for providing a wonderful enthusiastic group of youth to wash automobiles, for providing the vehicles to wash, and for every donation we received for our youth to attend this conference. You are our amazing, incredible God. Amen.

And this is the confidence that we have in him, that if we ask anything according to his will he heareth us. I John 5:14 KJV.

As days turned into weeks, my husband's appetite became less and less. It was very difficult to find anything that he would eat. Before he became ill, one of our favorite places to dine was B.J.'s Restaurant in Calhoun. Dale and Joan Bentley had an account opened there for us and called to tell me to go by and pick up family meals for us whenever I needed. It would give Randy a variety of meats and vegetables and would give us more time together when home. It was a wonderful, loving, thoughtful gesture on their part. The meals were delicious and saved preparation and clean-up time for the children and me. He continued to not be able to eat and became weaker. I was now spending almost all my time working from our home.

Dear Heavenly Father, I am still trusting you for my husband's total healing. You can do all things. There is nothing too hard for you Please give us mercy and grace in this dark hour. Amen.

Continue in prayer and watch in the same with Thanksgiving. Colossians 4:2 KJV.

Before Thanksgiving of 1996, Randy was readmitted to the hospital for an extended stay. I had not been home for several days and the children were worried about their daddy and missing both of us. God knows just what we need. Joan Bentley called me and said she and her husband Dale had arranged a nice hotel for me to bring the children to stay in so they could go to the hospital and visit their daddy and spend time with both of us. We had a wonderful time being together even though their daddy was very weak and in bed the whole time.

God always knows what we need. Often, he sends angels on earth to bless and meet the needs and sometimes the desires of our hearts also.

Dear Heavenly Father, when situations seem dark You come through for your children. I praise you for the friends you have blessed to be a blessing. What a difference they make. Amen.

JULY 14
HELP COMETH

Oh, that men would praise the Lord for his goodness and wonderful works to the children of men. Psalm 107:2 KJV.

My husband always loved the Great Smoky Mountains. He loved the deer, the elk, the turkeys, the bears, the mountains, the fog, and the abundance of waterfalls. Due to the illness, we had not been able to schedule a real vacation for a couple of years because we never knew when he would have a bad reaction to chemotherapy and have to be hospitalized. This particular year,1996, he had been in and out of the hospital twelve times from three-day stays to three weeks.

Our friends, Ellen and Robert Lee, owned a beautiful, three-story mountain home, totally furnished, 9 miles outside of Gatlinburg. They graciously offered it to us for a weekend. The oxygen, medications, medical supplies, and the children were all packed, and we were excited to be on an adventure. We did not get to see snow or bears but saw plenty of deer and wild turkeys. We had fun with the kids, playing game cards, watching movies, and enjoying popcorn and hot chocolate in front of a roaring fire in the fireplace.

Dear Heavenly Father, when illness strikes, having wonderful, thoughtful friends to bring smiles to your faces and alleviate some of the sadness and gloom is such a comfort. Please help us always remember how we were blessed. Help us to understand the impact and give us the desire to pay it forward in the future. Amen.

There is no fear in love, but perfect love casteth out all fear 1 John 4:18 KJV.

Christmas is the most wonderful time of the year! Our family has always decorated early for Christmas. When we came back from Gatlinburg, it was time to decorate. My husband loved Christmas, and so did the children and I. Putting up the Christmas tree was one of the highlights of our year. My husband was unable to take the lead this Christmas but the children and I decorated every room of our home. I discussed it with him and his family and decided to have the Holbert Family Christmas at our house this year. We had a good time with the family but certainly with sickness, not as loud or festive as usual .

Our son Isaac got so many gifts. In addition to gifts from family, Dale Bentley bought him his first set of golf clubs for a left-handed golfer. Butch and Chris Richards gifted him with three nice sets of steel tech to put together, and George Southgate gave him several sets of baseball cards and an incredible number of singles. Cicero Holbert helped him with his Pine Derby car race and accompanied him to the Boy Scout banquet.

Our daughter, Tiffany, also had a wonderful Christmas, getting lots of clothes, jewelry, cologne, and a designer purse. Jeremy Jackson, a wonderful longtime friend, elegantly treated her to the Dove Awards in Nashville, followed by a wonderful dinner.

Dear Heavenly Father, thank you so much for another Christmas together. Thank you to our immediate and extended families, who mean so very much to us, but most of all, thank you for sending your precious son, Jesus, to be our Savior. Even the Angel Gabriel told them to fear not that holy night in

Bethlehem, and that's what we are standing on Your Holy Word. Amen.

Oh, magnify the Lord with me and let us exalt his name together. I sought the Lord and he heard me and delivered me from all my fears. Psalm 34:3 KJV.

We attended the Christmas play at College Street Church of God, followed by finger foods in the church fellowship hall with friends. Randy was having difficulty breathing and we had to leave early. That was the last time he ever walked. We went to Gordon Hospital by ambulance for tests and X-rays the following week, and we learned the cancer had metastasized to his lung. When we went home, he wanted to hear scriptures playing all the time as he rested. When not listening to them, the Bill Gaither Homecoming Musical Videos or beautiful scenery videos with music and scriptures played 24/7 In our home as praise and worship went forth to our Lord.

Dear Heavenly Father I love you. I praise you. I thank you that, as a Christian family, you have removed all fear and doubt. I thank you for the sweet peace we feel in our souls and for the comfort of the Holy Spirit. Amen.

And God Himself shall wipe away all tears from their eyes and there shall be no more death, neither sorrow, nor crying, neither shall there be any more pain Revelation 21: 4 KJV.

One day, I was reading the Bible to Randy, and he was praying and worshipping the Lord. He started smiling and laughing and moving his hand in the air. I asked him what he was seeing. He said he just held our baby girl, that I had miscarried, and she was smiling and looking at him as he softly talked to her. "Oh, please tell me more, Honey!" I said. He said there were many babies in heaven, a huge number that had probably been aborted or otherwise murdered. He also said he had been welcomed by his Papa Tate and Reverend C. H, Chambley, who was a former pastor and close friend of the Holbert family. That was the day I engraved in my heart and memory.

Dear Heavenly Father, I saw our second baby girl once in a dream, but never have I held her. One day, I will hold her close when we are reunited in heaven, never to be separated again. Thank you for these wonderful glimpses you have given Randy of heaven and for allowing him to share them with me. I love you so much, Lord. Amen.

JULY 18
WHY SUCH SUFFERING

Heal me, O Lord, and I shall be healed. Jeremiah 17:14 KJV.

One morning in February 1997, my husband was so weak he could barely speak above a whisper. I called his home health nurse, and she called an ambulance. They arrived and put him in the ambulance and sat in the cul-de-sac in front of our home for thirty minutes, trying to stabilize him. I followed them in my car to the Gordon Hospital. They had to give him five units of blood. He was in tremendous pain and struggling to breathe. That day was the worst I have seen him suffer since his diagnosis.

He finally became calm and seemed to be resting around 7:00 p.m. I went to the nurses' desk and told them I was going to the prayer room. They said if he asked for me or they needed me, they would call for me.

When I got to the prayer room, no one was in there. Only a dim light shone softly, but I had a small flashlight with me so I could read my Bible. I turned to Isaiah 53 and read Isaiah's prophecy concerning our Savior coming to earth and what he would suffer for our sins. I wept for all Jesus had gone through and for what my husband was going through now.

Dear Heavenly Father, I do not understand why you had to suffer so, and I do not understand why my husband is having to go through what he is with this horrible, evil cancer. I have tried my best to trust you for his total healing, but he seems to get only worse. God, I know you are Jehovah Rapha, the God that heals. Amen.

JULY 19
GOD REVEALS HIS PLAN. PART 1

Continued from July 18

Wherefore, let them that suffer according to the will of God commit the keeping of their souls to him in well-doing as unto a faithful Creator. I Peter 4:19 KJV.

In the prayer room, the Holy Spirit mphatically said to me, "Read more!"

I got up, got a box of Kleenex, and laid down on the floor on my stomach. I opened my Bible and it randomly opened at Isaiah 54, exactly where I had left reading. My eyes went directly to Isaiah 54:5 KJV: For thy maker is thine husband. "No, God, please no! Do not do this." I begged.

Isaiah 54:6-10KJV: For the Lord hath called thee as a woman forsaken and grieved in spirit and a wife of youth. For a small moment have I forsaken thee; but with great mercies will I gather thee. In a little wrath I hid my face from thee for a moment; but with everlasting kindness will I have mercy on thee, saith the Lord thy Redeemer. For as I have sworn that the waters of Noah should no more go over the earth, so have I sworn that I would not be wroth with thee nor rebuke thee. For the mountains shall depart, and the hills be removed, but my kindness shall not depart from thee, neither shall the covenant of my peace be removed, saith the Lord that hath mercy on thee (my future foretold).

Isaiah 54:11,12 KJV: O thou afflicted, tossed with tempest and not comforted, behold I will lay thy stones with four colors, and lay thy foundations with sapphires. And I will make thy windows of agates, and thy gates of carbuncles, and all thy borders of pleasant stones (my husband in heaven foretold).

"But Lord?" I asked. "What about my children? What about their faith? They have believed in their father's healing here, not in heaven! Please do not let my children lose their faith!"

Isaiah 54:13 KJV: And all thy children shall be taught of the Lord and great shall be the peace of thy children. For ye shall go out with joy and be led forth with peace: the mountains and the hills shall break forth before you into singing, and the trees of the field shall clap their hands.

Isaiah 55:13 KJV: Instead of the thorn shall come up the fir tree (trees planted in our backyard) and instead of the briar shall come up the myrtle tree (Joan planted in the side yard), and it shall be to the Lord.

Isaiah 56:1 KJV. Thus saith the Lord, Keep ye judgment, and do justice: for thy salvation is near to come and thy righteousness to be revealed.

Isaiah57:1,2 KJV. The righteous perisheth and no man layeth it to heart: and merciful men are taken away from the evil to come.

He shall enter into peace: they shall rest in their beds, each one walking in his righteousness.

Isaiah 57:18 KJV: I have seen his ways and will heal him. I will lead him also and restore comforts unto him and unto his mourners (My husband healed eternally, and his family comforted).

Dear Heavenly Father, if You are going to take my husband home to Heaven to heal him eternally, You must tell him because we have trusted You for his healing here on earth. I cannot possibly break this news to him. Amen.

JULY 20
GOD REVEALS PART 2 OF HIS PLAN

Continued from July 19

Cast not away therefore your confidence which hath great recompense of reward Hebrews 10: 35 KJV.

After spending three hours in the Chapel at Gordon Hospital I went back toward my husband's room. I stopped by the nurse's desk and was told that he had been very peaceful and was resting. I had just gone inside his room and laid my Bible down when my husband said, "Honey, please don't be mad at me." I went to his bedside, took hold of his hand, and said, "Angel, I could never be mad at you." I climbed up into the bed with him and snuggled close to his left side.

We were looking into each other's eyes and holding each other when he said calmly. "Honey, I have asked the Lord to take me home. I am so tired, and I do not want to struggle anymore. I want to be well. God has answered me, and He will take good care of you and our precious babies. I hope you will find a godly man and remarry. You have too much love to give to not remarry. He must be good to you and our babies. I trust your judgment. I love you more than life itself. We will see each other again when everyone is well and happy and in a place where there are no more tears."

By this time, the tears were flowing from both of us. We lay there for a long time, holding each other and praying in the Holy Spirit. I called Margie Lee to tell them. Pastor Lee was in South Georgia. Margie called Pastor Keith Reed, Calhoun District Pastor of the Churches of God and he and George Seddon came to the hospital and had prayer with us. We planned to talk to our children tomorrow.

Dear Heavenly Father, we love You. We are trusting You. We know you hold all our futures in your hands. We are not letting go of your nail-scarred hands. They have brought all of us this far and we are trusting you to lead us safely all the way home. Amen.

BREAKING THE NEWS TO OUR CHILDREN

Let us hold fast the profession of our faith without wavering for he is faithful that promised. Hebrews 10: 23 KJV.

We came home in a few days from the hospital and picked up our children at my mom's house. We gathered in the living room, and there their daddy talked about how we had always trusted God as a family, how he would never leave us or forsake us, and how all of us had one ultimate goal, and that was to one day hear Jesus say, "Well done thou good and faithful servant. You have fought a good fight. You have kept the faith. Enter, therefore, into the joy of the Lord." Then he told them he had asked Jesus to take him home to Heaven. He wanted to be well, and he wanted all of us to see each other again in a land where there are no more tears. He also told them that Jesus had answered him and he would take care of his precious children and their mom. Then we held each other, with tears flowing, and spoke of our forever love.

Dear Heavenly Father, we are drained and weary. Please strengthen us to face the days ahead. Give us the courage to go on and not be afraid. We desperately want him to be well but God, how we love him and need him. Help me to be the wife that I need to be to my precious husband and the mother that my precious children so greatly need. GOD, I am certainly not feeling the part I have been thrown into. God, I need you more than I ever have before. Please do not allow my faith to fail me. Amen.

JULY 22
DAUGHTER'S AUTOMOBILE ACCIDENT

The eyes of the Lord are upon the righteous, and his ears are open unto their cry. The righteous cry and the Lord heareth and delivereth them out of all their troubles. The Lord is nigh unto them that are of a broken heart and saveth such as be of a contrite spirit. Many are the afflictions of the righteous; but the Lord delivereth him out of them all. Psalm 34:15,17-19 KJV.

One rainy afternoon on the way home from school, our daughter had gone by a friend's home. She had forgotten that she was to pick up her brother at middle school. When she remembered, she realized she was late and became anxious. She pulled out in front of a car, causing an automobile accident. Several people were hurt, including herself. She had a broken arm and cuts and bruises. My husband was dying, my children were barely holding on, and I desperately needed to be calm for all of them.

Dear Heavenly Father, you see my tears, and you know my broken heart. When I do not have the words to pray, please hear my heart. Amen.

JULY 23
DISTRACTION FROM SADNESS

Now the God of hope fill you with all joy and peace in believing that he may abound in hope through the power of the Holy Ghost. Romans 15:13 KJV.

The Board of Directors of the Child Abuse Council, where I worked as executive director, had come together and bought property for our offices. With a tremendous amount of community support, they completely remodeled the facility while I was working from home and caring for my husband with cancer. It was amazing the support, love, and prayers shown, not only by our family but by the council as well during this time. Our faith in God, hope, and love kept us going in the worst of times. The good news about the completion of this newly remodeled facility was certainly a pleasant distraction from all the sadness we were facing.

Dear Heavenly Father, none of us make it without You and the wonderful people You put in our lives. You strengthen our faith, You give us hope, and You let us feel Your wonderful love and that of others when we are running on empty. You fill us up just in time. Amen.

Plead my cause, O Lord, with them that strive with me: fight against them that fight against me. Take hold of shield and buckler, and stand up for mine help. Psalm 35:12 KJV.

A few days after my daughter's wreck, Tiffany and I received subpoenas to appear in Juvenile Court concerning the accident. My precious daughter was so scared. She had never even been in the principal's office, much less in front of a judge. I called the court and explained our circumstances, but the judge would not excuse us.

My husband's condition was worsening daily, and he did not want me to leave him. I called in a nurse to sit with him and assured him I would be back as soon as possible.

The court hearing only lasted a few minutes and we came back home. When we got there, my husband had gone into a coma. You can rest assured: CHOOSING FAITH DAILY is a must. It builds our faith muscles. We so desperately need a strong faith to stand when we do not have a choice. **REAL LIFE DEMANDS REAL FAITH.**

Dear Heavenly Father, if it was not for You and Your Word in our lives, our family would not have survived. Thank You, our mighty God Ameen.

JULY 25
HEALED ETERNALLY

For I know whom I have believed, and I am persuaded that he is able to keep that which I have committed unto him against that day. II Timothy 1:12 KJV.

My husband had been in a coma for several days and had been lying on his back in the same position during that time. I got up at 6:00 am that morning to give his shot that I gave every two hours. When I slipped back into bed, he moved his leg as close as possible and intertwined with mine. He had not walked since Christmas, and this was early spring. The kids were home for spring break. I lay there close to him and talked to him softly. His eyes were closed, and at exactly 8:00 am, he gave a big sigh, and he was gone. I believe that from 6:00 am to 8:00 am was a way of him telling me goodbye. I called the home health nurse, Cindy Edwards, my longtime friend, and told her he had passed. I went and woke the children, and they came and said their soft goodbyes to their daddy. Then, we went to the couch. I held them, and we cried and talked about how God had healed him eternally. No more pain, no more sickness. "Our Daddy has a new body!" Isaac reminded us.

Dear Heavenly Father, thank you for healing him completely and giving him what he had requested, the very desires of his heart, to live and be with you forever. Amen.

Because he has set his love upon me, therefore will I deliver him. I will set him on high because he hath known my name. He shall call upon me, and I will answer him: I will be with him in trouble, and I will deliver him and honor him. Psalms 91:14-15 KJV.

My husband's Homegoing Service held at the College Street Church of God was beautiful. Our youth group, the employees of Gordon County Farm Bureau, and the Board of Directors of the Child Abuse Council served as honorary pallbearers. Pastors Donald Lee and James Edmondson officiated. Pastor James Davenport, cousin, did the Internment Service at Chandler Cemetery. Lucretia Dykes was in charge of music. The songs chosen were The Anchor Holds, He's Been Faithful, and How Great Thou Art. After the internment, family and friends were served a buffet-style dinner at The College Street Church of God. After we went home, I assured my children that their daddy was healed eternally and we would be reunited someday. I

reminded my children that I loved them, and God loved us and held us in the palm of his hand. We would take life one day at a time and love and support each other. We were going to be fine and happy again because God assured their daddy and me that we would be.

Dear Heavenly Father, I praise You for loving my children and me and others who have lost a loved one here on earth. I thank You that You have provided Your Word to guide us and pray that we can take all of our needs, concerns, and hurts to You directly. Amen.

JULY 27
TIME FOR REST

And he said unto them, come you yourselves apart into a desert place, and rest a while: for there were many coming and going, and they had no leisure so much as to eat. Mark 6:31 KJV.

For this saith the Lord God, the holy one of Israel: in returning and rest shall ye be saved; in quietness and confidence shall be your strength. Isaiah 30:15 KJV.

After you have been through a crisis or great loss, such as losing someone you love to death or divorce, your body needs time to rest, grieve, heal, and restore. Grief presents itself differently in different people. Someone said that grief is love with no one to give it. Another friend told me that the deeper the love, the deeper you grieve. I am not a professional counselor, but I am a witness that my children and I needed rest. Every muscle and joint in my body ached after my husband passed.

Dear heavenly Father, thank you that your word advises us on how to take care of our bodies, minds, and spirits after going through a traumatic life crisis. We are dependent on you for healing and for restoration. Amen.

July 28
The Great Physician

Heal me O Lord and I shall be healed, save me, and I shall be saved; for thou art my praise. Jeremiah 17:14 KJV.

After going through an emotional trauma or great loss, it is a good idea to be seen by your personal physician. Stress over time can deplete the human body of valuable minerals and vitamins. Your physician can do blood work to determine if you are lacking in these areas. After our family loss, I had physicals completed on both my children and myself. The joint and muscle pain I had would not go away. After many tests and referrals to specialists and many diseases ruled out, I was diagnosed with fibromyalgia, spondylosis of the spine, and several protruding discs in my back and neck. I battled and was treated for fibromyalgia for twenty years after my husband's passing. God healed me at a lady's retreat.

Dear Heavenly Father, I praise you for being our divine healer. Often, you choose to heal with just a touch of your hand. Other times, You give doctors and surgeons the knowledge, or you may decide to take us home to Heaven and give us a new body. However, You decide to heal. We praise You for divine healing. Amen.

JULY 29
LIFE ALTERED FOREVER

*But thou, when thou, prayest, enter into thy
closet and when thou hast shut thy door, pray to the
Father which is in secret; and thy father which seeth
in secret shall reward thee openly. Matthew 6:6KJV.*

**It did not take long to realize my life had been
altered forever when my husband passed away. I
had instantly become a single person and single
parent through no desire of my own. I was now
making household, business, financial decisions,
and decisions concerning my children and their
well-being that their father and I would normally
make together. What I was facing was an incredible
responsibility, but I knew I had an incredible
Heavenly Father that I would now need to turn to
more than ever before.**

**If you are a single person and single parent,
especially, I encourage you to turn to Him often. I
am almost embarrassed to admit this, but I was
purchasing a piece of real property once and bought
the wrong lot. I sold it and it worked out fine, only**

471

because the Lord was taking care of me. We need the Lord in our decision-making.

Dear Lord, thank you for listening to my prayers and answering them when I do not know what to do in my new role as a Single Again. Please guide me and show me what I am to do. Amen.

JULY 30
DOES ANYTHING REMAIN THE SAME

Two are better than one; because they have a good reward for their labor. For if they fall the one will lift up his fellow: but woe to him that is alone when he falleth; for he hath not another to help him up. Ecclesiastes 4;9-10 KJV.

As mentioned before, my late husband and I were youth pastors at our local church. It had been a couple of weeks since his passing. The youth, including my children, had asked when we were going to go on a youth outing. I planned a cookout and games at Lake Allatoona. It did not take long to realize without his leadership and assistance. I was a square peg trying to fit into a round hole. I was the one who was called to teach Bible classes, but he was, undoubtedly, the youth pastor. Was anything to remain the same? Was anything to be unchanged in my life?

473

Dear Heavenly Father, I need your direction. I truly need you to lead and guide me concerning where and in what capacity I am to serve in the ministry without my partner. Amen.

JULY 31
WHO AM I

Jesus Christ the same yesterday, and today, and forever. Hebrews 13;8 KJV.

Since my husband went home to be with the Lord, my life is different. The only thing that has not changed is my identity in Christ. I am still the same born-again, spirit-filled Christian woman and the mother of Tiffany and Isaac Holbert that I was before. Knowing who I am in Christ is most important, but I seem to have an identity crisis at times. Some things seem so weird.

Before my husband passed, I was the same Christian woman but married. Because of marriage, my husband and I were a couple. Now that I am no longer a part of a couple, it seems I am not a part of the group. I am not invited to go out with them anymore, or if I am invited, I am not comfortable. Although they are still my friends, and I love them dearly, they treat me differently. It seems sometimes I feel like a fish out of water. The only one that has not changed is Jesus.

God seems to be giving me a new empathy for Singles and Singles-Again, whether they are unmarried, divorced, or widowed.

Dear Lord, I know that there are a lot of times of growth in one's life. We do not always remain the same. I pray for grace during the discovery of my new identity and my new place in you. Amen.

August

AUGUST 1
YOU ARE GOD

When I consider thy heavens, the work of thy
fingers, the moon and the stars, which thou hast
ordered; what is man that thou art mindful of him?
Psalms 8:3-4 KJV.

The God who revolves the earth around the sun knows every breath you take. The Creator who made every star in the universe knows the number of hairs on your head. The Everlasting One knew exactly where he would place you in human history. Our God, whose thoughts outnumber the grains of sand, is thinking about your all the time. He knows everything you think and say. He knows you going, and you coming. Nothing in your life is a secret to him. He has plans for your life now and for all eternity.

Dear Lord, I am so thankful you are God, and you know everything about us, yet you still love us. Amen.

AUGUST 2
BOLD, EXCITING FAITH

Have not I commanded thee? Be strong and of a good courage; be not afraid, neither be thou dismayed for the Lord thy God is with thee, whithersoever thou goest. Joshua 1:9 KJV.

Through the pages of your life, God will take you to unexpected places. You will encounter new relationships, new jobs, and new places of residence. Which aspects seem the most intimidating? In what way do you feel the most inadequate? What kind of disasters fill your imagination? Toss out your fears. God is in control. Grasp hold of the promise that God will be with you every step of the way.

Dear God, you are leading us down unfamiliar paths, a little scary, yet very exciting, a new adventure. Give us confidence in your presence as we follow you every step of the way. Amen.

AUGUST 3
CHILDLIKE FAITH

I drew them with cords of a man, with bands of love: and I was to them as they that take off the yoke or their jaws and I laid meat unto them.Hosea 11:4 KJV.

In our fast-paced society, children grow up in a hurry. Self-reliance is considered to be a success. Independence is a competitive edge. We are told if we have an education, money in the bank, and the latest technology there is no need for childlike faith. We are equipped to handle anything. We have a heavenly father who knows our need for nurturing and kindness. You do not have to be self-sufficient in tough times. You can cry out for help and loving comfort. When you are afraid, he loves you. He reaches and picks you up and holds you whenever you need him the most. Pray for your needs and problems. Bring him your sorrows and disappointments. Let him lead you by the hand and trust him to take you where you need to go.

Dear Lord, we try to be strong in every situation. Soften our hearts so we will remember how much we need you. Thank you for loving us more than our kind, dependable parents. Amen.

AUGUST 4
GIFT OF YOUR PRESENCE

So they sat down with him upon the ground seven days and seven nights, and none spoke a word unto him: for they saw that his grief was very great. Job 2:13 KJV.

It is so painful to see your loved ones hurting. You cannot ease their grief. You cannot erase cruel words of lies and slander. You cannot bring back a deceased loved one. You cannot restore a lost job. You cannot explain why they are suffering. You feel helpless in the midst of their pain.

Be still. Resist the urge to fix it or blame someone. Offer the gift of your presence. Stay close. Be ready to listen as they begin to process what has happened. Comfort with your touch and provide a shoulder to cry on.

Dear God, please bring comfort and peace. Give hope that you are going to do something. Amen.

But when Jesus saw it he was much displeased, and said unto them, suffer the little children to come unto me, and forbid them not: for of such is the Kingdom of Heaven. Mark 10:14 KJV.

Someone once penned: "Jesus loves the little children. All the little children of the world".

He wants to hold them, love them, and bless them. As parents and friends of children, we have the privilege of introducing them to Jesus. We are to do all we can to help, not hinder, children in coming to him. Pray for kids' salvation and protection from evil. Encourage them to bring him their problems, questions, and fears. Teach them God's word. Read Bible stories to them. Take them to church. Let them see you studying the word. Shield them from false doctrines and false teachers that do not teach the truth. Worship together along with worship music. Enjoy nature together, teaching them about God's creation.

Show love to others. Give kids chances to give and serve. Teach them to pray for their family and friends. Tell them to reach out to those that are hurting or left out.

Dear God, thank you for your example of love for little children. Show us how to love them so they will be drawn to you. Amen.

How can I say to thy brother, brother, let me pull out the mote that is in thine eye when thou thyself holdest not the beam that is in thine own eye? Thou hypocrite, cast out first the beam out of thine own eye, and thou shalt then see clearly to pull out the mote that is in thy brother's eye Luke 6:42 KJV.

It is so much easier to see someone else's faults than our own. The scripture teaches us to look within rather than outward. Let the Holy Spirit correct you. Be accountable for your sins, confessing your faults to God and the one you have offended. Study God's word diligently to know God's will for your life.

Dear Lord, please give me eyes to see clearly any sin in my life and repent of it before I try to exhort others. Amen.

Only by pride cometh contention. But with well advised is wisdom. Proverbs 13:10 KJV

Pride is at the root of every disagreement. We think we are right. We think our way is best. It would be easier if everyone cooperated with our plan. We do not want to slow down and listen to another person's perspective. We are so busy proving our point that people's feelings are left in the wind.

What conflict are you facing today? Take time to listen respectfully to the other person's ideas and opinions. Be acceptable to advice from others with greater experience and wisdom. Take your issues to God in prayer, asking him to open insight into what to do. There is no satisfaction in winning the argument if the relationship is lost.

Dear Lord, please forgive me for fighting to have
my own way. Teach me to communicate with
kindness and respect. Amen.

But avoid foolish questions, grudges, contentions, and strivings about the law; for they are unprofitable and vain. Titus 3:9 KJV.

Some people turn the scriptures God gave into an object of debate and division. Instead of responding to the word with a humble heart, they use it to condemn those around them. Does your Bible reading give you a sense of moral superiority to your neighbor? Do you study it to come out on top in a disagreement? Do you read your Bible because you want to earn God's love? If any of these are your reasons for studying the word of God, you are studying it for the wrong reason. Studying the Bible and praying to understand it will produce the fruit of the spirit-love, joy, long-suffering, gentleness, goodness, and faith in the reader. Ask God for a fresh perspective in his word. It should challenge you to love and obey the Lord. It should lead you to worship God. It should help you respond in mercy to those who are lost in sin. Pray for a pure desire for knowledge and understanding. Find freedom from legalism and conflict with others over the Bible. Allow the Lord's love and wisdom to fill your lips as you read it.

Dear Lord, please keep us humble as we seek to understand the Bible more and more. Thank you for your word that teaches us the way of salvation. Amen.

AUGUST 9
OUR HEAVENLY HOME

And there shall in no wise enter into it anything that defileth, neither whatsoever worketh abomination or maketh a lie; but which are written in the lambs book of life. Revelations 21:27 KJV.

Deceitful, shameful, evil. The words describe our world so well. Sex trafficking and pornography are rampant. Abortion, abuse, violence, and poverty cause pain and fear. Corrupt politicians use their power for selfish gain. Our peace and joy are buried under a world of suffering and sin. Thank you, Jesus, for the hope of eternity with you. You promise a picture of beautiful perfection. Purity, rest, truth, belonging, healing, life. The ugliness and death filling the headlines will disappear as he makes all things new. Our longing for Jesus will be finally satisfied. Allow God's promises for tomorrow to refresh your heart today. Trust him to hold on to you and bring you safely home.

Dear Lord, keep our eyes fixed on you. When the evil of this world is overwhelming, give us endurance and hope. As we wait for you, make us holy and fill us with your truth so we can shine your light in the darkness. Amen.

Here are a few scriptures that expound on the responsibility of parents and children in their relationship with each other.

Parents:

Train up a child in the way he should go, and when he is old, he will not depart from it. Proverbs 22: 6 KJV

And ye fathers; provoke not your children to wrath: but bring them up in the fear and the admonition of the Lord. Ephesians 6:4 KJV.

Not forsaking the assembly of yourselves together as the manner of some is, but exhorting one another: and so much the more, as you see the day approaching. Hebrews 10:25 KJV.

Tell your children of it, and let your children tell their children, and their children, another generation. Joel 1:13 KJV.

Pray without ceasing. II Thessalonians 5:17 KJV.

Children:

Children obey your parents in all things, for this is well pleasing unto the Lord. Colossians 3:20 KJV.

My son, keep thy father's commandments and forsake not the law of thy mother. Proverbs 6:20 KJV

Hearken unto thy father that begat thee and despise not thy mother when she is old. Proverbs 23:22 KJV

Children, obey your parents in the Lord, for this is right. Honor thy father and mother; which is the first commandment with promise; that it may be well with thee, and thou mayest live long on the earth. Ephesians 6:1-3 KJV

Dear Heavenly Father, the parent-child relationship is one of the most beautiful and rewarding relationships but one of the most exasperating. Please help us to be willing to follow the advice you gave us in your words. Bless our efforts so our families can be healthy, happy, blessed, and in heaven together. Amen.

AUGUST 11
HIGHWAY OF HUMILITY

But whosoever will be great among you, shall be your minister. And whosoever of you will be the chiefest shall be servant of all. Mark 10 43b- 44 KJV.

I had the privilege of learning under a much-anointed Bible teacher, Bert Brooks, at the North Rome Church of God. He once said if you want to achieve success, you must get on Humbleness Highway and turn right. Bert was a very successful businessman. He said when he first came to Rome, Georgia, everything he owned filled one pasteboard box. I went into his business one day to buy a new set of tires. In the customer waiting area, I witnessed a scene I shall never forget. A single mom with small children was inquiring about the cost of a new set of tires. When she found out what they cost, she broke into tears and said there was no way she could purchase a new set of tires. Bert handed her some money and told her to go and take the children across the street for a meal. When she returned, she would have a new set of tires on her car to drive safely. By that time, I was in tears.

Dear Heavenly Father, thank you for blessing my life with examples of godly people like Bert Brooks. He not only ministers spiritually, but in other ways as well. Thank you for the example and the godly blessing he was that day. Amen.

Every good gift is from above. James 1:17 KJV.

I once owned a triple golf course lot in Bent Tree, a beautiful, gated community in Jasper, Georgia, in the foothills of the Blue Ridge Mountains. It is gorgeous there, complete with waterfalls. After my first husband passed, I would drive up there, take my Bible, and sit for hours in the swing, praying in front of Lake Tamarack. It was so nice to be there, meditating on the goodness of God. After taxes and amenity fees became so expensive, and I had two kids to get through college, I sold the property. I thought of Bent Tree often but had not been back in years.

I was about to celebrate a milestone birthday. My husband had often heard me speak about Bent Tree. For my birthday, he rented a home there for us to stay in to celebrate my milestone. Bent Tree boasts many beautiful houses and properties. My husband knew nothing about a particular little alpine chalet there that was always my favorite. I always thought it would be the perfect property for a writer or an artist to live. My husband knew nothing about the alpine chalet at Bent Tree. He made the reservations, and when the confirmation came, it showed a picture of our rental. To my surprise, it was the little alpine chalet on Alpine Dr. that I had always loved.

Is that not just like our heavenly father? His Word says in Psalms 37:4 KJV, "Delight thyself also in the Lord; And he shall give thee the desires of thine heart."

Dear Heavenly Father, I praise you for loving me and blessing me. I usually do not ask for my desires when I have so many in need. I did not ask for this special blessing, but you knew the desire of your daughter's heart. Because of your love for me, you

teamed up with my precious husband and gave me my milestone birthday in a very special alpine cottage. I shall never forget. Why would everyone not want to serve you? Amen.

AUGUST 13
WHO CHRIST SAYS I AM

The next time the devil comes knocking on your heart's door and tells you that you are not good enough, tell him that you would like to share who Christ says you are. When you give him the word of God, he will flee.

All scriptures in KJV.

I am God's child John 1:12. I am Christ's friend John 1:15. I am united with the Lord I Corinthians 6:17. I am bought with a price I Corinthians 6:19-20. I am a saint set apart for God Ephesians 1:1. I am a personal witness of Christ Acts 1:8. I am the salt and light of the earth Matthew 5:13-14. I am a member of the body of Christ I Corinthians 12:27. I am free forever from condemnation Romans 8:1-2. I am a citizen of heaven Philippians 3:20. I am free from any charge against me Romans 8:31-34. I am a minister of reconciliation for God II Corinthians 5:17-21. I have access to God through the Holy Spirit Ephesians 2:18. I am seated with Christ in the heavenly realms Ephesians 2:6 I cannot be separated from the love of

504

God Romans 8:35-39. I am established, anointed, sealed by God II Corinthians 1;21-22.

I am assured all things work together for my good Romans 8:28. I have been chosen and appointed to bear fruit John 15:16. I may approach God with freedom and confidence Ephesians 3:12. I can do all things through Christ who strengthens me Philippians 4:13. I am the branch of the true vine, a channel of his life John 15:1-5. I am God's temple I Corinthians 3:16. I am complete in Christ Colossians 2:10. I am hidden with Christ in God Colossians 3:3. I have been justified Romans 5:1. I am God's coworker I Corinthians 3:9, II Corinthians 6:1. I am God's workmanship Ephesians 2:1. I am confident that the good works of God he has begun in me will be perfected Philippians 1:5. I have been redeemed and forgiven Colossians 1:14. I have been adopted as God's child Ephesians 1:5. I belong to God. This is who He says I am in Christ!

AUGUST 14
BECOMING A BETTER CHRISTIAN WIFE

(Husbands' Standpoint at Marriage Seminar taught by my Husband and Me.)

Whoso findeth a wife findeth a good thing, and obtaineth favor of the Lord. Proverbs 18:22 KJV.

Less spiritual superiority, less worry, less tardiness, less superficial communication, less materialistic, less stubborn, less emotional attachment to parents, more understanding, more open regarding beliefs and convictions, more faith, more humble, more flexible, more realistic in goal setting, more honest in making me aware of my shortcomings, more understanding of my silence, more asking God for guidance, more respect, more submission, more prayer for your husband, more understanding of the husband's moods, more familiar with Ephesians Chapter 5, more help organizing our home, more sensitive, more responsive to the physical and sexual needs of the husband, more coordination of daily schedule with the husband, more meaningful communication, more

506

listening, more acceptance, more moral support concerning work, more patience with children, more prayer together, more studying God's word together, more letting God lead our lives, share God's love to neighbors, and better housekeeping.

Dear Lord, we certainly have our work cut out for us, but we can do all things through you. You are our strength. Amen.

August 15
Becoming A Better Christian Husband

(Wives' Standpoint at Marriage Seminar taught by my Husband and Me)

Therefore shall a man leave his father and his mother, and shall cleave unto his wife: and they shall be one flesh. Genesis 2:24 KJV.

Be more loyal to me than your parents, be sensitive, pay attention to body language, be spiritual leader of the home, be sensitive to a woman's role as housewife and mother, be responsible, have pride in our home and yard, be more helpful with domestic work, set a Christian example for non-Christian friends, talk with me in the evening, listen and communicate better, take the initiative in family devotions, be honest, even if it hurts, discipline the children when you are home and see the need, spend more time with me discussing our relationship, set goals for our marriage and family, spend more time alone with me, do not spend more time at work than necessary, accept a woman's emotional makeup,

ask how can I be a better husband, give the wife a weekly spending allowance and monthly clothing allowance without having to ask for it, realize that sex begins in the morning and not when we go to bed at night, hold me after we make love, don't be personally threatened by my desire for a written budget, don't grab the newspaper, mail, or phone when you walk in the door, understand you are not the only one who has had a hard day, relieve me when you come home, take me on a date weekly, come up with creative suggestions, surprise me, occasionally with a small gift, plan time during the week exclusively for the kids.

Dear Lord, you know what is needed for each couple to achieve a better marriage. It is going to

take work, but oh, the rewards can be heaven on earth with your special blessing! Amen.

AUGUST 16
CALMING AN ANXIOUS SPIRIT

Thou draw us near in the day that I called upon thee: Thou saidst fear not. Lamentations 3:57 KJV.

Shortly after the passing of my husband, my sixteen-year-old daughter, Tiffany, flew to Florida with her Calhoun High School debate team. That morning, I had picked up breakfast biscuits and went to work early to put on a pot of coffee for my staff. Just when the phone rang, the lady on the line asked if I was Jan Holbert and had a daughter, Tiffany Holbert, traveling on flight 427 from Atlanta to Fort Lauderdale. I panicked with fear.

"Yes. Yes! What has happened?" I asked. The lady said, "Oh, nothing is wrong. Quite the contrary. I am so sorry I startled you." She said she had an athletic team to cancel on another flight leaving later and could offer our debate team a much cheaper rate on that flight if the debater's parents were agreeable. I have never been more thankful, not for the cheaper rate, but for the safety of my precious daughter and the other teens.

Dear Heavenly Father, thank you for the safety of our teens that day and for calming my anxious spirit and frightened heart. Amen.

AUGUST 17
GOD'S WORD MAKES SATAN FLEE

For God hath not given us the spirit of fear but of power and of love and of a sound mind. II Timothy 1:7 KJV.

After my husband passed, I battled fear for a long time. I was very protective and constantly concerned about my children, their well-being, and their safety. My son Isaac played the saxophone in the Calhoun High School Band. One Friday night, there was a football game in another city, and I was too tired to drive. Before the game, I received a phone call from Brad Johnson, a friend of Isaac's, who told me there had been a caravan of buses leaving Calhoun and there had been an accident. My son was on the bus that had been involved. They were taking the students on the bus to the Floyd Medical Center.

I jumped in the car, praying, and headed for Rome, Georgia, so uneasy about what I might find. When I got there, the parents were lined up, waiting for medical reports. I shortly learned that my son was fine and had gone on to the game.

That night, I decided, "No more Satan!" I rebuked the devil in the name of Jesus. I told Satan the word of God said to submit yourselves to the Lord, rebuke the devil, and he would have to flee. From that night on, my faith in God's protection of my kids was greater than the fear Satan tried to put on me.

Dear Heavenly Father, thank you for the power of your word over Satan and for your protection over my children. Amen.

AUGUST 18
SECOND CHANCES

Behold, I will do a new thing; now it shall spring forth shall ye not know it? I will even make a way in the wilderness, and rivers in the desert. Isaiah 43:19 KJV.

I had read that if widowed, you should make no major life decisions until well over a year has passed. Supposedly, by then, you would be more aware of what would be best for you and your family without making decisions based on emotions only.

My children and I had prayed about changing churches and had started attending East Calhoun Church of God. Pastor Keith Reed called me and said he would like to appoint me over the Single and Single Again Ministry, men and women over college age who had never been married, the divorced and the widowed. He gave me a list of twenty-five names and phone numbers of those eligible. I planned a Bible study with a chili supper in my home and began calling, introducing myself, and inviting them over. One of the 25 was not home, but

515

I left a message. When he returned my call, we talked for four hours by long distance. Not only was he a dedicated, spirit filled Christian, but he had two children, almost the same age as mine, and he loved Mustang cars! Talking about much in common, we were married the following year with our four children as our attendants.

Dear Heavenly Father, you are so good to your children. I praise you for loving us, directing our footsteps, bringing special, unannounced blessings into our lives, and for giving all of us second chances you determine that we need. Amen.

GRADUATION AN IMPORTANT MILESTONE IN LIFE

Happy ithe man that getteth wisiom and the man that getteth and that getteth understanding. Proverbs 3:13 KJV.

Graduation is one of the first and most important milestones a person reaches in life. It signifies the finishing of a course of study at a school, college, or university and the receiving of a diploma or other document certifying so. But it means so much more than a mere piece of sheepskin. It means determination, perseverance, ambition, and commitment to the cause. It also signifies commitment to a new life. The beginning of a new and wider dimension. Other decisions must be made, decisions that will affect the outcome of your life. If you can look back on your career as a student and can say you studied hard and tried to make the most of the opportunities your education has afforded, then you can feel confident that you are prepared to face the future. You can feel confident in your abilities and have faith that the

Lord above will help you through future situations because you have done your very best to prepare.

Proverbs 4:7 KJV says, "Wisdom is the principal thing. Therefore, get wisdom and with thy getting get understanding. But most importantly, don't forget to trust in the Lord with all thine heart and lean not unto thine own understanding. In all thy ways acknowledge him, and he shall direct thy path." Proverbs 3:5-6 KJV.

Dear Lord, thank you so much for the opportunity to further our learning. I thank you for the opportunities our children, and now our grandchildren, have had to continue their education. I thank you for every scholarship that has been awarded and for being with them every step of the way. Amen.

Wisdom is the principle thimg .Proberbs 4:7 KJV.

Graduation is so wonderful. It is such an exciting event in life and something to really look forward to. It signifies great accomplishment and honor. Along with it comes a newfound freedom as you enter the adult world. When I graduated from high school, I felt so ready to go out there and set the world on fire. I wanted to show them just how much I knew and just how things should be done. It did not take long until I realized just how much I did not know and how much more was waiting to be learned in that great horizon of knowledge. What is so fantastic about life is that it is an everyday learning experience, and you will never stop learning until you are 6 feet under.

Success is something too. With hard work, it comes one step at a time. It is hard to realize you have reached it because there are always higher goals to be set and achieved. A great secret to a happy, successful life can be found in Matthew 6:23

KJV: "But seek ye first the Kingdom of heaven and his righteousness and all these things shall be added unto you. What a promise, graduate. Now is the perfect time in your life to claim it for your very own. If you will always strive to do God's will live close to him, and allow him to guide you, success and happiness will follow."

Psalm 37:4-5 KJV says, "Delight thyself also in the Lord, and he shall give thee the desires of thine heart. Commit thy way unto the Lord. Trust also in him, and he shall bring it to pass."

Dear Heavenly Father, thank you so very much for the wonderful milestones in our lives that we can work toward. How exciting and rewarding life can be. Amen.

AUGUST 21
LOVE IS IN THE AIR

Be thou an example of the believer. I Timothy 4:12 KJV.

Neither was the man created for the woman; but the woman for the man. I Corinthians 11:9 KJV.

Love is in the air, the time set aside for blushing brides, wedding bliss, and couples in love beginning a new life together as one.

Marriage is one of the greatest steps in life that you will ever take. It should not be taken lightly. Just what does the Bible say about marriage anyway? In the biblical story of creation as creation unfolds, we read in Genesis 1:27-31 KJV, "God created man in his own image and in the image of God created he him; male and female he created them, and God saw all that he had made, and behold it was very good."

Genesis 2 tells us, "God wanted to provide proper companionship for man, so God created

woman. God saw that his creation was good. Marriage was planned by God."

In John 2 we read of a wedding feast in Cana of Galilee Jesus. Jesus performed his first miracle there when helping the host out of an embarrassing situation. His presence and helpfulness placed the stamp of approval on marriage. To further demonstrate God's blessing upon marriage, the New Testament is filled with teachings pertaining to the honor of marriage. One of them is found in Hebrews 13: 4 and stated very plainly. Marriage is honorable in all, and the bed undefiled. But whoremongers and adulterers, God will judge. Marriage is holy and blessed by God.

What should your attitude be? Should the vows be taken lightly? Do you really love each other? Do your marriage plans include forever thoughts? Pray together about your wedding plans. God is concerned.

Dear Lord, you see each couple that is about to take the step of marriage. I pray that you will guide their thoughts as they approach this important step in life. Enter their hearts with your wisdom and your will for them. Amen.

AUGUST 22
CHRISTIAN MOTHERS

In all things showing thyself a pattern of good works. Titus 2:7 KJV.

There is no greater or nobler influence in the world today than the influence of a Christian mother. Carolyn Davenport, Pastor's wife and dedicated praying mother,related a story once about the mother of Alfred Tyng. She was known for her force of character and her strong faith in God. When grasping for breath in her dying hours, she heard her husband express some anxiety about the future welfare of their children.

She confidently replied, "My dear, do not be uneasy about my children. God will bring them all to himself. This is his covenant with me."

This woman was on more than just speaking terms with God. She had prayed for her children, and she knew the master was going to take care of these children. Soon to be motherless, the secret of a successful and good mother was with her. She

knew the power of prayer when trying to rear children.

Dear Lord, thank you so much for the privilege of being a mother and for the opportunity to bring up my children in covenant with you. Amen.

August 23
Mothers-In-Law

For I have given you an example. John 13:15 KJV.

Mothers-in-law have been joked about and cut down probably as far back as Eve. The Bible does not record any disputes or misunderstandings in that sense in that family. They were human, so I am inclined to believe they had them back then also.

I have heard a lot of people talk about their mothers-in-law, and to hear them say I am surely one of the few who was blessed with a good one. I thanked God for her, and I loved her dearly. I did not say we got along perfectly, without any differences of opinion. That would be a slight misrepresentation of the truth. She and I were of different generations with different views and ideas on certain subjects, and of course, we disagreed at times, but we loved each other, and we respected each other's viewpoints. From the time I became a member of the family by marriage, she made me feel at home and treated me as a daughter. I appreciated it with

526

all my heart. I am thankful and grateful to my mother-in-law because if it had not been for her, I would not have met and married the man of my dreams. She gave her son, then my husband, the gift of life. I realize it was through her teaching and training, her prayers, and her sacrifices as a mother that he grew up to be the wonderful man he was. So, the next time you get a little aggravated at your mother-in-law, just think of that person you married and how much you love him. Then call up your mother-in-law if she is still living and tell her just how much you appreciate her for being the mother and mother-in-law she is.

Dear Lord, I praise you for the mother my husband had, the nannie my grandchildren had, and for the mother-in-law she was to me. Amen.

WHAT WAS YOUR FATHER?

Sixteen teenagers were attending a home Bible study. While there, they were asked the question what was your father? One of them said he was a loving, tender person. Another commented that her dad was a dedicated Christian who loved her very much. While another said that his father was a pillar of strength. One said his father deserted them when he was small and therefore, he never had the chance to really get to know him. Another said sadly that her father was a drunkard. So on, around the room, the question was asked.

Not one mentioned his father's profession, possessions in life, or the position he held. If the Lord tarries and you depart this life before your family, what will they say about you? They are not impressed by what you do for a living or how much money you make.

What kind of father are you? After answering the question yourself, are you pleased with your answer? If not, the Bible is the best place to turn as a source of strength and guidance toward becoming the father that God intended for you to be. For beginners, how about Ephesians 6:4? It says fathers provoke not your children to wrath but bring them up in the nurture and the admonition of the Lord. This passage of scripture admonishes the father to love his children and discipline his children so that they will grow up to be contributors to the betterment of our society. What better time than today to begin fulfilling the role that God intended for you as a father?

Dear Heavenly Father, good fathers are so needed in our world and in our families today. You have so beautifully mapped out the way for them. Please help them turn to you. Amen.

August 25
Storing Sweet Memories

I thank my God upon every remembrance of you, always in every prayer of mine for you all making request with joy, for your fellowship in the gospel from the first day until now; being confident of this very thing, that he which hath begun a good work in you will perform it until the day of Jesus Christ. Philippians 1:3-6 KJV.

When God created people

they were made in such a way

That they could store sweet memories

as they lived day by day

And what a blessing that has been

for memories of the past

Are stored for many, many years

as treasures that will last.

Of course, the people who are smart

will occasionally review

The things that mean the most to them

it kind of' helps them through

The rainy and the cold days

when loneliness sets in

And with sweet memories to think about

they feel peace within.

Some thoughts may refresh a weary soul

and can even bring a smile

And when they see how blessed they are

it makes their life worthwhile

So, cherish your sweet memories

God gave us power to store

A lot of good things in our heart

And still have room for more.

Dear Lord Jesus, I praise you for my sweet,
memories that you have given me and allow me to
revisit occasionally. I love you, Sweet Jesus. Amen.

Therefore, all things whatsoever you would that men should do to you, do you even so to them. Matthew 7:12 KJV.

Pastor Charles Green, told a story once about a couple who was passing through Philadelphia. It was pouring rain, and they had been driving for hours. They spotted a hotel, but the sign read "no vacancy." They drove on for several blocks and passed several other signs with the same message. Finally, in desperation, they pulled into a third-class hotel and went inside. The elderly gentleman said to the young man at the desk, "Please, son, do you have a room? My wife and I have been driving for hours, and we are so tired and hungry." "Sir I'm sorry", the young man said, "I rented the last room hours ago." The man turned and started sadly to walk away. After seeing the look on the couple's faces, the young man could not bear to turn them away. "Sir," he said, "I am on duty tonight, and my room is vacant. It is not as nice as the others, but it is clean. You are welcome to stay in it for the night." "Oh, thank you, thank you, young man," the couple responded, "You are so very kind. How can we ever repay you? The next morning, while eating breakfast in the dining room, the couple had the young man paged. As he smilingly approached their table, he told them he hoped that they had a restful night. "Young man," the elderly gentleman said, "You are much too good at your job to work in a place like this. How would you like it if I built a first-class hotel in New York City and asked you to come to work in it for me?" "Oh, Sir, that would be wonderful and far beyond my imagination." the young man said. The couple the young man put up for the night was Mr. and Mrs. William Waldorf Astoria. Afterwards, the hotel was erected, and the young man became the first manager of the great Waldorf Astoria in New York City. The young man did not have to put them up for the night. He had a valid reason to turn them away, but this young man was different. He was kind-hearted and wanted to be of help to others. He remembered the Lord's command, and he was greatly rewarded for his kindness.

Dear Lord, I love this story my pastor related. It would be so wonderful if kindness was sprinkled all over the world like confetti. There would not be enough volumes to hold the uplifting stories written to talk about it. Amen.

Dale Carnegie once said, "One of the most tragic things I know about human nature is that all of us tend to put off living." How many of us dream of some magical little cottage in a rose garden over the horizon instead of enjoying the roses that are blooming in our own backyard?

Write in your heart that every day is the best day of the year. He is rich and owns the day. No one owns the day who allows it to be invaded with fear and anxiety. "Finish every day and be done with it," said Ralph Waldo Emerson. You have done what you could. Some blunders and absurdities, no doubt, crept in. Forget them as soon as you can.

Tomorrow is a new day. Begin it well and serenely with a high spirit. A brand-new day is too dear with its hopes and aspirations to waste a moment of yesterday.

Dr. Paul Conn, Psychology instructor at Lee University, said Psychologist William Marston asked 3000 persons what have you to live for? He was shocked to find that 94% were simply enduring the present while they waited for the future, waited for something to happen, waited for children to grow up and leave home, waited for next year, waited for another time to take a long dreamed about trip, waited for someone to die, waited for tomorrow without realizing that all anyone has is today because yesterday is gone. There is nothing you can do about it, and tomorrow never comes.

Dear Lord, please help us live today and be present in it. Amen.

AUGUST 28
BLESSING OF GRANDPARENTS

We will not hide them from their children,
shewing to the generation to come, the praises of the
Lord. Psalm 78:4 KJV.

I will never forget how special and how loved my grandparents made me feel the minute I walked into their home. Yes, grandparents are important people. I doubt anyone would disagree with me pertaining to that subject. Some of them are called Mimi, Granddaddy, Papaw, Mamaw, Nana, Papa, Gigi, Grammy, and the list goes on, but whatever the pet name, they all stand for the same thing. A very special person that possesses the heart of a grandchild somewhere that thinks the sun rises and sets in their grandparents.

Grandparents always remember the most interesting stories about you when you were small. They always seemed to know just how to have the best of times regardless of the occasion. They have a way of letting you by what your mother terms "murder," and if there is anything your heart desires within their reach, you can be sure it is yours for the asking.

On birthdays or Christmas, we can always count on grandparents to come through with something very exciting. When you go to their house, they are so excited and proud to see you. Even an ordinary weekend seems like Christmas. A grandmother will always be sure to cook that favorite chocolate cake or those half-moon apple pies just because they happen to be your favorite. Oh, to wake up on a cool, crisp morning at Mamaw's house to smell ham frying and see those fluffy biscuits rising that go so well with her yummy gravy and scrambled eggs. When you hear those fire logs snapping and crackling, you know you are at Mamaw and Papaw's house in the country.

Oh, don't ever underestimate the power of a grandfather, either. He is the one who always has time to go fishing or take you for a long walk. He tells the most interesting stories about his younger days. As you are walking along, all the while, he is whittling on an old piece of wood or a rock, but in no time, he produces a tiny carved treasure all your own to take home with you. Yes, grandparents are special people. The good Lord knew no child should ever grow up without them, and that is why he made grandparents. Grandparents are more than yesterday's mothers and fathers.

Dear Lord, thank you so much for our grandparents. They have meant so much to us through the years. They have poured love and instilled knowledge in us that has helped make us who we are today. Amen

As we have thereof opportunity let us do good unto all men. Galatians 6:10 KJV.

When you think of our present-day world situation, peace on earth and goodwill toward men seem to be as far away as the Christmas season itself. Peace and goodwill should be found within us every day of the year. Peace begins in the home and in the heart. You cannot fight for peace with bombs and missiles and through a battle of words. Greedy and warlike men hungry for power will never contribute to bringing this world closer to peace. The fortress of peace comes from within the heart.

Dear Heavenly Father, please help us to walk in an atmosphere of peace, leaving goodwill wherever we exit. Amen.

If you abide in me, and my words abide in you,
ye shall ask what you will, and it shall be done unto
you. John 15:7 KJV.

My husband and I, my two children, and two of
their friends were vacationing on Tybee Island. I
was putting sunscreen on my son's back and
noticed two very large brown moles that I had not
noticed before. I called immediately and got the
first available appointment with a dermatologist. My
husband and I began praying and fasting
immediately for a good medical report.

When the dermatologist examined Isaac's back,
she said that she was going to sedate him,
surgically remove the moles and send them for
biopsies. She said it was stage 4 and appeared to
be cancer. When my husband heard the word
"cancer," he passed out and hit the floor! He
regained consciousness quickly. While the nurse
took my husband out and gave him a wet, cool
cloth, the dermatologist allowed me to remain by

543

my son's side during the procedure. I had spent prior time in prayer, and he and I remained calm. The dermatologist said the biopsies would determine if we had to do a plan of treatment. I had already rebuked the devil for placing fear on me concerning my children. Isaac experienced some discomfort that following week from the moles being cut out, but the area soon healed. When the biopsy results came back, they were benign. He now has the area checked annually during his physical.

Dear Heavenly Father, I praise you for answering our prayers. The moles were not cancerous. You gave Isaac and me peace in the office that day and I thank you for my husband, Henry, caring so much for my children and me. As Isaac

continues to have his back monitored, we continue to trust you for good reports. Amen.

A FRIEND'S HEARTY COUNSEL

Ointment and perfume rejoice the heart: So doth the sweetness of a man's friend by hearty counsel. Proverbs 27:9 KJV.

Everyone needs at least one true friend in life. Eleanor Roosevelt said, "Many people will walk in and out of your life, but only a true friend leaves footprints in your heart."

In 1969 my parents started construction on a new home in a different community and school district from where we were living. I began praying for the Lord to give me a special friend there so that I could build a friendship. I asked him to please let her be a dedicated Christian with convictions like mine. Cindy Dutton, n/k/a Edwards, was the answer to my prayer. From the first day of high school to college, she and I were almost inseparable. We have shared most of our lives together: crushes, broken hearts, romances, graduation, college, weddings, children, losing spouses, and losing our parents. We have shared many joys and heartaches. I am so

thankful for wonderful friends to share our lives, especially Christian friends whom we can pray with and encourage each other in the Lord. Recently, the graduating class of 1972 celebrated our 50th high school class reunion.

Helen Keller said, "True friends are never apart, maybe in the distance but never in heart."

Dear Heavenly Father, I cannot praise you enough for the special friendship you placed in my life. Please bless everyone with at least one special friend like you did me. Amen.

September

And he hath put a new song in my mouth: even praise unto our God: Many shall see it and fear and shall trust in the Lord. Psalm 40:3 KJV.

Have you reached the age where you are always looking for a new technique to remove wrinkles or at least hide them? I have.

I refuse to spend money on every new cream that comes out, so I am always reading about home remedy recipes or new techniques to make me more beautiful.

Did you know the Master Creator has the perfect process for beautifying your face? By his touch, wrinkles of worry can be smoothed away. Shadows of shame and doubt can become portraits of grace and trust. He relaxes clenched jaws and smooths furrowed brows. His touch can smooth the bags of exhaustion from beneath your eyes. He turns tears of sorrow into tears of joy. How does he do it? It is a process called prayer and praise. Prayer removes

549

heavy burdens when we lay them at Jesus' feet. It takes off pounds. Praise is the grandest hydration and moisturizer. When you brag about him, it makes your eyes light up. It totally revitalizes and rejuvenates. The master's well of living water never runs dry. The Master Creator takes pleasure in making his technique known and available at no monetary cost.

Dear Lord, thank you for loving us. Your love alone puts a shine on our face that beautifies the homeliest. I have never seen a person who had an encounter with you leave the same as they came. Amen.

SEPTEMBER 2
A HEART AT PEACE

These things have I spoken unto you, that in me ye might have peace. In the world ye shall have tribulation: but be of good cheer; I have overcome the world. John 16:35 KJV.

The older I get, the more I yearn for peace. Jesus was loved by the multitude yet content to live a simple life. Women adored him, yet he never had a lustful affair. He was scorned and ridiculed by his own brothers but was ready to forgive them before they asked. Jesus was at peace. When the waves became tumultuous, he slept soundly. When the disciples became frantic at not having enough to feed the crowd, Jesus saw it as an opportunity for a miracle. Peter cut off the arresting soldier's ear, and Jesus healed him.

Peter travelled with Jesus and described him as a lamb without a spot or blemish. If you enjoy being at peace, you will love spending more time with Jesus. He is the peace speaker.

Dear Lord, I love you! I enjoy being with you. You are good for my health and mood. You calm my heart and lower my blood pressure. Amen.

If any of you lack wisdom, let him ask of God that giveth to all men liberally, and upbraideth not; and it shall be given him. James 1:5 KJV.

So, your options are clear. You can choose the safe side. You can build a fire in the hearth. Stay inside, stay warm, and stay dry. You cannot fall if you do not take a stand. You cannot lose your balance if you do not climb. So, do not try it. Take the safe route.

Or you can choose adventure. Instead of building a fire in your hearth(fireplace), build a fire in your heart. Adopt the baby. Move overseas. Take the class. Change courses. Change careers. Run for office. Make a difference. It is not safe, but what is?

I am glad you asked. It is safer to pray for wisdom from God first. I opened a Christian bookstore once without praying first, and I lost my investment.

Dear Lord, I am feeling a little adventurous now. Is it an impulse from you? If I am not to make this move, please stop me and redirect me. Amen.

Rejoice in the Lord always: again, I say rejoice.
Philippians 4: 4 KJV.

Let's go back a couple of thousand years. We are in a cold, drab, dingy, stone room, rat and roach infested with a terrible stench. The only light is coming through the metal bars on the window. We see a man in poor physical condition struggling to write a letter. He is seated on the floor in chains and bound to a Roman guard.

He must surely be a horrible criminal. No, wait, it is the apostle, Paul.

He must be writing a complaint letter about the horrible circumstances he has found himself in serving God. No, he is writing a book, two thousand years later, a well-known piece of Roman literature called the Book of Philippians- Treatise on Joy.

Dear Lord, I am ashamed of my attitude at times. Especially when I read and enjoy the book of Philippians about joy and remember it was written in such horrible conditions. Please help me to rejoice always. Amen.

SEPTEMBER 5
NO SECRETS FROM GOD

He that covereth his sins shall not prosper: but whoso confesseth and forsaketh them shall have mercy. Proverbs 28:13 KJV.

When we fall, we can dismiss it, we can deny it, we can distort it, or we can deal with it.

We keep no secret from God. Confession is not telling God what we did. He already knows. Confession is simply agreeing with God that what we did is wrong.

God does not forgive what we deny. God does not grant pardon when we do not admit what we did. Is guilt what we avoid? Is not guilt what we detest? Why is guilt so bad? Does guilt not imply show that we know right from wrong? Does guilt not aspire to be better than we are? Is guilt not regret for telling God one thing and doing another?

557

Dear Lord, when we fall, please help us to admit it to you and ask your forgiveness so that you can restore us. Amen.

SEPTEMBER 6
GENTLE LAMB

For the lamb which is in the midst of the throne shall feed them and shall lead them into living fountains of water: and God shall wipe away all tears from their eyes. Revelations 9:17 KJV.

Some people live with a hidden fear that God is angry at them. Somewhere, sometime, someone convinced them that God has a paddle in his hand or back pocket and he is going to nail us when we have gone too far.

No concept can be more wrong. Our savior's father is very fond of us and only wants to share his love with us. We have a father who is filled with compassion, a loving father who hurts when his children hurt. We serve a God who, when we are under pressure and feel that nothing is going to go right, is waiting to embrace us whether we succeed or fail. He does not come stomping and forcing his way into anyone's heart. He comes like a gentle lamb.

Dear Heavenly Father, please help us have the right idea of who you are. You are not an abusive father, but you are like a gentle lamb. Thank you so much for your gentle love. Amen.

Ask, and it shall be given you; seek, and ye shall find; knock, and it shall be opened unto you. Matthew 7:7 KJV.

Thomas came with doubts. Did Christ turn him away?

Moses had reservations. Did God tell him to go home?

Job had struggles. Did God avoid him?

Paul had his hard times. Did God abandon him?

No, God never turns away the sincere heart. Your questions do not stunt God. He invites our asking. God never turns away the honest seeker. Go to God with your questions. You may not find all your answers, but in finding God, you find the one who does have the answers.

Thomas had doubts. Christ did not turn him away.

Moses had reservations. God did not send him home.

Job had a lot of struggles. God did not avoid him.

Paul had his hard times. God did not abandon him.

Dear God, I praise you that we can come to you with our hard questions. They are hard for us, but they are not hard for you. You invite our coming. Amen.

But without faith it is impossible to please him: he that cometh to God must believe that he is, and that he is the rewarder of them that diligently seek him. Hebrews 11:6 KJV.

Be diligent in your search for God. Be hungry in your pursuit. Be relentless in your quest. Study the Holy Bible. Let this devotional book be one of the dozens you read about Jesus. Avoid puny pursuits of possessions and positions and seek your Savior!

Do not be satisfied with studying angels. Do not be content with stargazing in the sky. Seek him out as the shepherds did. Long for him as Simeon and Anna did. Search for him and worship him as the wise men did. Do as John and Andrew did. Ask where he resides. Do as Matthew and invite him into your home. Imitate Zacheus and scale whatever heights it takes to seek Christ.

Dear Lord, thank you so much that we can
diligently seek you and find you for ourselves. Amen.

But my God shall supply all your need according to his riches in glory by Christ Jesus. Philippians 4:19 KJV.

If the Lord is one of many options, he is no option. If you can fix your own problems and carry your own burdens you have no need for a problem solver. If your life brings you no grief, you have no need for comfort.

If you love only yourself, you have no need for someone to love and someone to love you in return.

If you can take him or leave him, you will have to leave him because he will only be taken wholeheartedly. When you are at the point of no return in your life, when you mourn because of your sins, when you have no one else to call on, and you have no other option, then cast all your cares on him. He is waiting for you with open arms. Amen.

Dear Lord, please help sinners realize that you are their only option. Amen.

These things I have spoken unto you, that in me ye might have peace. In the world, ye shall have tribulation; but be of good cheer, I have overcome the world. John 16:33 KJV.

God has kept no secrets from us. He has told us that on this journey called life, we will encounter troubles, tribulations, and heartaches.

People will be hurt by divorce, widowed by death, and hungry because of poverty. War will cause destruction, and cancer will afflict bodies.

When Satan shows up and laughs at our pain, we do not have to panic. Just remember, Satan's days are numbered. One day, his inflictions will be no longer. Keep the faith! It will be worth it.

Dear Lord, we can be cheerful and keep the faith despite Satan's attacks. You have overcome the world. Amen.

For he hath not despised nor abhorred the affliction of the afflicted; neither hath he hid his face from him. But when he cried unto him, he heard. Psalms 22:24 KJV.

When my daughter Tiffany and her husband Eric were expecting their first child, Eric was away in the military. Tiffany stayed with us near her due date. She went into labor, and we took her to the hospital. Randyn Lewis Burns, my first grandchild, was born. He was so cute and totally precious. I could not wait to hold him.

The nurse was suctioning his mouth, and he began having difficulty breathing. They did X-rays and confirmed he had been born with a condition called choanal atresia. His face was perfectly formed but he had no openings inside his nose to breathe. It was a solid bone forcing him to breathe through his mouth only. They immediately transported him from Hamilton Medical Center to T .C. Thompson Children's Hospital in Chattanooga.

We got in touch with the proper military authorities, and my son-in-law was allowed to come home on family emergency leave. Our family and church began praying immediately for this precious baby and his parents.

Dear God, I am so thankful for the faith our family possesses in you. You are our God of miracles, and we are standing in need of one right now in little Randyn's life. Amen.

OUR AMAZING MIRACLE CHILD

This poor man cried, and the Lord heard him, and saved him out of all his troubles. Psalms 34:6 KJV.

God brought grandson Randyn through two surgeries, and he came home on oxygen. My daughter Tiffany, who worked in radiology, went back to work on the weekend shift, Friday through Sunday nights, to allow her the most time possible with the baby.

I was keeping Randyn on a Friday night. He completely stopped breathing for a short time, but what seemed like an eternity to me. I prayed earnestly for God to save that precious baby. He then caught his breath and continued breathing. His parents took him to Children's Miracle Network Hospital in Atlanta. He underwent another surgery, and with much prayer and fasting, God blessed that child immensely. He went on to play football and to graduate with honors. He has accepted the calling of God in his life to preach the gospel. Our God is so great. He is a God of amazing, answered prayers and miracles.

Dear Lord, I could never praise you enough for the prayers you heard and answered on behalf of our miracle baby. You enter our world in our circumstances and do for us that we cannot do for ourselves. Amen.

SEPTEMBER 13
YOUR PASSION

I delight to do thy will O my God: Yea, thy law is within my heart Psalm 40:8 KJV.

Are you seeking God's will for your life? What is within you and ignites your heart? What are your passions? Abused children, pediatrics, the elderly, the hungry and needy, those emotionally abused, teaching, medicine, banking, business, the ministry? What is it that you have to do? What is it that you feel you must do? You simply cannot get away from it.

I have always had a passion for learning and studying God's word. I was saved at the age of eleven. I read my complete Bible for the first time in one year. When I was fourteen years old, my pastor handed me a Bible commentary and asked me to teach the adult Sunday school class the following week. I have been studying God's word and teaching since. I am passionate about teaching God's word. It is my ministry.

I worked as a legal secretary, studied, and became a paralegal. Helping abused children was my passion. As Executive Director of the Child Abuse Council for ten years, I worked to prevent child abuse and neglect. It was my second passion, my career.

Whatever sets your heart on fire and you cannot get away from doing is probably what God has placed in your heart, and it is likely his will for your life. Seek him until you know for sure.

Dear Lord, I thank you for passion, like a fire within our hearts, to perform your will in our lives. Help us to obey you because it is what will fulfill and make us happy. Amen.

God is love. I John 4: 8 KJV.

For God so loved the world that he gave his only begotten son that whosoever believeth in him should not perish but have everlasting life. John 3:16 KJV.

Thou shalt love the Lord thy God with all thy heart, with all thy soul, and with all thy mnd. Matthew 22:37 KJV.

A new commandment I give unto you, that ye also love one another; as I have loved you, that ye also love one another. John 13:34 KJV.

Every person born into this world will eventually ask what is the purpose of my life. In every heart, you will find a longing for purpose and a quest for meaning.

Some search for meaning in a career. My purpose is to be an architect. Great vocation but hardly a reason for existence. Others search for meaning in houses, cars, and land. Good for the

575

economy but bad for their budgets. Others seek entertainment, sports, cults, and illicit sex. You name it. Simply mirages in the desert of purpose.

In meditating on the above scriptures, I believe our purpose in life is to love God, others, and ourselves and to accept love from God, from others, and from ourselves.

Dear Lord, please give everyone the capacity to love and receive love. Amen.

MAKING DISCIPLES OF OTHERS

*By this shall all men know that you are my
disciples if ye have love one to another John 13:35
KJV.*

Recently, my son Isaac posted a vacation picture of him making footprints in the wet sand, and my grandson Hudson striving to follow in his dad's footprints. I thought about what a great devotion for Father's Day this would make. I then thought about us striving to follow in Jesus's footprints and what a good picture of discipleship this is.

In our faith, we follow in someone's steps: a parent, a grandparent, a pastor, a pastor's wife, a youth pastor, a Sunday School teacher, or a special hero. None of us are the first to walk the path alone. All of us have someone that we follow.

In our faith, we leave footprints to guide us. There is a grandchild, a friend, and a recent convert. None should be left to walk the path alone. It is the process of discipleship.

Dear Lord, please help all of us Christians be willing to disciple others, just as we were guided along the way by someone else. Amen.

SEPTEMBER 16
GOD WILL SEE YOU HOME SAFELY

While we look not at the things which are seen but at the things which are not seen: for the things which are seen are temporal, but the things which are not seen are eternal. II Corinthians 4:18 KJV.

For some of you, the journey has been long and hard. The road has been rocky. I do not wish to minimize the things you have had to face along the way. I know the hard times I have gone through, but I look around every day and see others who are so much worse than I have been. Some of you have shouldered burdens that few of us could ever carry. Some of you have had to say goodbye to a lifelong partner. You may have had a precious baby taken just when you were enjoying it so much. You may have been robbed of an opportunity or a dream in life that was rightfully yours. You may be living in a failing body that cannot sustain your spirit. You may be married to someone who absolutely detests your faith. You may have bills that outnumber paychecks and challenges that outweigh your strength. God did not say the journey would be easy, but he did say that the arrival would be worthwhile.

Dear Lord, I pray for those who are going through trials and tribulations that I cannot imagine. I pray for your strength to see them through and for them to arrive home safely and say it has been well worth it! Amen.

SEPTEMBER 17
LOVE DETESTS EVIL

All we like sheep have gone astray; we have turned everyone to his own way. And the Lord laid on him the iniquity of us all. Isaiah 53:6 KJV.

People often ask why a loving God would send anyone to hell. He does not. He gives people a choice. He even provided his utmost, his beloved son, as the sacrifice in their stead. People make their own choice. They accept Christ for the remission of their sins and choose to go to heaven, or they deny him and choose to go to hell for their sins. Sin is costly, and it must be paid. God honors their choice.

If there was no hell, God would not be just. If there is no punishment for sin, heaven would be apathetic toward the pillagers, rapists, and violent murderers of society. If there is no hell, God is blind toward the victims and has turned his back on those who pray for justice. If there is no wrath toward evil, then God is not love. For love detests that which is evil.

581

Dear Lord, I pray that you will open blind eyes and let sinners see that there is a purpose for hell, but they do not have to go there. Help sinners realize it is their choice. Please help them to quit listening to Satan and to accept Christ while they still have the chance. Once they experience Christ for themselves, none will ever be able to change their mind about him. Amen.

For thus saith the Lord God behold I even I will both search for my sheep and seek them out. Ezekiel 34:11 KJV.

God is waiting for you. God is standing on the portico of heaven, expectantly hoping and searching the horizon for a glimpse of his child. You are the one he's looking for.

God is the waiting father, the caring shepherd in search of his lamb. His legs are scratched. His feet are sore, and his eyes are burning. He scales the cliffs and combs the meadows. He explores the caves. He cups his hands to his mouth and calls into the canyon. The name he calls is yours. The message is simple. God gave up his son to rescue all his sons and his daughters to bring his children home. He Is listening to your answer.

Dear Lord, please let the answer of sinners be yes this very day. Amen.

Lay not up for yourselves treasures upon earth where moth and rust doth corrupt and where thieves break in and steal: but lay up for yourselves treasures in heaven...for where your treasure is, there will your heart be also. Matthew 6:19,21 KJV.

It is mind-boggling how you spend almost a lifetime collecting things, and one day, you realize if you die tomorrow, your kids are not going to want but a minute amount of it. It will be a burden to them to dispose of unwanted items. So, I have set out to inquire about what my kids want, and I am tagging those specific items with their names. I am also giving a tremendous number of items away and donating other items to charity.

It has created a simpler life, less dusting, and freed up time for more important and enjoyable tasks. The most powerful life is the simple life that knows where it came from, where it is going, and what its purpose is now. The main source of man's weariness is the pursuit of possessions. They are dead things and cannot satisfy When we try to get life out of possessions, it results in dissatisfaction because they are non-living.

Dear Lord, please help us to achieve a heart, a home, and a life free of clutter. Help us to lay our treasures in heaven. Amen.

Who shall change our vile body that it may be fashioned like unto his glorious body according to the working whereby he is able even to subdue all things unto himself. Philippians 3:21 KJV.

What will our resurrected body look like? We do not know, but I am hoping for a perfect figure, size 10. Just kidding! You might not recognize me then! Will we still bear the marks of the pain of life, the wrinkles from worry, the scars from war, the disfigurements of disease, the wounds from violence? Jesus kept his wounds for at least forty days. No, I don't think so. Our wounds will be removed and remembered no more. Only the wounds of Jesus are worthy to be remembered.

Dear Lord, it is exciting to know we will have a new, glorified body with no signs or remembrance of past sins or anguish. Amen.

September 21
Our Defender

He only is my rock and my salvation: he is my defense; I shall not be moved. Psalm 62:6 KJV.

Have you ever wondered what God is doing when you are in a real dilemma? When the last penny is gone, and there are no groceries in the house, when the lifeboat springs a leak, when the rip cord snaps. I know what we are doing, ringing our hands, biting our nails, pacing the floor, but what is God doing?

If we call on him, he steps in, points us to the side, and takes over. He fights for us. Last night, our area suddenly came under a flash flood watch. We live on a terraced hill with a short retaining wall behind us. It had rained for hours, and the water was about to come over the retaining wall. There was nowhere to get sandbags in the middle of the night. My husband was standing watch, and we began to pray and call upon the Lord for help. The rain stopped shortly thereafter. Our house was not

flooded, and we went to bed and slept the rest of the night.

Dear Lord, I praise you for answering prayer, just in the nick of time. Amen.

Let not your heart be troubled; ye believe in God, believe also in me. In my father's house are many mansions: If it were not so, I would have told you. I go to prepare a place for you. And if I go and prepare a place for you, I will come again. And receive you unto myself; that where I am, there ye may be also. John 14:1-3 KJV.

Our finite minds are not capable of comprehending our future. When it comes to a future with no boundaries of space or time, we simply do not have the references required to explain it. God takes on the role of a parent and says trust me.

Do not be troubled by the return of Christ. Do not be anxious about the path or the parts you cannot understand. For Christians, the return of Christ is not a mystery to be solved or a code to be broken but rather a day to be anticipated with great joy.

Dear Father, you are in control. Please help us to trust you completely with the things we do not know or cannot comprehend. Amen.

He that hath an ear let him hear what the spirit sayeth unto the churches; To him that overcometh will I give to eat of the hidden manna, and will give him a white stone, and in the stone a new name is written, which no man knoweth saving he that receiveth it. Revelation 2:17 KJV.

I am intrigued by names and the meanings behind them. When a new baby enters the world, I cannot wait to hear what the parents have named it. I have written poems for all eight of our grandchildren, spelling out their first names with characteristics I pray that my grandchildren will develop and eventually possess.

Did you know that God is going to give each of us in heaven a new name that he and only the recipient will know what it is? There is more to your story than you ever thought. How exciting!

Dear Lord, you never cease to amaze me. The more I learn about you, the more I am enthralled by you. Amen.

September 24
In The Service

For as we have many members in one body and all members have not the same office; we being many are one body in Christ, and every one member one of another. Romans 12:4-5 KJV.

Just imagine we have been enlisted in God's Navy and placed on his ship. The vessel has one purpose, and that is to get us safely to the other shore.

This is no vacation cruise. We are on a battleship. We are not called to a life of leisure but a life of service. We all have different jobs, some concerned with those drowning or snatching people from death. Others are concerned about the enemy, so they use cannons for prayer and worship. Others devote themselves to the crew, feeding and training the new crew members. Though different, we are the same branch. Each had had a personal encounter with the captain. Each had received a personal call. We all followed him across the gangplank onto the same ship. There is one captain

595

and one destination. Though the battle is fierce, our vessel is safe, for God is our captain.

Dear Lord, there is no concern about the vessel sinking with you on board and in control. Amen.

Whatsoever thy hand findeth to do, do it with thy might. Ecclesiastes 9:10 KJV.

Time slips away, days go by, and years fade. What we have come to do, we must do now.

As we get older, our vision should improve, not our earthly vision but our vision of heaven. We have looked for it for a long time. As we get a glimpse of it, we should skip our steps. If there is something you hope to do, something you wish to say to someone, do it now. What we come to do must be done while there is still time.

Dear Heavenly Father, we never know how much time is left. So please let us do whatever we

plan to do. Do it now with urgency while there is still time. Amen.

SEPTEMBER 26
QUEST FOR EXCELLENCE

For we are his workmanship, created in Christ Jesus unto good works, which God hath before ordained that we should walk in them. Ecclesiastes 2:10 KJV.

My husband, Henry, strongly believes that if you are going to do something for God, you should do it with excellence. He has taught classes on it and given devotions concerning the pursuit of excellence.

The desire for excellence is a gift of God that is much needed in society today. It is characterized by respect for quality and a yearning to use God's gifts in a way that pleases him. Doing your very best to glorify God is a mark of spiritual maturity.

Dear Lord, whatsoever our hands find to do, may we do it with excellence to bring honor and glory to your name. Amen.

Blessed be the Lord who daily loadeth us with benefits, even the God of our salvation. Selah. Psalm 68:19 KJV.

What do you do when you make mistakes and fail? Even when you fall and everyone else rejects you, Christ will not turn away from you. He came first and foremost to those who had no hope. He goes to those no one else will go to and gives them life more abundantly. You are the only one who can surrender your concerns to the father. No one can do it for you. Only you can cast all your anxieties on the one who cares for you. What better way to start another day than to bring your cares to him and lay them at his feet? Amen.

Dear Lord, you know how I have failed and what a mess I have made. I am bringing all my cares and concerns, failures and flaws, and laying them down at your feet. Please show me where to go from here. Amen.

Knowing that whatsoever good thing any man doeth, the same shall he receive of the Lord, whether he be bond or free. Ephesians 6:8 KJV.

Although we're limited as to what we know about the next life, one thing is for sure. It will be a day of reward. Those who went unknown on earth will be known in heaven. Those who have never heard the cheers of men will have the cheers of angels. Those who missed the blessing of a father here will have the blessing of their heavenly father there. The unnoticed will be crowned, and the faithful will be honored. The Glory Club is not reserved up there for the elite but for all the Children of God.

Dear Heavenly Father, we do not know a lot about what is to come in heaven, but we know you said that eyes have not seen, nor ears heard what you have prepared for your children who love you. Amen.

And will be a father unto you, and you shall be my sons and daughters, saith the Lord Almighty. II Corinthians 6:18 KJV.

It is very difficult to understand, but no one in this world can hurt you like your family. Maybe because they are the closest to you, or you expect them to always have your back and be in your corner or to be proud of you, happy for you, and want the very best for you, but that is not always the case. If you have been hurt by family, Jesus totally understands. His brothers made fun of him and his mission; they even said he was a maniac. Jesus never reprimanded them or tried to change their views. He showed them love and went on doing what he was called to do. If you have never had the support of a loving family, let your heavenly father heal your pain. Also, never underestimate his power to change hardened families. One of Jesus' brothers became an apostle (Galatians 1:19), and the other brothers became missionaries (I Corinthians 9:5).

There is absolutely nothing our God cannot do when we ask and believe.

Dear Lord, thank you for loving us. Please bless and move on families and help them to become what you intended. Amen.

The way of the wicked is an abomination unto the Lord: but he loveth him that followeth after righteousness. Proverbs 15:9 KJV.

Perhaps the wound happened years ago: a person to be trusted tried to take advantage of you, your spouse ran off with your friend, and your father left you out of his will.

Maybe it's a fresh wound: you were lied to and slandered, a boss promised you a promotion but gave it to someone else. Part of you is broken, and the other part is angry. Part of you wants to cry, and the other part wants to fight.

You are left with decisions. Yes, you were mistreated. You can get over it, or you can get even. Do you ask God to heal your heart, or do you let it turn to hate?

Dear Heavenly Father, there are so many hurting, wounded, broken people. Please let them turn to you for healing. Please deliver them from anger. Set them free from the pain that holds them hostage. Amen.

OCTOBER

LITTLE IS MUCH WHEN GOD IS IN IT

Better is a little with righteousness than great revenue without right. Proverbs 16:8 KJV.

Nestled in the beautiful foothills of the Blue Ridge Mountains sits an elegant little snow-white country church with newly added rock on the front. Two welcoming springtime wreaths adorn the double wooden doors. A white steeple pointing toward the sky reminds the viewer that God is sitting high on his throne in heaven with Jesus, his son, and our Savior, seated at the right hand of the Father.

The church grounds are immaculate in keeping with this country setting. A fellowship hall welcomes members and their guests to come and enjoy showers, wedding receptions, holiday gatherings, homecomings, and other social events. There is also a huge marble table under a shelter outside for the congregation to enjoy in case of crowd overflow, picnics, cookouts, or other outside

activities. In the back of the church is a well-kept cemetery for families in case of need.

To the left of the church property is a beautiful playground area to accommodate the children, a vital part of this congregation. The church sign in front of the complex introduces the Ludville Church of God as the church that love is building. To all who attend, it is a beautiful reminder that this church has been a beacon of light and love in this community.

For over one hundred years, this church has preached the gospel of Jesus Christ, had new converts, baptized them, taken in new church members, married them, dedicated their babies, buried their deceased loved ones, and set some forth in the ministry. It has truly ministered to its members, their friends, and the Ludville, Pickens County, Georgia community at their point of need. I can attest to this because I am one of those converts. If you attend this church or one like it that preaches the gospel and loves people, it will totally alter the outcome of your life.

Dear Lord, thank you for guiding our footsteps to a church where we can be a part , be loved, be used where needed, and be ministered to so our faith will grow strong. Amen.

OCTOBER 2
MAMA'S HOMEGOING

For we know that if our earthly house of this tabernacle were dissolved, we have a building of God, an house not made with hands, eternal in the heavens. II Corinthians 5:1 KJV.

My Mama had mentioned several times over the years that the hardest part about getting older was losing your independence and not being able to remain in your own home. Mama still owned her little house with her furnishings all in place. She had fallen a few times, and my sister Barbara had taken her to her house. Mother's Day was coming up in a week, and my sister and I decided to celebrate Mother's Day at Mama's home because that was Mama's desire.

We cleaned the house thoroughly and took Mama home that night. I stayed with her and helped her get ready for bed when she passed out. I slowly lowered her onto the carpet, and she regained consciousness. I called an ambulance, and she was taken to the hospital, where she underwent tests and was placed on oxygen.

Her condition worsened, and a few days later, the doctor told us there was no more he could do. He sent her home on oxygen and with the services of Hospice Care. My sister had gone home that night to rest, and my daughter and I stayed. The hospital bed was in the living room, and I slept beside Mama on the sofa. I gave her meds and moistened her lips several times through the night.

The next morning, I heard a knock on the front door and thought it was Hospice Care but it was my daughter's pastor. He was on his way to spend the day with his daughter when the Lord impressed him to come by and check on us. At that time, our sweet Mama gave a big sigh and took her last breath.

Mama had received her wish to come back to her home. She had spent her last night in her home amidst familiar surroundings she loved. She was then carried to Jesus' arms by a band of heavenly angels, just in time to spend Mother's Day in heaven with Daddy and other beloved family.

Dear Heavenly Father, it is so difficult to give up a parent, especially your mother. She has been closer to you than anyone. She cared for you and nurtured you. But when you know she is in heaven with Jesus and healed eternally, you would not bring her back, even if you could. Amen.

OCTOBER 3
WHAT IS A DADDY?

And he shall turn the heart of the fathers to the children and the heart of the children to their fathers. Malachi 4:6 KJV.

Any man can be a father, but it takes someone special to be a daddy. From my experience as a daughter and having seen the relationship between my own daughter and her dad, and now viewing my oldest granddaughter, Abigayle, and her dad's relationship, I can truly say that there is no love more angelic than that which exists between a father and a daughter. At the request of a few close friends, I am including my version, written in memory of my daddy, the late Mr. Dean Watson, and dedicated to every father who has ever known the joy of raising a daughter.

WHAT IS A DADDY?

A daddy is a little girl's friend, someone to play with when mom is too busy in the kitchen.

He is daring and will let you do more exciting things than Mom because she is not so nervy.

He is the one who decides all little girls should have a horse, even when mom objects.

Daddy is the one who boasts the most when his daughter makes all A's.

He tells her she should always strive to do her best in everything she sets out to accomplish.

If she should fall short, he is always there to encourage her to try again.

A daddy is the one who gives his daughter driving lessons just to spare the Drivers Ed teacher a heart attack.

A daddy is the one who makes the final decision about whether his daughter is old enough to have that first date.

A daddy is a provider, the one that makes piano lessons, prom dresses, and summer camp possible.

A daddy is a daughter's confidant, the one she goes to for advice or counsel when making important decisions in life because his approval and advice are very important to her.

A daddy is the person the daughter respects and looks up to. When he speaks, she listens because she knows daddy will never let her down.

A daddy is a person you are never afraid to call. Even when it is his fender, you have dented.

A daddy is the one who drops you an unexpected check in the mail when you are away at college with only a little note attached saying Love, Daddy.

A daddy is the one who voluntarily picks up the payments on that new stereo and piano you bought just to help you out.

A daddy is the one who goes with you to pick out your very first car, changes the oil, and checks the tires for you until you leave home.

A daddy is the one who possesses Christ-like qualities and traits the daughter looks for in the man she marries.

A daddy is the one who tells your fiancée on the night you announce your engagement that you cannot boil water just to discourage him.

A daddy is the one you want to escort you down the aisle and give you away because only he has the right. After all, everyone knows that a daughter's heart belongs to her daddy.

OCTOBER 4
IMPACT YOU MAY NEVER KNOW

For ye are all the children of God by faith in Christ Jesus. Galatians 3:26 KJV.

While earning my college degree, I worked in various volunteer and paid positions at numerous special services and nonprofit agencies. I knew I wanted to work with people in need. This allowed me to acquire specialized training in many areas while being a blessing to those in need. It certainly did not help my bank account, but it gave me many valuable experiences.

In one home where I worked, there was a young man whom I will call Hal, who had a diagnosis of mental retardation with bouts of anger and violence. His mother was deceased, and his father's whereabouts were unknown. The only thing we knew for sure was that his dad had a criminal record for domestic violence and cruelty to children.

When I began working with Hal, I immediately picked up on the fact that he enjoyed helping. He loved taking out my trash bag and replacing it with a new one. He responded to praise. I found out he liked peanut butter and cheese crackers and ginger ale. I promised to bring him a snack daily to help me. The first day I gave him snacks, he could not believe that I kept my promise.

I had worked with Hal for over a year with no episodes of aggression, and it was documented in his chart. The day came when I had scheduled to leave. He was slightly upset. I promised him I would talk to my director and make sure he was aware that Hal was a good helper and worthy of recognition. When he learned, I was going to work with children, he said he could be one of my children. That brought tears to my eyes. If you love people and show them respect and dignity, you may never know if you had an impact on them, but you will certainly know the impact they had on you.

Dear Lord, we may never know the influence we have on others, but you know, and that is what matters. May we always strive to be a blessing, no matter where we are or what we are trying to accomplish. Amen.

OCTOBER 5
SAY NO TO ABUSE

For we are his workmanship created in Christ Jesus unto good works which God hath before ordained that we should walk in them. Ephesians 2:8-10 KJV.

When a child has been abused, he grows up with more problems than physical pain. He may live with the anger that no one helped him, no one intervened on his behalf, and no one stepped in and rescued him. Others may have known, but they did not do anything to stop it. He feels like a baby that was thrown away, unwanted, and not good enough.

The abused may not be the only ones who feel this way. The rejected and the abandoned may have issues also. Almost everyone goes through at least one of these experiences at some time in their life.

When people reject you, it is very difficult to feel good about yourself. You start thinking that if they do not think I am worthy, maybe I am not. I must be of no value. This must be my fault.

Please do not allow another person's view of you to control the way you see yourself. That is too much power to give to another person. If people do not have the discernment to know the truth and value the riches inside you, that is their problem. If you sit at home and wallow in hurt and self-pity, then it becomes your problem. Do not believe Satan's lies.

Dear Lord, I pray for the ones who are dealing with low self-esteem because of the pain of rejection. Please heal the hurt, let them know the truth, and see themselves as you see them. Amen.

OCTOBER 6
THE WIDOW'S HEART

Is my hand shortened at all that it cannot redeem or have I no power to deliver? Isaiah 50:2 KJV.

My heart hurts with pain like I have never known before. I need hope, and I need help. Loving friends come with offers of lunch invitations and other opportunities for distraction. Even their love cannot reach the pit of my soul. My loss has left me feeling lost and alone. His death ended what we had together and that we were together, one flesh, one mind, one spirit.

I do not want to face life by myself. Pull me back to life from this grave of grief. Heal the aching in my heart. Soften the piercing stabs I feel when everything I see reminds me of the one, I lost. Deliver me from feeling guilty over things I wish I had said or done.

Dear God, please speak to me the living words
that only you can say. Send me the kind of comfort
that only comes from heaven. I am leaning on your
love. Bring the light of your presence to this dark
abyss. Restore me with the tenderness of your mercy
until I am strong and whole again. Amen.

OCTOBER 7
WORSHIP IS WARFARE

The angel of the Lord encampeth around about them that fear him, and delivereth them. Psalms 34:7 KJV.

When you are praising the Lord, he is fighting your battles in the heavenlies. He is dealing with the enemy of your soul. He is pulverizing the demonic powers that sought to oppress you, blind you, and keep you from God's blessings.

Your praise is not just an expression of your joy. It is actual warfare in the spirit while you are praising God. Do not fear the fluttering in the atmosphere. The war angels of the Lord are coming into your hospital room. The fighting angels of the Lord are surrounding your children and protecting them. The war angels of the Lord are scattering your enemies. God's angels encamp around us when we revere and fear the Lord.

Dear Lord, thank you for the privilege of praise. We are not only expressing our joy in praise, but we are initiating spiritual warfare against the enemy of our souls. Amen.

But my God shall supply all your need according to his riches in glory by Christ Jesus. Philippians 4:19 KJV.

How on earth did I get myself in so much debt? I am totally strapped. It seems like every time I pick up the phone, there is a bill collector on the other end. I am not only out of money. I am totally out of energy. I never realized how important money was to me until I spent much more than I had. Now, I am trapped in a cycle of debt that is spiraling out of control.

Dear Lord, I am calling on you for financial management. I repent of the unwise spending choices I have made. I repent of the lack of discipline that got

me into this mess. Lord, please work a miracle in my finances. Please give me creative ways to earn money and the ability to discern how to use it. I commit to walk with you, Lord. With your help, I will pay faithfully toward this debt until I owe no man nothing but to love him. And, oh yes, I am going to research tithing. I know it all belongs to you, Lord. I want to honor you in my finances. Amen.

I will give him unto the Lord all the days of his life. I Samuel 1:11 KJV.

Life is easier to give your children back to God when they are older if you realize from the beginning that they are not yours to keep. This is incredibly difficult but possible. Your authority changes. You will move from diaper changer to decision maker and discipline enforcer to confidant, cheerleader, and champion. This is not promoting disrespect but development. If you respect yesterday's child and recognize that she has become today's adult, she will always love you for your tremendous contribution to that independence.

When Jesus was found teaching in the temple, he returned home with his mother and continued to submit to them from that time on. He increased in wisdom and stature and in favor of God and man. He was not embarrassed to be seen with his mother. His love followed him all the way to the cross. Although their roles changed, and he became

increasingly independent, his love and care for her continued to the final moments of his life. She would always be his mother.

Dear Heavenly Father, sometimes we feel we are treading some rough waters, but we know that you are in control and that you love us. We pray for your divine guidance and your wisdom as we continue as parents of adult children. Amen.

A FEW POSITIVE QUALITIES OF DELILAH

(Taken from my notes of a sermon by Bishop T. D. Jakes)

Marriage is honorable in all. Hebrews 13:4 KJV.

Marriage is best when both parties can be vulnerable to each other and not be ashamed. There is no resting place for the man who must hide in his own home.

Let's talk about Delilah. Most women do not like her. Her morals are inexcusable, but there are a few things wives can learn from her.

If your husband is in a high-ranking position, if he is powerful and full of purpose, you should learn from Delilah. Where can this mighty man lay his head? Where can he take off his armor and rest for a few hours? Is your home a peaceful place? Is it clean and neat? Is it warm and inviting?

If not, Delilah's place is ready, and Sampson does not have to solve her problems the minute he

walks through the door. She knows he is tired after fighting the Philistines all day. So, she says, "Come lay your head in my lap."

Delilah knows that all men are little boys. Somewhere deep inside, they started their lives by being touched by a woman. A woman sang your husband's first lullaby with her tender voice. A woman gave him his first bath. When he was tired, he laid his head against her warm breast and went to sleep. A woman soothingly talked to him, touched him, and made him feel safe, not criticized, not ostracized, just safe.

Men respond to praise. Praise will make a weary man perform. For all your husband's fears and tears, he needs your arms, your soothing touch, and your song.

Dear Heavenly Father, thank you for pointing out a few positive excerpts in the Bible story of Samson and Delilah that a husband and wife can beautifully apply to their Christian marriage. Amen.

Likewise, you wives, be in subjection to your own husbands; That if they obey not the word, they also may without the word be won by the conversation of the wives; I Peter 3:1 KJV.

When you and your spouse are having problems do not suppress the gentle side of you to avoid being hurt. If you do, you may fall into depression. Do not fight fire with fire. The best way to fight fire is with water. You can win with a gentle, soothing character, like pouring water on blazing coals, not with heated words that will only fan the flame.

In fact, if you do not say a word, you may even be able to lead an unbelieving husband to the Lord. Believe in God for your marriage. Marriage was his idea, to begin with. It will not be your feelings that heal your relationship. It will be your faith. The power to unleash your marriage is in your faith. Dare to believe that God will do what he said he would do. Trust God. He will soothe your wounds. He will resurrect your marriage. Believe it!

Dear Lord, please help husbands and wives to lay down their egos, give up the need to have the last word, and simply decide to love and take good care of each other. With faith, marriage can be a marriage made in heaven, just as you intended. Give me soft-spoken words in times of marital conflict. I trust and believe you will revive my marriage in this way. Amen.

OCTOBER 12
BLESSINGS OF SINGLENESS

Upon the handmaids in those days will I pour out my spirit. Joel 2:29 KJV.

Did you know your single or single-again years should be the most spiritually productive years of your life? Some of you do not understand the benefits of being single. While you are not married, take advantage of being involved with God. God ordained that single people would have the free time to minister to him because when you get married, you minister to your spouse. This is the way God ordained it.

When you are single, you can wake up at 5:00 A.M. and stay in bed for two more hours praying in the spirit. You can soak in the bathtub for as long as you like, reading God's word or listening to praise and worship songs. There is nothing wrong with wanting to be married. When you are married, you will have a husband to minister to.

638

Simply take care of the Lord while waiting. Minister to him. Let him heal you and mature you. Single women ought to be the most consecrated women in the church. You are the ones whose shadows ought to fall on people, and they should be healed. You are in a position and posture of prayer. Miracles should abound in your prayer life.

Dear Lord, in my time of singleness, please guide me. Help me to pray and to seek your will. Help me to fall deeply in love with my Savior. Amen.

And God shall wipe away all tears from their eyes. Revelation 21:49 KJV.

I have had losses in life. I had a miscarriage of a baby I never got to hold in this life, and I grieve. To lose a child you have loved, nurtured, bonded, and laughed with, I cannot imagine any grief more consuming.

Dear Lord, I have no words to say. They must feel numb. It is difficult to imagine being real and permanent. As the parents, it must be so hard to release that child to the father. For those of us who want to reach out but feel so inadequate, show us

ways that will be helpful. Lord, please be these parents' deepest friend and help them cling more closely to each other. Bring them through these devastating days. Give them grace through this grief. Help them to survive, and when it is time, help them to get stronger and more compassionate. Help them know this child is safe with you, and so are they. Amen.

Thanks be unto God for his unspeakable gift. II Corinthians 9:15 KJV

Marriage is having someone to curl up against when the world seems cold and uncertain. It is having someone as concerned as you are when the children are sick. It is having a hand that keeps checking your fever when you come down with covid. It is having a shoulder to cry on when they are lowering your parent's body into the ground. It is rapping a swollen knee in a warm blanket. Him giggling without his teeth at the sight of you with cold cream on your face.

To the person you marry, you are saying, when it comes my time to go, it is you I want to kiss goodbye, it is your hand I want to hold, and your eyes I want to investigate deeply and know that I really did matter to someone.

Cherish the moment. Lift the glass and drink deeply of life. If you can look back and catch a

glimpse of a few of those moments or trace a smile back to a memory, you are blessed. You could have been anywhere, doing anything, but the waiter seated you at a table for two with an ocean view.

Dear Lord, thank you for your precious love and your special blessings on us. Amen.

To everything there is a season, and a time for every purpose under the heaven. Ecclesiastes 3:1 KJV.

I miss them more than I ever dreamed I would. The last child is gone off to chase his dreams and sail the uncertain waters of adulthood. In days gone by, I yearned at times for peace and quiet, but this silence, this stillness, is more deafening than any children's noise could ever be.

Dear Father, every day in my household now is a new season in the life you have given me. It is time for us, this lady and her Lord. It is time for me to know you in ways I could not when children and teenagers were coming and going in and out. It is

644

time to worship, time to seek your face. Time to find a brand-new ultimate place in you. It is time for this home to belong to you in ways it never has before. Come and fill the empty rooms where songs of children and teens once were heard. Now, let my heart sing to you. Where little voices gasped and giggled, now let me find wonder and delight in the lover of my soul. Lord, I welcome this new season, even with its challenges. I welcome you in my heart and my home as never before. Amen.

And be renewed in the spirit of your mind.
Ephesians 4:23 KJV.

I am so thankful that Jesus medicates all the areas in our lives that cause us emotional pain and frustration. He will virtually eliminate the entire struggle in the hearts of those who trust in him. His presence helps men and women alike to avoid obsessions and extremes that accompany disorders and dysfunctions. Jesus is the balm for every woman and every man whose life has been impaired by something they received. He even provides for those whose hurt stems from the reminders of what they were refused. He is the bread of heaven and the water of life. If you take him in, he will satisfy your very soul.

Dear Lord Jesus, I am so thankful that you provide the remedy for whatever is emotionally and spiritually missing in men's and women's souls if taken as prescribed. Amen.

A friend loveth at all times. Proverbs 17:17 KJV.

Before I sat out on my journey to write this book, I was a part of a Tuesday Morning Ladies' Bible Study Group. God wants to bring friends together. Every Mary needs Elizabeth. Throw down the walls you have built around yourself for protection. God put something in your friends that you need and something in you that your friends need. We saw prayers answered and miracles happen in our small Tuesday morning group. When you come together for prayer, Bible study, and mutual support, things start happening. Jesus said that if two of you agree on earth concerning anything that they ask, it will be done for them by my Father in heaven, for where two or three are gathered, there am I in the midst of them. Matthew 18:19-20 KJV.

If you are not a part of a Bible Study and Prayer Group, I highly suggest you find one and become involved. You will be glad you did.

Dear Lord, thank you for answering prayers when people come together to study the Word of God and pray together. Amen.

OCTOBER 18
ABOVE AND BEYOND WHERE WE ARE

Then shall we know, if we follow on to know the Lord: his going forth is prepared as the morning, and he shall come unto us as the rain, as the latter and former rain unto the earth. Hosea 6:3 KJV.

In your thoughts, do you see something above and beyond where you are? If you see a goal, a dream, or an aspiration that others would think impossible, you may have to hold it. Sometimes, you may have to hide it, and most of the time, you will have to water it as a farmer waters his crops to sustain life in them. But always remember they are your fields. You must eat from the garden of your own thoughts. So, do not plant anything you do not want to eat. As you ponder and daydream, receive grace from the Lord for places that are hard and healing for the damaged soil. Just know that when your children, your friends, or anyone else comes to the table of your wisdom, you can only feed them what you have grown in your own fields. Your wisdom is so flavorful, and the texture is so rich

that it cannot be store-bought. It must be homegrown.

Thank you, God, so much for giving me goals, dreams, and aspirations. You plant them as seeds in my heart. They come forth because of you. I must do the pruning and the uprooting of weeds. You then send the rain, and they grow. I am blessed, and as I bless others, you are glorified. Amen.

GRANDCHILDREN AND HOT COCOA

As the cold of snow and the time of harvest so is a faithful messenger to them that send him; for he refresheth the soul of his master. Proverbs 25:13 KJV.

Every season of your life brings new challenges and joys to look forward to. I am now in the autumn season of my life and enjoying my grandchildren immensely. I see my children when they were little in them so much. I just prepared Natalie and me a hot cup of cocoa and we are drinking out of porcelain Beatrix Potter teacups that belonged to her Aunt Tiffany when she was a little girl.

My granddaughter Natalie is such a people person, and she loves to share her faith. We had a discussion today on how God's Word tells us that our faith can be just like a warm, refreshing treat when we share it with other people.

Dear Lord, I pray that my granddaughter's faith will be an encouragement to everyone she meets. May she know that you are pleased when she seeks you and that her faith can be like a refreshment to others. May she be known as a friend to all and a steadfast messenger of your Word. Thank you for saving her at such a tender age. Amen.

In the fear of the Lord is strong confidence and his children shall have a place of refuge. Proverbs 14:26 KJV.

My grandchildren loved to build fortresses together out of Lincoln logs, Legos, and other building blocks that belonged to their dad, Isaac when he was a little boy. They could be entertained for hours as I talked to them about how fear or reverence for the Lord is like a fortress or safe place of protection in times of storms.

Dear Lord, you are our refuge, and we praise you for your protection. My grandchildren have embraced you at a young age and are learning to

trust you as their Savior. Help them to understand that your promises are like a strong fortress providing safety and security for your children in an ever-changing world. Amen.

Trust in the Lord with all thine heart and lean not unto thine own understanding. In all thy ways acknowledge him and he shall direct thy path. Proverbs 3:5-6 KJV.

Randyn, Abi, and I were walking from our townhome up on the hill down to the pool. On the way down, we discussed the best path to take to arrive at our destination. Randyn, my eight-year-old grandson, wanted to go down the steepest hill through the landscape. It was the shortest route but certainly not the safest. His sister and I had him outnumbered, but he only changed his mind when I pointed out that some of the bushes had briars.

Dear Heavenly Father, it can be tempting for your children to take detours, especially if the detour takes less time to arrive at your destination. I pray that my grandson will trust you to always keep his feet on a straight and safe path. Thank you for giving him this Bible promise that as he trusts and acknowledges you in everything he does, you will guide him safely to his destination. Amen.

The way of life is above to the wise that he may depart from hell beneath. Proverbs 15:24 KJV.

It was a beautiful starry, starry night to be outside. We were on the patio, making s'mores at the fire pit. Granddaddy was discussing with the grandchildren how God's ways and thoughts are so much higher than ours. His Majesty is proclaimed throughout his creation. There are so many fun, teachable moments to take advantage of when you are hanging out with your grandchildren.

Dear God, your word tells us that just as the heavens are higher than the earth, your ways and thoughts are so much higher than ours. I pray that your Holy Spirit will cause our grandchildren's

minds and affections to dwell upon Jesus, who sits in heaven at your right hand. Please give them the power to be faithful in pursuing a life here on earth that is controlled by a heavenly focus. Amen.

*The Lord is a man of war: the Lord is his name.
Exodus 15:3 KJV.*

I read the Bible story of David and Goliath to my grandchildren before tucking them into bed. God greatly blessed David, a mere lad who was not even strong enough to hold up the warrior's armor. He killed his nine-foot foe when he came in the name of the Lord God Almighty instead of trusting in worldly weapons, physical strength, and skill.

Dear Heavenly Father, please help us to teach our grandchildren not to trust in their own strength. Instead, help us teach them to put their confidence in you, the only stronghold that will forever endure. Amen.

A wise man is strong; yes a man of knowledge increaseth strength. Proverbs 24:5 KJV.

My husband, Henry, and my grandson, Hudson, while in arm wrestling, were discussing the different strengths one can gain with a faithful exercise regimen-physical, mental and spiritual. Hudson, who is also an avid baseball player, commented on the similarities of what it takes to be a good baseball player. Granddaddy told him that he also needed to build spiritual muscles. It takes regular church attendance, daily Bible reading, and daily prayer to build strong spiritual muscles. Hudson said that that requires a lot of discipline which is needed in playing your best in any sport.

Dear Lord, there is no one as strong and powerful as you. This verse tells us that wise people gain knowledge and wisdom by also increasing strength and power. I pray that my grandson will come to understand that while worldly knowledge is important to a certain kind of success, faith, and godly wisdom bring strength of character and please you. Amen.

The king's favor is toward a wise servant but his wrath is against him that causeth shame. Proverbs 14:35 KJV.

At the dinner table, we discussed what Natalie would like to do when she grows up. She hopes to become a marine biologist. One question that came up was what happens when people make wise decisions on their jobs. Some of the answers were familiar. A fireman rescues people and animals from burning buildings and homes. A police officer keeps us safe and himself alive. A doctor cures people with diseases and prolongs lives. Natalie sees herself caring for marine life and striving to make a safe environment for them to thrive. Our discussion led to how important it is that people make good choices and wise decisions in their line of duty. It is very important for all involved.

Dear Lord, thank you for your faithfulness to your children. I pray that you will enable our granddaughter to be a wise and loyal servant in your kingdom. Please help her faithfulness to you overflow into every area of her life. Help her to sense your delight as she makes wise and prudent choices every day. Amen.

OCTOBER 26
HE HAS BIG PLANS FOR YOU

For I know the thoughts that I think toward you, saith the Lord, thoughts of peace, and not of evil, to give you an expected end. Jeremiah 29:11 KJV.

I love to discuss life and scriptures with my grandchildren and hear their take and opinions on the matter. Jeremiah 29:11 is one of my favorites to talk about with Randyn and Abigayle, my young adult grands. They are college-aged, in training, and almost ready to step out onto the stage of adulthood. I can hardly wait to see how God continues to use them and what he has in store for them.

Dear Heavenly Father, we acknowledge you as the God of all hope and comfort. I pray that my

grandchildren will never envy or want to be involved with those who break your laws. Help them instead to zealously pursue you and to know that your greatest hope for their future is Jesus. Please prosper them, give them hope, and may they always be protected by you. Amen.

OCTOBER 27
FORMING GOOD DAILY HABITS

Bow down thine ear, and hear the words of the wise, And apply thine heart For it is a pleasant thing if thou keep them within thee; they shall withal be fitted within thy lips. Proverbs 22:17-18 KJV.

This morning, before breakfast, our grandchildren and I discussed the importance of forming good daily habits such as washing your face, combing your hair, brushing your teeth, drinking plenty of water, and getting fresh air and exercise. Natalie reminded us of the importance of daily Bible reading and prayer as good spiritual habits that must be formed in our lives.

Dear Lord, please help my grandchildren to be receptive to learning your word today. May they

learn to love the dailiness of trusting you, spending time with you, and knowing that your mercies are new every morning. Please help them faithfully establish a regular time to read your word and listen to your voice for interaction. May they store these nuggets of wisdom in their hearts so that they may not sin against you. Then, have all of them at their access and be ready in their lives to share with others. Amen.

Every word of God is pure. He is a shield to them that put their trust in him. Proverbs 30:5 KJV.

At Easter, I presented my grandchildren with new, age-appropriate Bibles. There is no better gift than they could ever receive. I included a personal transcription reassuring them of our love and God's great love for them.

Dear Lord, we are grateful that your holy scriptures are perfect. You have given them to our grandchildren to show them how to live. Please give them a love for your word and a desire to live a life governed by your principles. As they hide your word in their hearts, please help each of them to feel

completely protected and shielded from all harm and danger. Amen.

Hearken unto thy father that begat thee and despise not thy mother when she is old. Proverbs 23:22 KJV.

Today, Hudson and Natalie snipped a beautiful bouquet of red roses from my garden for their mother. They then painted a special rock paperweight for their daddy. They said that these were special "just because we love you" gifts for their parents.

Dear Lord, I thank You for my grandchildren's thoughtfulness and how I praise You for each of their godly parents. I pray that all our grandchildren will continue to appreciate their fathers and mothers and that early in life, they will value relationships with

extended family members across the generations. Help them to respect their father and listen to his advice and to show love and understanding always for their mother. Amen.

My son attend to my words; incline thine ear unto my sayings. Proverbs 4:20 KJV.

Tonight, my grandchildren and I found an easy, favorite recipe and made this special treat. We discussed the importance and the benefits of following the instructions closely. "In making a recipe, if you do not follow the instructions, you will not get the results you desire," Natalie added.

MIMI'S EASY FUDGE

1 14 oz. can of semi-sweet dark chocolate morsels

1 3.5oz can of sweetened condensed milk

¼ tsp. of vanilla flavoring

Turn the stovetop eye to medium. Add the above ingredients to a small boiler.

Stir constantly until all morsels are melted and the ingredients are blended.

Pour and smooth into a 4X4 Rubbermaid container until fudge sets and cools. Cut into squares. Makes 16 pieces easily. Enjoy!

You can use different kinds of morsels, different flavorings, different candies, sprinkles, and marshmallows. Add peanut butter or your choice of nuts. Go simple or as creative as you like. Have fun!

Dear Lord, I pray the instructions from my grandchildren's godly parents will always be wise and gracious. I asked that you help them be consistent models in their words and actions. Please help my grandchildren to be willing to listen and live out their parents' instructions. Amen.

HAVE MERCY ON THOSE IN NEED

He that despises his neighbor sinneth; but he that hath mercy on the poor happy is he. Proverbs 14:21 KJV.

Twice annually, my grandchildren and I go through clothes, shoes, coats, household items, books, toys, etc. (with the approval of their parents), and we have a yard sale, pricing gently used items way below what they are worth. After the yard sale, we usually have a truckload of items to be given to the needy. Granddaddy takes them to the Voluntary Action Center or Providence Ministries, where we donate them to the poor. We always have a discussion on what the Word of God says about giving to the poor. My grandchildren and their parents are all givers to those in need. I am so proud of my entire family, and just like the Word of God says, "Happy are they!" Your family can be happy givers as well.

Dear God, I pray that my grandchildren will enjoy friendly relations with their neighbors always. I pray that they will be sensitive to the needy around them and extend kindness and help to them. Please let the words that they speak be winsome and full of grace so that others will be drawn to you through them. Amen.

NOVEMBER

So likewise, ye, when you shall have done all those things which are commanded you, say, we are unprofitable servants. We have done that which was our duty to do. Luke 17:10 KJV.

The process of godliness has taken place as I learned godly responses to people's ruffled feathers. Have you ever been given general instructions to do something, and you did it? You fulfilled your responsibility, but it did not meet the approval or expectations of you by others. Did you know that even Jesus did not always meet the approval of others? In Mark 1, Peter asked Jesus to come back and heal more people. Jesus said he would not because he had other priorities and must be about his father's business. Jesus went on to preach in other towns. His example has helped me realize that I need not always meet others' expectations. It gave me the courage to say "no." To others' demands on my time and energies that

conflict with the priorities I have already set with God.

Dear Lord, I am so thankful I have an intimate relationship with you, and I am learning to do your bidding without feeling guilty instead of meeting others' demands. Amen.

Moreover, Lord Jesus Christ himself and God even our own father which hath loved and hath given the everlasting consolation and good hope through grace comfort your hearts and establish you in every good word and work. II Thessalonians 2:16-17 KJV.

Did you know God made a man and a woman in marriage to need each other? Men will often avoid situations in which they do not feel competent. A man may be sure of himself in his work and unsure of his skills in deeply personal relationships. If he feels unsure, he may compensate by coming on even stronger. I remember taking a drive with my parents that should have taken an hour, and it took three hours. My mother would tell my dad to stop and ask for directions, and he would tell her to keep reading her book. When Daddy finally realized it was not a sign of weakness to admit a need, he came up with a good plan. He would drive; Mom would navigate. He had the wheel; Mom had the map. Our trips became more enjoyable and faster.

Dear Lord, please help couples lay down their egos and learn to take advantage of their individual strengths as you intended. Amen.

In everything give thanks for this is the will of God concerning you. I Thessalonians 5:18 KJV.

I had a pastor friend who had been in the ministry for many fruitful years. When he found himself getting up every morning dreading facing another day, he took a sabbatical from his church.

A member of the church sent him a gift basket. His wife asked him if he would write a thank you note for the beautiful gift. He wrote the thank you card. Then, he wrote a note to his pianist, who had not missed a Sunday in fifteen years. Then, he wrote a thank you note to the janitor, the board of deacons, and his secretary. He began feeling so good about his life that he was now beginning his day in worship and closing it in praise. He had moved outside himself, and his life had been renewed. He returned to his church a whole new person, restored by the spirit of thanksgiving.

Dear Lord, it is so amazing what being thankful will do for our spirits. Thank you so much for your word that tells us to give thanks always. Amen.

Two are better than one; because they have a good reward for their labor. Ecclesiastes 4:9 KJV.

Probably the most widely believed of all marital myths is that marriage will ensure your happiness. It might and it might not. This myth is ridiculous indeed when you consider the math of marriage: one self-centered sinner plus one self-centered sinner equals two self-centered sinners, a double dose under one roof. Add two young sinners, and you have quadrupled the trouble under one roof.

Even mature, well-adjusted, spirit-filled believers have to work through countless areas of differences. He wants to travel. She needs a dishwasher. She likes to go out occasionally. He is a homebody. He is romantically inclined tonight; she was romantically inclined last night. She enjoys her friends, but he prefers his family. Every time you turn around, there is a new potential for disagreement. Do not misunderstand me. Marriage can be wonderful. It can be deeply satisfying and mentally fulfilling, but if it becomes that, it is because both partners have paid a very high price over many years to make it so.

Dear Lord, please help couples realize their marriage can bring them much happiness and fulfillment. But it will take both parties' commitment to make it so. Amen.

And I seek not mine own glory. There is one that seeketh and judgeth. John 8:50 KJV.

A competitive spirit is often initiated by a dissatisfied spirit. If we learn to accept God's place and plan for us, we will not need to compare ourselves with someone else. Having developed the use of gifts with humble service as our goal, we will be able to serve quietly without envy. We will be able to work in the church nursery in a spirit of service and contentment rather than wishing we were gifted like the one leading a large Bible class. Servants in either situation can feel confident and grateful for the opportunity to serve wherever God has called them.

The bottom line may be who gets the glory for our service, our self or God. When we learn to hand the accolades back to God, we will not need to compare ourselves with anyone else.

Dear Lord, I thank you for every opportunity I receive to serve you in my call. Amen.

NOVEMBER 6
THE BEST FOR KIDS

Let the deacons be the husbands of one wife ruling their children and their own houses well. I Timothy 3:12 KJV.

Marriage and family experts agree that a good marriage is the best thing parents can do for their children. If the parents love each other and the marriage is primary, it is amazing the effect it has on the children. In every family, the parenting relationship should be subordinate to the marriage relationship. If the parents' relationship is unstable, usually the kids will blame themselves for causing the problem. If a child sees love and care between his parents, he has a sense that he can go out and take on the world because, as a family unit, they stand strong. A loving family can overshadow the negative, destructive influence in a teenager's world. On the other hand, if the parents are not walking with the Lord and loving each other in front of their kids, the teenagers become fair game for discord, drugs, alcohol, the misuse of sex, and all

688

the other lies our culture tries to tell them. When parents are at war with each other it plays on their children's insecurities. They do not know from one day to the next if their parents are going to be together. That affects their sense of well-being greatly.

Dear heavenly Father, please help parents put their marital relationship second only to you so that their children will grow up to be secure in their parents' love. Amen.

When Jesus, therefore saw her weeping and the Jews also weeping which came with her, he groaned in the spirit and was troubled. John 11:33 KJV.

If your spouse comes home and she is upset with her boss, she may be about to project that anger onto her husband. An understanding spouse can help by saying, "Wait a minute. I really think you are about to project your anger on me, and it is inappropriate. Do you want to tell me about whatever it is that your boss did today?"

Empathy says, "I cannot feel your pain, but I want to understand it. Will you share it with me?" That gives your spouse an opportunity to unburden herself, and it prevents you from taking on her anger, hurt, or pain. That can be the best way to deal with a work-related problem.

Dear Lord, my spouse has a difficult job at times. I hope to be a blessing and a help to her. Please give me wisdom and empathy. Amen.

FIGHTING EMOTIONAL MALNUTRITION

And let us consider one another to provoke unto love and to good works. Hebrews10:24 KJV.

Everyone needs encouragement, especially from their spouses. How can we tell our partners I believe in you? A good place to start is with encouragement. Give them the benefit of the doubt and think the best of them. It is scary to criticize but much more rewarding to encourage.

Dear Lord, please help us as spouses to fight emotional malnutrition in our world and our community, but mostly in our homes and in our marriages. Amen.

Confess your faults one to another that you may be healed and pray one for another. The effectual fervent prayer of a righteous man availeth much. James 5:16 KJV.

An important aspect of a Christian prayer life is praying with your spouse. Prayer is the super glue that holds a marriage together. Anger hurts, and misunderstandings melt away in the presence of a holy God. There is power in your marriage and in your lives as the two of you pray together. Praying is a humble experience when you kneel, hold hands, and invite the Holy Spirit into your marriage, into your home, and into your bedroom. It will always draw you closer. Living a life of prayer is the power source of all Christians. It provides us with the power and the resources to be the person God would have us to be, for Him and for each other.

Dear Lord. Thank you for the privilege and the power of prayer. Amen.

A friend loveth at all times. Proverbs 17:17 KJV.

An elderly lady went to her pastor and said, "Pastor, I am so lonely. I have no friends." Her pastor asked her what she was looking for in a good friend. She said, "Someone who would accept me, someone I could count on, and someone I could share my hopes and dreams."

Her pastor told her to find someone and be that kind of friend to them, and they would be that kind of friend to her.

We do not need to be lonely. It all depends on how we choose to respond to others.

Dear Lord, please help the person who is feeling lonely today. Give them the courage to make new friends. Please make them good friends. Above all, Lord, help them realize you are the best friend they could ever have. Amen.

He shall call upon me and I will answer him: I will be with him in trouble; I will deliver him and honor him. Psalm 91:15 KJV.

Veteran's Day is an important day set aside on November 11 of each year to express honor and gratitude for the sacrifices and dedication of military veterans who have served our country. It was on November 11 that World War One ended. I always become emotional on Veteran's Day when I especially think of our veteran Eric Burns, our son-in-law. I have no idea, and I can only imagine what he went through fighting in a foreign country. I do know first-hand the sacrifices his wife and children made while he was away in Iraq serving our country. I am so thankful for Eric and all the other brave veterans God protected and allowed to return home to their families.

Dear Lord, please protect our military and bless and keep their families while they are deployed. We thank you for them, their families, and the sacrifices they make to keep our country free. Amen.

The Lord God said it is not good for man to be alone. I will make him an help meet for him. Genesis 2:18 KJV.

It is impossible to overemphasize the need people have to be listened to, to be heard, to be taken seriously, and to be understood. No one can develop freely and find a full life without being understood by at least one person. Being misunderstood, one loses his self-confidence. He loses his faith in life or even in God. He who would see himself clearly must open up to a confidant. This is why God says it is not good that man should be alone.

Dear Lord, thank you for your plan of marriage between one man and one woman. Please help couples everywhere strive to make their marriage all you intend it to be. Amen.

NOVEMBER 13
GROWING TOGETHER

Wherefore laying aside all malice and all guile, hypocrisies, and envies, and all evil speaking, as newborn babes desire the sincere milk of the word that ye may grow thereby. If so be ye have tasted that the Lord is gracious. I Peter 2:1-3 KJV.

Being married can grow you up as a person. You do not have the luxury of being self-centered when you constantly have your spouse's personality and needs to consider.

You can both be a dedicated Christian when you marry, but marriage will change you. In fact, marriage will always have a profound effect on the development of both parties and both spouses' spirituality. The great evidence of spirituality is love. What better area for practicing love than in a marriage?

Dear Lord, nothing can strongly encourage a couple to grow up quicker than getting married and having a strong desire for marriage to be successful. Every married couple needs your grace and assistance please. Amen.

And in that day thou shalt say, O' Lord, I will praise thee: though thou wast angry with me thine anger is turned away and thou comfortest me. Isaiah 12:1-2 KJV.

God's patience with us is unfathomable. How many times did the children of Israel turn their backs on God to worship idols? How many times did he punish them, only to welcome them back later with open arms?

We can learn two important lessons from God's patience with his wayward children. One, although our sin angers him, he always makes mercy available to us when we seek his forgiveness. Two, we should extend the same kind of patience and mercy to our fellow man. If a holy God can bear with us despite our daily failures, why can't we extend to each other a large dose of mercy and acceptance? No matter how frustrated we may become, approaching others with a large dose of mercy and acceptance presents a clearer picture of God's patience with us.

Dear Lord, you have forgiven us. Please help us to show mercy and grace to others and forgive them. Amen.

NOVEMBER 15
RELYING ON GOD

Trust in the Lord with all thine heart and lean not unto thine own understanding. In all thy ways acknowledge him and he shall direct thy path. Proverbs 3:5-6 KJV.

God demands that we rely totally on him. Anything less is disobedience. No concern is too small, and no issue too complex to bring to him. Through the ups and downs of life, I have felt fundamentally confident about the future. I have tried to rise above the good news/ bad news syndrome, which is feeling great when things are good and despairing when they are not. Those emotions come and go. God's peace, which settles deep inside you, will not fluctuate, and it is available to every one of us who trusts in him wholly.

Dear Lord, please help us trust you fully and not try to work things out ourselves. Amen.

NOVEMBER 16
SEEKING GOD IN PRAYER

We know that all things work together for good to them that love God, to them who are the called according to his purpose. Romans 8:28KJV.

A faithful prayer life is a costly life. It may mean loss of sleep, missing my favorite Hallmark movie, or missing having lunch with my best friend. It may even mean going through some deep waters so that we can learn trust.

Through one dark trial I went through, I latched on to Romans 8:28. To believe that promise, I had to learn to know who made it. I had to learn to get in my closet and pray.

I took that promise of faith, and for fifty years, I have watched it work in my life. It is my rock and my anchor. I know I can trust him because I know who he is. He is the God of the universe, whom I have met face-to-face in prayer.

Dear Heavenly Father, thank you for the tremendously difficult seasons in my life that I have learned trust through seeking you in prayer. Amen.

Beloved if God so loved us, we ought also to love one another. I John 4:11 KJV.

When I stop to think of all that love should be except forgiving, supporting, and strengthening, God is all that and more.

I must laugh when I think back over the early letters and poems, I wrote years ago when my idea of love was so idealistic. The expectations I had were so lofty, so unfair, that only the Lord himself could live up to them. When I realize all that love is or could be, I visualize everything I thought was the perfect picture of the love God has for me, and that is refreshing.

Dear Heavenly Father, your love for us is so beautiful. Thank you for the example you have set before us of perfect love. Amen.

My little children let us not love in word, neither in tongue; but in deed and in truth. I John 3:18 KJV.

It is unrealistic to assume that two completely different personalities can blend together in marriage without going through difficulties, but if both marriage partners want to make it work, a miracle as great as bringing down the walls of Jericho can happen. Our feelings can change from day to day and hour to hour. As a result, there are times when we must, will to affirm and express our love to our mate. There are times when we do not feel very loving. Misunderstandings over matters like money, the disciplining of children, or work-related pressures can create rifts. In the heat of those disagreements, if harsh words are spoken, they can cut deeply. It is in the moments when feelings of love change to anger and hostility that true commitment holds us in place.

Dear Lord, when we disagree with our spouses and angry words come forth, may the anchor of commitment hold us steady. Amen.

Naked came I out of my mother's womb and naked shall I return thither: the Lord gave and the Lord hath taken away; blessed be the name of the Lord. Job 1:21 KJV.

Americans believe they have certain rights: the right to be happy, the right to an acceptable standard of living, the right to a satisfying marriage and a fulfilling job.

But according to the Bible, we really do not have any rights: whatever we are blessed with is because God, in his grace and generosity, has given it to us. When we realize this, joyous gratitude comes into our lives, and we are freed from resentment and anxiety over what we do not have.

Dear Lord, thank you for your blessings to me. I am grateful of every one of them. Amen.

But if from thence thou shalt seek the Lord thy God thou shalt find him if thou seek him with all thy heart and with all thy soul. Deuteronomy 4:19 KJV.

Points of change are points of stress to me. Rarely do I welcome change. My skin took on wrinkles, my friend's marriage turned sour, and my company was bought out.

Sometimes, the change is a package I would like to return to the sender. My four-year-old neighbor succumbs to leukemia, and I grieve over the loss of her.

In my quest for stability, I remember Job caught in chaotic upheavals. Currents of change that blew hard against all that he had and was. But when all was said and done, he came face to face with his changeless God. The stress points or the changes in Job's life moved him toward God and opportunities to discover new dimensions of God.

Dear Lord, your ways are so much higher than mine. I certainly do not understand it all. I do know this, I choose unwavering faith daily, and I choose to trust you explicitly Ameen.

O' taste and see the Lord is good. Psalms 34: 8 KJV.

There is no way to take the first step toward the Christian life, which is accepted by faith. Just as a baby starting its new life must have blind baby trust in his parents, we must accept the fact of a personal relationship with Jesus Christ by faith. Just as children accept the fact of parental love for the child as well as the new Christian, understanding comes later. Jesus said to the woman, your faith has saved you. Go in peace in Luke 7:50 KJV. Faith, then, can be defined as stepping out of trust.

If you believe, you will receive whatever you ask in prayer. Matthew 21:22 KJV.

Dear Lord, please help those who are not living for you to taste and see that you are good. I can tell them all day how delicious my pumpkin roll is. But until they taste for themselves, they will never know. Please help them to step out and take the first bite. Amen.

I can certainly tell Thanksgiving is almost here. My mind is on giving thanks, and I am looking forward to family gatherings and food! Here is one of my family favorites I would love to share with you.

MIMI'S PUMPKIN ROLL RECIPE

Oven Temp: 375°.Time: 13 to 15 minutes. Serves: 16

Cake:

1/4 cup powdered sugar(to sprinkle on towel)

3/4 cup all-purpose flour

1/2 teaspoon baking powder

1/2 teaspoon baking soda

1/2 teaspoon ground cinnamon

1/2 teaspoon ground cloves

1/4 teaspoon salt

3 large eggs

1 cup granulated sugar

2/3 cup pure pumpkin

Filling:

1 8-ounce package of cream cheese at room temperature

1 cup powdered sugar sifted

6 tablespoons butter or margarine, softened

1 teaspoon vanilla extract

Powdered sugar to sprinkle for decoration

For cake: Preheat oven to 375°. Grease 15 by 10-inch Jelly roll pan. Line with wax paper. Grease and flour paper. Sprinkle a thin, cotton kitchen towel with powdered sugar.

Combine flour and baking powder. Baking soda, cinnamon, cloves, and salt in a small bowl. Beat eggs and granulated sugar in a large bowl until thick. Add pumpkin and beat. Stir in the flour mixture. Spread evenly into the prepared pan.

Re-roll cake. Wrap in aluminum foil and refrigerate for at least one hour. Sprinkle with powdered sugar before serving if desired. Be sure to put enough powdered sugar on the towel when rolling up the cake so it will not stick.

This can be made, frozen, and then served for up to 10 days. This is delicious, hot or cold. I prefer to cut a piece and put it in the microwave for 20 seconds. Serve with coffee and a lot of love! Enjoy!

NOVEMBER 23
JOYFUL NOISE

Oh come, let us sing unto the Lord. Let us make a joyful noise to the rock of our salvation. Let us come before his presence with Thanksgiving and make a joyful noise unto him with psalms. For the Lord is a great God, and a great king above all gods. In his hand are the deep places of the earth. The strength of the hills is his also. The sea is his and he made it, and his hands formed the dry land. Oh come, let us worship and bow down: let us kneel before the Lord our maker. For he is our God, and we are the people of his pasture and the sheep of his hand. Psalm 95:1-7 KJV.

In just a few days, people everywhere in America will again be observing Thanksgiving Day. It is a great time for family gatherings. Turkey and dressing, pumpkin pies or pumpkin rolls, and many other mouthwatering goodies, exciting parades, and football games on TV. In all the hustle and bustle of this wondrous, joyful day, let us not forget the most important thing. The very reason for this day is to give thanks to God above for making it all possible

and for blessing our lives and our families. And our country, as he so abundantly has.

Dear Heavenly Father, we cannot praise you enough for this Thanksgiving season and for all your wonderful blessings to us. Amen.

NOVEMBER 24
YOU BE THE SALT

For this reason a man will leave his father and mother and be united to his wife and they shall become one flesh. Genesis 2:24 KJV.

Holidays can become a tug-of-war between husbands and wives who wish to celebrate like their family did when they were at home. There is no need for it to become a time of arguments and hurt feelings. You may want to come up with a few different ways and establish some of your own traditions. When my children were growing up, it seemed we had too many places to go to celebrate. Now that time has passed, our children's grandparents are deceased, and there are only a few places that we can go, and we miss our past celebrations terribly.

The main thing during holidays is to be flexible and try to enjoy your time together. So, what if the potatoes have lumps in them? Just be glad you have potatoes. You can volunteer to bring the potatoes next year!

724

My point is loving your family. That is what truly matters. Make good memories and take a lot of pictures.

Dear Heavenly Father, this Thanksgiving please help us be the salt, light, and calm and set the mood for a blessed Thanksgiving with our precious family. Amen.

NOVEMBER 25
GIVE THANKS TO THE LORD

Make a joyful noise unto the Lord all ye lands. Serve the Lord with gladness. Come before his presence with singing. Know ye that the Lord he is God. It is he that hath made us and not we ourselves. We are his people and the sheep of his pasture. Enter into his gates with Thanksgiving and into his courts with praise. Be thankful to him and bless his name. For the Lord is good. His mercy is everlasting and his truth endureth to all generations. Psalm 100 KJV.

Our country has certainly come a long way since that first Thanksgiving feast spread in America. Thanks to God's abundant blessings and his providential care, our country is what it is today. Even in the 1980s, when our country was in recession, many American people could not tell the difference as far as enjoying three tasty, well-balanced, nutritional meals a day. Our country is great, and it will continue to be if we realize and acknowledge that the Lord is God. It is he that hath made us and not we ourselves.

Dear Heavenly Father, please help each of us realize all the abundant blessings that we have come from you and only you. Lord, we praise you. Amen.

Pure religion and undefiled before God the Father is this: to visit the fatherless and widows in their affliction. James 1:27 KJV.

I recall one Tuesday night prior to Thanksgiving, our youth at the College Street Church of God took fruit baskets to the nursing home as part of a Thanksgiving project. As we were visiting different patients, talking to them about the goodness of God, and having prayer with some of them, the spirit of Thanksgiving seemed to really fill our hearts. There were many who were in pain, and others were completely bedfast. Seeing this helped us to really be thankful for good health and the privilege of being active and up and on the go. One little lady particularly, Mrs. Dupree, seemed to steal our hearts. She had been serving the Lord for years. She had been active in her home church prior to the loss of sight in one eye and a stroke, which left her partially paralyzed. She told us she used to sing in her church. Her favorite song was "Jesus is

Precious to Me." She said that when she had the stroke and could no longer sing, it really hurt her. Then she proclaimed with a beautiful big smile, "But I can still pray!" We left the nursing home that night with greater determination than ever to live for the Lord all the days of our lives. Thank God for our precious elderly people. They hold a special place in my heart because they have paved the way for us as younger generations. God help us not to forget them, especially on holidays such as Thanksgiving and Christmas. They seem to enjoy our visits so very much. One thing for certain, you can never give of yourself without receiving more in return. Our elderly people have so much to give. Why not take advantage? If you have not visited them in the past, this Christmas would be a great time to get started.

Dear Heavenly Father, as we come before you, we are bringing our elderly people and holding them up to you. Lord, please strengthen them. Take away their pain. Help them to know you still have them here for a reason. Lord, help us to love them more, show more respect, and show more honor to them. Amen.

Rejoice evermore. I Thessalonians 5:16 KJV.

Time flies so swiftly. It is hard to believe it is Thanksgiving already. It seems like only yesterday we were enjoying those carefree summer picnics at the park. Then vacations were over, school began, and here it is, Thanksgiving!

This year, let us propose in our hearts to slow down and take in the sights, sounds, and smells of the season: leaves of red, gold, and brown dancing in the wind as the teens play football in the yard, sounds of laughter and giggles of the little ones playing in the den, and oh, those heavenly smells coming from the kitchen! May your turkey be plump and juicy, your mashed potatoes creamy without lumps, and your pumpkin roll ever so delicious. As you relax and take it all in, enjoy the time with your family around a table of plenty, and give God thanks for all He has given you.

Dear Heavenly Father, we praise You for all the
many bountiful reasons You have given us to be
thankful. We are such blessed people. Amen.

NOVEMBER 28
SO MUCH, SO UNDESERVED

Give thanks and bless his name. Psalm 100:4 KJV.

I bless the name of the Lord Jesus Christ with every fiber of my being. I rejoice in my salvation and my healing of fibromyalgia. I am thankful for my husband, my children, my grandchildren, and a few wonderful friends. I am so undeserving.

What are you thankful for? Do you demonstrate your gratitude to God daily? If God took everything away from you that you have not thanked him for, would you be in trouble? Most of us would be because we often take our blessings for granted. During this season when our country sets aside a time to be thankful, look around you, and see what God has done for you.

Dear Heavenly Father, thank you for all the many blessings you have given me. I could never praise you enough for so many things, so undeserved. Amen.

Let your moderation be known unto all men.
Philippians 4:5 KJV.

Even a man or woman who is in tune with God's leadership will struggle to maintain a balanced life. There are going to be times when we will be out of step at work or in our personal lives. Just be loving, just be open and receptive to the fact that life is not going to be perfect always. It helps bring perspective back into a busy person's life. God may not always provide us with a perfectly ordered life. But what he does provide is himself, his presence, and open doors that bring us close to being productive, positive, and realistic Christians.

Dear Lord, during the times when we seem so busy, and our lives seem out of balance, please let us know that you are here. This is your will, and this season is not going to last forever. There will be peace and calm again, as well as time with my family and friends. Amen.

Now faith is the substance of things hoped for, the evidence of things not seen. Hebrews 11:1 KJV.

When my first husband passed away, he had been in a coma for the week prior to his passing. I was saddened that we did not actually get to say our goodbyes the day he passed. But the Lord assured me that in our twenty years of marriage we had and during his illness that we had spoken and shone our love amply to each other.

A widowed friend told me that God takes the awfulness out of each situation and sets us forth to be able to continue our journey. That is the amazement of faith. A born-again Christian trusts God every day through the good and the bad. When tragedy hits, what seems like it would be totally unbearable somehow becomes bearable. That way, when the floods rush in, we will not be swept away.

Dear Lord, how can we ever say thanks for all the things you have done for us? You have carried us through so much. When you sit me down, and I then arise, I am still able to stand. That is the amazement of faith. Amen.

DECEMBER

Rejoice evermore in everything give thanks for this is the will of God in Christ Jesus concerning you. I Thessalonians 5:16,18 KJV.

One cold, dreary December day, I stood in the kitchen peeling vegetables for homemade soup. I could hear Henry in the garage hammering nails as he was working on a bird feeder for the birds he enjoys in our backyard. Natalie and Hudson were spending the night. Natalie was at the dining room table writing a short story, and Hudson was reorganizing his baseball cards in an album on the rug in the living room. Suddenly, I saw us just as we were Mimi, Granddaddy, granddaughter, and grandson, happily doing the things we enjoyed. A surge of joy went through me. Paul told the Thessalonians to be joyful always. Give thanks in all circumstances. Most of the time, we think of this scripture when going through difficult times, but there we were, all safe, happy, and content, just doing ordinary things that we enjoy. But the same grace that blesses our deepest pain can work in ordinary times to remind us that every day is a new gift from God. Any love that we have, to bring to a hurting world is always nurtured at home with those we love.

Dear Heavenly Father, I thank you for a warm, comfortable, loving home with my husband and my grandchildren here, just doing ordinary tasks and enjoying them. Every day is a new gift from you. Amen.

December 2
Approaching God's Throne

Let us therefore come boldly unto the throne of grace, that we may obtain mercy, and find grace to help in time of need. Hebrews 4:16 KJV

King David was a man who encountered many family problems as well as spiritual ups and downs. When he or his family sinned, they inevitably reaped the consequences of their wrong choices. Yet even with all the trouble he endured, he was known as a man after God's own heart. Obviously, David had experienced God's love and forgiveness enough that he felt confident when he took his problems to God in sincerity of heart that God would hear him, forgive him, and again bring good things to David and his household.

Like David, we can ask God to protect and bless our families through Christ. We have the freedom to approach God's throne. Jesus is our advocate. We can pray to God in confidence on behalf of our needs and those of our family.

Dear Lord, I am so thankful that we can approach God's throne through you with all our needs and our concerns for ourselves and for our families. Amen.

Blessed be God which hath not turned away my prayer, nor his mercy from me. Psalm 66:20 KJV.

In today's world, where most people are too busy and self-absorbed to even notice someone else, much less show kindness and love, aren't you glad our heavenly father is not like that? When his children come to him with a need or a problem, he is quick to listen, and he never turns us away. That is the God we serve. Aren't you glad to be serving a God like that? I sure am.

Dear Lord, thank you so much for always being kind and loving and having time to listen to the problems of your children. I love you, Lord. Amen.

The Lord taketh pleasure in them that fear him,
in those that hope in his mercy. Psalm 147:11 KJV.

Have you ever noticed how much joy grandparents get from their grandchildren and how grandchildren seem to think their grandparents are the most special, loving, and kindest people in the whole world? That is because of the special love between them.

It is the same way with God. He delights in us as His children. He is happy to answer our prayers, and He likes us to expect Him to be loving, kind, and generous. God has been so gracious and good to me that nobody could ever convince me that He could be any other way. He deserves our love and respect, and I am so happy to be serving Him.

Dear Lord, I want to give You joy today and every day by honoring and serving You. I expect Your love and kindness in my life. I have confidence in You as Your child. Amen.

In the fear of the Lord is strong confidence, and his children shall have a place of refuge. Proverbs 14:26 KJV.

Whether you are a male or female believer, a single parent raising a child, or raising children with your spouse, the verse above says you can have deep strength. To gain this strength, all you have to do is reverence God. Love and fear Him—not in a negative way, but with great respect.

When your children sense that deep strength in you, they will feel safe and secure. I encourage parents today to reverence and love God. A great way to do this is by getting involved in a Bible-believing church. Your failure to love God and become involved in a church that preaches the truth could ruin your life and your children's lives as well.

Be a man or woman of deep strength and help your children feel secure in a world where so many are struggling with insecurity. You can raise wonderfully secure kids who know they have peace and safety in God.

Dear Lord, for their sake and the sake of their children, please turn parents' hearts toward You so they can receive the strength they need to raise secure children in a world where there is no peace and safety apart from You. Amen.

DECEMBER 6
OPEN PLEASE?

Behold, I stand at the door and knock: if any man hear my voice and open the door, I will come into him, and will sup with him, and he with me. Revelation 3:20 KJV.

God respects your right to choose, and He will never push His way in, but He continually stands at the door and knocks, hoping you will allow Him to come in and fellowship with you. He is patiently waiting for you, longing to fellowship with you as His child. If you open the door and respond to His love, you will experience the most wonderful relationship in your life. What an awesome opportunity.

Heavenly Father, thank You for loving me and patiently knocking on my heart's door. I open wide the door of my heart and ask You to fellowship with me daily. I look forward to developing a close relationship with You so I will hear You when You call and not be afraid. Amen.

DECEMBER 7
PEACE IN PERILOUS TIMES

Now the Lord of peace himself give you peace always by all means. The Lord be with you all. II Thessalonians 3:16 KJV.

If you read the newspaper or watch TV, then you know what a mess this world is in. We are living in perilous times, and God is the only source of true peace. Many things come against us in life. Psalm 34:19 tells us that the righteous will suffer many afflictions, but the Lord delivers us out of them all. Even if you lived a wicked life before you met Jesus, you are now the righteousness of God through Christ Jesus, and you are entitled to His peace.

If your world is chaotic and you are not experiencing God's peace, ask Him for it now. When He gives it to you, thank Him for it.

Dear Lord, thank you for allowing me to have your peace today in every situation. Help me to remember that whatever comes my way, you are with me. Amen.

DECEMBER 8
GOD KEEPS HIS PROMISES

Happy is he that hath the God of Jacob for his help, whose hope is in the Lord his God. Psalm 146:5 KJV.

Whatever happens today, know that God can handle it. His Word is packed with promises that everything is going to turn out for good to those who love Him.

Enjoy the beauty of God's wondrous world today. Hope in the Lord and rejoice in the fact that His promises belong to you.

Dear Lord, I rejoice today in all Your creation. Thank You for Your promises that I can be happy because my hope is in You. I am thankful that You keep all Your promises, and they are all mine. Amen.

753

The Lord is merciful and gracious, slow to anger, and plenteous in mercy. Psalms 103:8 KJV.

Have you ever felt that you did not deserve God's tenderness or His mercy? I have. That is God's very nature. He simply cannot be harsh and unmerciful to His family.

You might say, "I never thought of myself as being a part of God's family." If you are born again, you are a very important part of God's family. You are welcome at God's table. You are heir to a great inheritance of peace, love, joy, patience, kindness, goodness, gentleness, faithfulness, self-control, and more. These are the fruit of the Holy Spirit, and He has promised they belong to you.

Isn't it time you start to let yourself enjoy God's tender feelings toward you? Isn't it time to allow His mercies to cover you? See yourself as God sees you for a change. You will never be the same.

Dear God, what a joy it is to be a part of Your family. Your gift of salvation and eternal life is glorious. As an inheritance, You have given me the fruit of Your Spirit. I am so thankful for Your tenderness and mercy toward me. Amen.

December 10
Obedience Brings Success

Whoso despiseth the word shall be destroyed: but he that feareth the commandment shall be rewarded. Proverbs 13:13 KJV.

If you have known God in the past but do not have as close a relationship with Him as you once had, you are miserable. Aren't you? But when you go back and begin serving God again—living by His Word, being both a doer and a hearer of His Word—you feel good inside, and your obedience brings success, according to Proverbs 13:13 KJV.

I encourage you today to obey the Word of God. Do not waste another minute being separated from your Creator. He loves you, and He is always willing to forgive you and welcome you back. His loving, outstretched arms are reaching out to you today. Stay on the road of obedience to God, and you will always enjoy success.

Father, I desire to be successful, and I know that obeying Your Word is one of the keys to success. I commit myself to be obedient to Your Word. Please strengthen me daily as I walk this journey of faith. Please be by my side. Amen.

DECEMBER 11
STRENGTH AND VICTORY

Blessed be the Lord my strength, which teacheth my hands to war, and my fingers to fight. Psalm 144:1 KJV.

Have you ever noticed how the tide of the battle seems to turn when we pray and ask God for assistance? His Word promises He will be with us in the heat of our battles—with health, finances, jobs, relationships, and any other challenge.

But how do you obtain the strength and skill to fight those battles? By knowing the Word of God, trusting in His wisdom, and believing that God desires to help you. Let God become your rock by knowing what His promises are. He will give you strength and victory.

Dear Lord, you are my rock, my fortress, my strong tower. My enemy must face the Rock who stands with me in battle and gives me the strength to fight and win the victory. Amen.

DECEMBER 12
GUIDED SAFELY INTO THE HARBOR

They reel to and fro, and stagger like a drunken man, and are at their wits' end. Then they cry unto the Lord in their trouble, and he bringeth them out of their distresses. He maketh the storm a calm, so that the waves thereof are still. Then are they glad because they are quiet; so he bringeth them into their desired haven. Psalm 107:27-30 KJV.

Sailors sometime encounter tremendous storms and huge waves and are tossed to and from until it seems they will sink. Life often brings us storms like this when we are at our wits' end.

But the Bible says when they cried to the Lord in their trouble, He saved them, calmed the storm, stilled the waves, and brought them safely into harbor, bringing the stillness of peace.

Dear Lord, you are my safety in times of trouble. I will forever cry out to you for help in the storm. I know you will calm my fears and guide me to safety. Amen.

TELL GOD YOUR LONGINGS

Trust in the Lord at all times; ye people, pour out your heart before him: God is a refuge for us. Selah. Psalm 62:8 KJV.

All our hearts have longings. Many people have longings that no one can fulfill in this life except God. Some people long for their spouses or children to be saved. Some long for peace that passes all understanding. Some lonely people long for second chances at a long-lost love. Sick people long for healing. Our longings are varied and without end.

If you pour out your longings to God, He will bless you and help you according to Psalms 62:8. This chapter concludes with, "For thou renderest to every man according to his work." (Verse 12).

I love knowing that just because God loves me, He will bless and help me when I pour out the longings of my heart to Him. He loves to answer the prayers of His children. Why not have a "heart-to-heart" talk with God today?

Lord, you alone know my innermost longings.
You alone can satisfy the deepest desires of my heart.
I trust you, Lord, to bring about the best in my life.
Amen.

In the day when I cried thou answerest me and strengthened me, with strength in my soul. Psalm 138:3 KJV.

Christmas, the most wonderful time of the year, is swiftly approaching! In today's fast-paced world, it is easy to get overworked, become tired, and even discouraged if not careful. I encourage you to do as much preparation in advance as possible for the holidays. I also try to simplify our celebration somewhat, as I am getting older and not as energetic as I used to be. Instead of cooking every dish everyone likes as I did in the past, I am now making a menu and sticking to it as much as possible.

The integral parts of the Conner Christmas Celebration, like preparing a special Happy Birthday Jesus cake (with singing included) and having Granddaddy read the Christmas story from Luke chapter 2 before opening gifts, will always be included.

When we feel weak, we need to go to God and draw from his supernatural strength. II Corinthians 12:9 tells us his strength is made perfect in weakness. God likes to answer the prayers of his children. His Word says he will encourage you and give you the strength you need.

Dear Lord Jesus, as the wonderful Christmas season is upon us, please help us stay focused on having a celebration that glorifies you. Please keep us strong and well and give us energy so that we can fully honor you with a celebration you so deserve. Happy Birthday, Jesus. We love and adore you! Amen.

December 15
Mimi's Rudolph Ranch Cheeseball

Ingredients:

1 tsp. sour cream

1 (1 oz.) package of buttermilk ranch dressing mix

1 (8 oz.) package of Philadelphia cream cheese

½ lb. cheddar cheese, shredded

½ cup finely chopped pecans

2 green pickled olives (for eye decoration)

1 cherry tomato (for nose decoration)

2 curlicue pretzels (for antler decoration)

Directions:

Mix sour cream with ranch dressing mix in a bowl until smoothly combined.

Add cream cheese and cheddar cheese and mix together with your hands until thoroughly blended.

Chill the mixture for 5 minutes and shape it into a ball.

Place pecans into a shallow bowl and roll all sides of the cheese ball in pecans to coat.

Place the pretzels on top of the cheese ball for the antlers.

Place the two green pickled olives in place for the eyes.

Place the cherry tomato for the nose decoration.

Serve immediately with buttery Townhouse crackers to those you love and hold "deer". Enjoy!

DECEMBER 16
HAPPIEST TIME OF THE YEAR

And she shall bring forth a son, and thou shalt call his name Jesus: for he shall save his people from their sins. Matthew 1:21 KJV.

Christmas. The happiest time of the year, the dawning of the yuletide season. I don't suppose there is anyone who loves Christmas more than my husband and me. Thankfully, he shares my excitement. If he did not, I would really be in trouble. Christmas is just so special in our house. I remember when I was first married and, by standards, a full-fledged adult, but I was thinking then I hoped I would never see the day that I was too old to enjoy Christmas. As I sit here writing, sipping a hot cup of cocoa, and playing Christmas carols, the tree is already over to the side, fully decorated and beautifully aglow. I suppose Christmas is so very special to me because I am a Christian, and I love the Lord. Without him in my life I guess the Christmas season would not have much meaning, after all.

768

It hurts me so much to hear someone say, "Oh, it is almost Christmas, and what a bother. Oh, the hustle and the bustle of buying and preparing. Things are so outrageously expensive!"

I feel so sorry for people that feel that way. They just do not understand what the true meaning of Christmas is.

I never will forget the first year my husband and I were married. We put our Christmas tree up on the 7th day of November and kept the drapes drawn in our apartment so our neighbors would not think we had completely lost our minds. We really did not intend to decorate that early, but we had ordered a large seven-foot Canadian pine. We could not afford it, but it proved to be one of the most enjoyable investments we have ever made. The tree came in on the 7th of November, and we just had to see what it looked like when it was decorated. So, it stayed up until after the first of the year in all its splendor and glory.

Since my first Christmas married, our Christmas tree is always up by Thanksgiving or that night at the latest. Now, I know that it is early for most people, especially if they enjoy a real live tree. But Thanksgiving just seems to prepare my heart for the Christmas season. Thanksgiving through the dawning of the new year is a religious celebration to me. With every piece of garland I put up, with every candle I light, it is all in honor of Jesus' birthday, the one who gave his life for me. He is my reason for living. I truly hope that you have experienced the touch of the Lord in your life also because without him, Christmas is mere commercialism, lonely and empty, but with him, Christmas is truly the happiest time of the year.

Dear God, thank you for sending your son and giving us such a happy cause to celebrate. We praise you for the greatest gift ever given. Amen.

For unto us a child is born, unto us a son is given: and the government shall be upon his shoulder: and his name shall be called Wonderful, Counselor The mighty God, The Everlasting Father, The Prince of Peace. Isaiah 9:6 KJV.

It is that time of year again when the magic of Christmas begins to unfold right before our very eyes. Christmas, the birthday of our Savior, what a cause for celebration! I don't suppose there's anyone except Santa himself who loves Christmas any more than I do. Christmas is just so special at our house. Now, with little ones around, it seems even more magical. Even the lights on the tree seem brighter. Someone said Christmas is for children. I agree but they should not tag an age limit in their statement. I hope I never get too old to enjoy the beauty of this season. It is a tradition at the Holbert home to begin early, and I do mean early, like Thanksgiving night, for instance. Not only does the tree get decorated, but the whole house gets decked out at its finest. Christmas is a holy time and what better time to begin getting ready than on Thanksgiving when our hearts have already been prepared to give thanks to the Lord? So, now you have heard the Holbert philosophy (Conners have continued it.) behind celebrating Christmas. Christmas is Christ's birthday, and if you love him, then you have cause to celebrate. Every part of our decoration becomes symbolic. Even our little ones know what every item stands for. The evergreen is symbolic of life, so the tree, the outdoor wreaths, and the greenery that decks the entryway all stand for eternal life through Jesus Christ. When we see the lights twinkling on the tree, we are reminded of how we are letting our light shine in the world. The red bows that deck the tree and other places in the house stand for the blood of Jesus. The white snow reminds us of how we have been made pure through that blood, the cleansing of our sins. The doves on the tree represent the Holy Spirit. Our dated Hallmark ornament collection, which we add to every year, reminds us of the special occasions in our lives. Our first Christmas together and the baby's first Christmas ornaments will be family heirlooms for ages to come. The other ornaments dated in between and thereafter remind us of how the Lord has blessed us and kept us as a family. Many special ornaments, such as crocheted snowflakes, angels, and crosses, have been made and given to us by special friends and are priceless family treasures. The star that adorns the top of the tree reminds us that Christ is the light of the world. The gifts under the tree are symbolic of the gifts of love the wise men brought on that first Christmas. Our nativity scene in the den was a wedding present from our now-deceased Papa Tate, reminding us anew and afresh of the humble birth of God's son. As the candlelight in the living room filters through the beautiful stained-glass nativity set, another gift from a dear friend, Bob Collins, an attorney that I previously worked for, reminds us of the beauty of it all, the true meaning of the Christmas season, the birth of our savior, the greatest gift ever given to mankind. What a cause for celebration!

Dear Heavenly Father, thank you for Christmas

Ameen!

DECEMBER 18
THE WAY WAS PAVED

Blessed art thou among women. Luke 1:28 KJV.

Three months before the birth of John the Baptist, God sent the Angel Gabriel to the city of Nazareth to visit a meek and lowly home. A young maiden directly descended from King David was the object of his visit.

She was alone in the house, and the angel said: "Hail thou that art highly favored, the Lord is with thee: blessed art thou among women." (Luke 1:28). When Mary saw and heard the angel from heaven, her mind whirled. "Why me, Lord? What is the meaning of all this?" She was stunned beyond words.

But the angel reassured her: "Fear not, Mary: for thou hast found favor with God. (Luke 1:30) There was no mistake about this visit. The angel had called her by her first name. She listened intently as he delivered his prophetic announcement:

775

"And, behold, thou shalt conceive in thy womb, and bring forth a son, and shall call his name Jesus. He shall be great and shall be called the son of the Highest, and the Lord God shall give unto him the throne of his father David: And he shall reign over the House of Jacob forever; and of his Kingdom, there shall be no end". (Luke 1:31-33).

Thus, the way was paved for a union of deity and humanity. Soon, the ancient prophecy would be fulfilled. After the fall of man, the Lord God had told the serpent: "I will put enmity between thee and the woman and between thy seed and her seed. It shall bruise thy head, and thou shalt bruise his heel Genesis 3:15. Soon, the seed of the woman, Jesus Christ, would enter the world to destroy the works of that old serpent called Satan.

Dear Heavenly Father, Mary must have been very dedicated to have been highly favored, and she had to have trusted you explicitly. Thank you for her example to other women. Amen

Glory to God in the highest and on earth peace goodwill toward man. Luke 2:14 KJV

There is a mystery and a miracle of motherhood that demands adoration. Mary was given an experience no other will ever share. She knew her baby was different. Gabriel had explained it to her earlier: "Hail thou that are highly favored. Behold thou shalt conceive in thy womb and bring forth a son and shall call his name Jesus. He shall be great and shall be called the son of the highest, and the Lord God shall give unto him the throne of his father David, and he shall reign over the house of Jacob forever and of his Kingdom, there shall be no end. The Holy Ghost shall come upon thee, and the power of the Highest shall overshadow thee: therefore, that holy thing which shall be born of thee shall be called the Son of God." Luke 1:28,31-33,35).

Our heavenly father means for the Christmas season to be joyous. It centers around the babe.

That babe introduced a new race on earth, and the apostle called it a seed that is incorruptible." God himself, ordered the birth announcements: "Glory to God in the highest and on earth peace goodwill toward men." Luke 2:14

Dear Heavenly Father, we praise you for the miracles of Christmas on so many levels. Amen.

I am the root and the offspring of David and the bright and morning star. Revelation 22:16 KJV.

The star that many of us place at the top of our Christmas tree is symbolic of the star in the heavens that shone high over Bethlehem. Stars speak of other worlds. Their radiance comes from afar, and they witness a realm beyond our earth. Christmas holds just such a message for each of us. Above our busy lives, high over our varied activities, especially this time of year, and even above our doubts and fears, there is a Holy Spirit that presides and counsels, plans, and guides. Stars are most clearly seen when it is night. When the earth seems the darkest, it shines with the greatest brilliance. When we are overwhelmed by clouds of despondency and when our lives are shrouded in a night of fear, then we see most clearly the light of God's gift in his truth and the brightness of his all-comprehending love. Could God have chosen a more suitable and appropriate symbol for Christmas than a star? The wise men were guided by a star from their homes. They traveled in its light. They did not know the way and were not sure of their destination, but they believed the star. To them, the star represented God's guiding hand. In their hearts was a compelling faith that is a prerequisite for such journeys. In life, if we believe in God, he will guide us in taking the right steps. When we trust him, he will brightly light the way ahead because he remains the bright morning star.

Dear Lord. We praise you that you remain the bright morning star, guiding our footsteps aright. Amen.

Behold, there came wise men from the East to Jerusalem. Saying, where is he that is born king of the Jews, for we have seen his star in the east, and are come to worship him. Matthew 2:1-2 KJV.

Christmas stars and lights are used all over the world as Christmas symbols. The star, which we often use to top the Christmas tree, represents the star in the East mentioned in the Bible in Matthew 2:1-2.

Pastor Charles D. Green, in his sermon, once said that Martin Luther was perhaps the first man to use lights on a Christmas tree. According to a popular story, Luther put lights on his tree to represent the glory and the beauty of the stars above Bethlehem. On the night of Christ's birth, we place single tapers in our windows to light the way for the Christ child on Christmas Eve.

When our youth go Christmas caroling, they carry single-lighted tapers in honor of Jesus Christ, the light of the world, a light that will never burn out.

Dear Heavenly Father, we praise you for sending Jesus, the light of the world. Amen.

There were in the same country shepherds abiding in the field, keeping watch over their flock by night, And lo, the Angel of the Lord came upon them. And the glory of the Lord shone round about them. And they were sore afraid. Luke 2:8-9 KJV.

Palestine has been and still is the land of the shepherd. Christ even identified himself with this group of people when he said I am the Good Shepherd. The shepherds were the first to recognize and acclaim him at birth. These common working people believed the message.

The shepherd said to one another, let us now go even unto Bethlehem, and see this thing, which is come to pass, which the Lord has made known to us. Luke 2:15 KJV.

They became evangelists before the fishermen of Galilee were even called, and when they had seen it, they made known abroad the saying. Which was told them concerning this child. Luke 2:17 KJV. The Lord really blessed their efforts.

784

And all that heard it wondered at those things which were told them by the shepherds, Luke 2:18 KJV. The Christmas story just would not be complete without the shepherds.

The main shepherd has arrived on earth. We have promise that he will come again and the commission to tell others until he comes.

Dear Heavenly Father. We praise you for the Chief Shepherd, and when the Chief Shepherd shall appear, we shall receive a crown of glory that fades not away. Amen.

DECEMBER 23
WISE MEN STILL RESPOND

Behold, there came wise men from the east to Jerusalem saying Where is he that is born King of the Jews? Matthew 2:1-2 KJV.

The Christmas story would not be complete without the wise men who journeyed long days and weary nights across wasteland and desert and came at last to Bethlehem to worship the newborn King Jesus. They were called wise men because, by profession and study, they had mastered both textbooks and the wisdom of the heavens.

They were philosophers and astrologers. On that day, astrologers observed the heavens to determine the will of God. The wise men were accustomed to looking above the world of men for guidance from the Highest. The wise men of old believed because their hearts were tuned into God's. Wise men today kneel at the crib of Christ Jesus, spiritually speaking, and surrender their human wisdom and will to the influence of the greater wisdom of God. Their wisdom must be

added courage because they challenged the winds and dangers of the desert. Also, they possessed faith, a faith that got them there safe, a faith that caused them to recognize the baby as being the son of God, the newborn King, and thirdly, a faith that led them back to their homes by another way. In the birth of Christ, all the wisdom of the ages is fulfilled. The wise men knew that the heavens declared the glory of God. We, too, are wise men when, like them, look upward and follow where He leads. God often makes known His will to men, but only those who are wise respond to his guidance.

Dear Heavenly Father. We praise You, and we know that wise men today are still seeking your guidance. Lord, we pray that more eyes will be opened, and more people will come to you while there is still time. Amen.

For I am not ashamed of the gospel of Christ. For it is the power of God unto salvation, to everyone that believeth, to the Jew first, and then to the Greek. Romans 16:1 KJV.

If you have not already read the Christmas Story from the Bible this season, why not take time to read it before the day is over? One of the most beautiful accounts of the Christmas story is taken from the 2nd chapter of the book of Luke. Luke's account of the Christmas story is one of the best-loved passages of literature ever written. But this story possesses more than mere beauty. It was the beginning of power, the power to become the sons of God without going through the sacrificial rights of offering up a burnt sacrifice.

Today, we live in a world where the Word of God is challenged by those who do not believe in the virgin birth of Jesus or the power of his blood that was shed to give hope for eternal life. Some study the Bible only as history or literature without receiving its message that gives them the abundant grace and mercy of God. But to them that believe it is the power of God unto salvation. If you have not yet discovered the true meaning of Christmas, then why not accept the Lord Jesus as your personal Savior? The true spirit of Christmas will come to live in your heart this holiday season. What a reason to celebrate!

Dear Lord, how we praise you for the blessed Christmas season, for the Word of God, and for all your many blessings to your children. Happy Birthday, Jesus. We love you so much! Amen.

Thanks be unto God for His unspeakable gift. II Corinthian, 9:15. KJV.

The twinkling lights on the evergreen towering in the corner of the living room match the glistening in my eyes. The fragrance of the season seems to overwhelm me with feelings of love, excitement, and a touch of nostalgia. It's late. The house is quiet with sleepiness. I turn out the lights, leaving only the Christmas tree standing aglow. I curl up on the carpet in front of the tree, toasting my toes in its warmth. I don't want these tender and peaceful moments on this late eve in the Christmas season to escape me.

My thoughts drift dreamily. Just a moment ago, I tiptoed quietly into their rooms to peek at my little angels sleeping soundly in their beds. Sprawled out flat on their backs with arms outstretched, they reminded me of cut-out angels I made as a child. It's hard to believe this will be her sixth and his first Christmas. I remember the awe and the wonder of her first Christmas just a few short years ago. What a special Christmas it was, our little package sent from heaven. And I think how magnificent the gift God gave to all of us over 2000 years ago. The baby born in a stable sent to redeem us. In my human reasoning. I try to imagine the depth and the spectrum of God's love brought into focus in the form of baby Jesus. As a human parent, I know how deeply I care for these children of mine. So, I try to comprehend the multiplied and perfect love the father had for his son born in Bethlehem that night so long ago.

My thoughts drift to the plans and dreams I have for my children. I think about the choices they will have to make in the future. A mother has the right and privilege to dream about the wonderful opportunities that may be afforded her children. But her children have the right to choose which paths to take. So, as I sit here quite cozily in front of the tree, I think about the bright hopes they have for this Christmas.

Once again, my thoughts bounce back to that baby in the manger, Jesus. I wonder if Mary really knew what would happen to her son during his lifetime on earth. She knew that he was God's Son on a magnificent mission to save us all from our sins. But did she know how he would do this? Did she know just how much he would suffer and die so utterly alone on that cross?

But God knew. All his love had been poured out into the form of that baby Jesus lying in the hay among the cattle that night. All the compassion and tenderness he must have felt. As he gazed down upon his little son and as the panorama of Jesus's life flashes in front of him. What terrible anguish God must have felt. He knew what was already planned for that baby lying so peacefully asleep. How much God must love us to allow His beloved Son Jesus Christ to suffer and die a torturous death on the cross for you and for me, for everyone, all the generations of the world that have been and are yet to come.

Just a soft glow remains as I turn out the Christmas lights and tiptoe up the stairs. I stopped at each door to make one last check before going to bed. I stooped over their beds and planted a kiss upon each tousled little head. Again, I think of their futures. I love them so much, but my love for them does not even begin to compare with God's beautiful and tender love for them. And that is the greatest gift they will ever receive: God's love in the form of that precious Lamb, Jesus.

Heavenly Father. How can I say thanks for all the things you have given me? Gifts so undeserved. Amen.

Therefore, the Lord himself shall give you a sign. Behold, a virgin shall conceive and bear a son, and shall call his name Emmanuel, meaning God with us. Isaiah 7:14 KJV.

Everything concerning Christ coming into this world was unusual. How many people have you read about or heard of whose birth was predicted hundreds of years before it occurred?

Isaiah 53:2-12 foretold. For he shall grow up before him as a tender plant and as a root out of dry ground. He has no form nor comeliness, and when we shall see Him, there is no beauty that we should desire him. He is despised and rejected by men. A man of sorrows and acquainted with grief, and we hid, as it were, our faces from him. He was despised, and we esteemed him not. Surely, He hath borne our grief and carried our sorrows. We did esteem him stricken, smitten of God, and afflicted, but he was wounded for our transgressions. He was bruised for our iniquities. The chastisement of our

peace was upon him, and with his stripes, we are healed. All we, like sheep, have gone astray. We have turned everyone to his own way, and the Lord hath laid on him the iniquity of us all. He was oppressed, and he was afflicted, yet he opened not his mouth. He is brought as a lamb to the slaughter. And as thy sheep before the shearers is dumb, so he openeth not his mouth. He was taken from prison and from judgment. And who shall declare his generation, for he was cut off out of the land of the living. For the transgression of my people, was he stricken? And he made his grave with the wicked and with the rich in his death because he had done no violence, neither was any deceit in his mouth, yet it pleased the Lord to bruise him. He hath put him to grieve. When thou shalt make his soul an offering for sin, He shall. To his seed, he shall prolong his days, and the pleasure of the Lord shall prosper in his hand. He shall save the travail of his soul and shall be satisfied. By his knowledge shall my righteous servant justify many, for he shall bear their iniquities. Therefore, will I divide him a portion with the great, and he shall divide the spoil with this

795

strong, because he hath poured out his soul unto death, and he was numbered with the transgressors. And he bared the sin of many and made intercessions for the transgressors.

Was this not the world's most unusual child? Who else had prophecies concerning his whole life? This included his conception, birth, life, and death. No other person has ever been born of a virgin. There were others visited by angels and manned by them in biblical times, but none were conceived by the Holy Ghost. Other children have been born, but no parents have ever been so carefully instructed by angels as were Jesus's mother and Joseph. The prophecy concerning his birth at Bethlehem and his living at Nazareth were carried out to the letter. His whole life here on earth was lived. He came to an end fulfilling those prophecies only so those who accept Him as Lord and Savior could have a glorious new beginning.

Dear Heavenly Father, thank you so very much for the unique life of Christ and for what it has meant to the world. Amen.

Follow after charity and desire spiritual gifts. I Corinthians 14:1 KJV.

I love people and desire to help everyone I meet. I want the best for their lives. I believe God wants to use me to reach others. And He wants the same thing for you. You can win souls. You can bring people back to God. You can see the sick healed, broken hearts and homes mended by His power, and you can see miracles performed. You are probably asking me, "How can God use me?" Through love. If you read much about Jesus in the Bible, you will soon find out that he was moved by divine compassion rising in his heart. He felt love flowing out of his spirit. The result was that the healing love of God brought deliverance to the suffering people of that day., The divine flow of God's love can move you toward the people God wants to reach. We need to watch for the rise of this supernatural love and be ready to follow wherever it flows.

Father, thank You for the powerful gifts of your Spirit that all operate through your love. The flow of your love as you minister through me is what your gifts are all about. your word says now abide, faith, hope, love, these three, but the greatest of these is love. So, I will make Love my greatest aim. Teach me to love others as you love them and use me as your vessel of love. Amen.

DECEMBER 28
REFLECTIONS ON OLD AND NEW

Gather up the fragments which remain that nothing be lost. John, 6:12. KJV.

As I look back on this swiftly passing year, I think of all the resolutions, dreams, and aspirations that I had at the beginning of the year, and when realizing how very little I have accomplished, it leaves me with a feeling of deflation.

But someone once said every cloud has a silver lining. So, to look on the brighter side, if I had not dreamed those dreams and possessed those aspirations, I would probably have accomplished even less.

John 6:12 reminds me of the long list of things that linger in my mind, things that I still want to accomplish, and projects that were thought out almost a year ago. An unknown author once said those very yearnings that linger on within you are the comforting evidence that the Holy Spirit is still tenderly ministering within you, causing you to still hunger and thirst after higher things. Several years ago, the young man who was a ministerial student at Lee College and a member of my home church, Jim Searcy, while in a discussion about God's will for your life, once told me that he had found it to be true that when something was God's will in your life, you never really got away from it until you had set out to fulfill that dream or accomplish that task. It would constantly be brought to your attention. He said that he had found it true that when the Lord intended for you to do something, your subconscious mind would harbor that thought, and you would be reminded of that idea repeatedly until you got up and did something about it.

It is interesting to know that just as John 6:12 tells us, we can gather up those remaining aspirations and turn them into new prayers. We are dealing with an understanding Christ who forgives the past and offers new enablement for the new year. Just as he turned the loaves and fishes into twelve baskets of food, he can turn our regrets into a new promise.

Then again, we should gather up the fragments of the old year's lessons. Experience may be the greatest of teachers but sometimes experience really costs. If we gather the lessons we have learned during the past year, it will fill our baskets with wisdom for the new coming year. Thirdly, there are the fragments of the old years of lost opportunities, opportunities for making things right between us and others, but most importantly, opportunities for making things right between our Heavenly Father and ourselves. With that accomplished. We can look forward to confidence and reassurance of a happy and prosperous New Year.

Dear Heavenly Father, as we once again look forward to a new year, we need you more than ever

before. We need Your guidance. We need the Holy Spirit leading us as we set out to accomplish. Amen.

DECEMBER 29
NEW YEAR DAWNING

I will instruct thee and teach thee in the way which thou shalt go: I will guide thee with mine eye. Psalm 32:8 KJV.

As another new year dawns, most of us are busy making New Year's resolutions. Sometimes, it's rather discouraging thinking of how many we have made in the past only to lay them aside. But without guidelines and resolutions, I guess less would be accomplished than what it is. So, let's face it: these guidelines and resolutions certainly have a valid place in our lives. Our daughter lives in Colorado. There is a picturesque mountain trail in Colorado with such inviting scenery as to be positively breathtaking. However, it's also known for its treachery. Lives are lost along its trail every year.

Strangely enough, no one ever falls when danger is greatest and the trail most narrow. Those who fall are always at the top, where the space is as large as two football fields.

So, it is along the trail of life. It is not when we are carefully following good directions and meeting our obligations and commitments that we get lost. It is when we can do anything, go anywhere, and be so broad-minded that we can look at and participate in almost anything that we become spiritual fatalities. The spiritual, mental, and physical guidelines we set for ourselves will never prove so valuable as when life seems easiest, and our problems are farthest from us. For these are our moments of greatest danger. As a new year dawns. If we set guidelines along our trail of life for the discipline of body, mind, and spirit, then we will be sure to keep on course and go right.

Dear Heavenly Father, as the New Year dawns, please help us to stay in Your word, follow Your guidelines and do Your will. Amen.

The Lord is my strength. And he will make my feet like Hinds feet, and he will make me to walk upon mine high places. Habakkuk 3:19 KJV.

Second only to the human mind and body, in my opinion, a mountain is probably the greatest masterpiece God ever created. When I view a mountain huge and tall, I am reminded anew and afresh of how great God is who placed it there.

There is something mysteriously awesome and powerful about a mountain that demands respect and admiration. I stood in awe for hours on end and enjoyed the view from the top of the mountain only to go away spellbound.

What a challenge a mountain presents to mountain climbers, hikers, sightseers, and nature lovers alike. What dangers lurk within? Falling rocks? Wild animals? Steep slopes and curves? What beauty and unmatched majesty as it stands tall and proud in all its splendor and glory. Take the ocean if you please, but please give me the mountain.

As Christians, spiritually speaking, we often must walk through many valleys. But we need the mountaintop experience. When I say mountaintop experience, I am not referring to the times in our lives when we are carefree and without problems, but rather, I am referring to the need to stand high to see far. As Christians when we look around us and view things in our lives that are happening and developments in our society that are coming to pass, we need to look at it from a high altitude. In Revelation 21:10, when John was to be shown the New Jerusalem descending out of heaven, he was carried away to a great, high mountain. Just prior to this, in Revelations 13:1, he had stood down by the seashore and seen the beast rise out of the deep. We see too many beasts today. It does not help in our troubled lives because too many of us tend to have a seat to live at sea level. There are many influences to keep us there: average television program, average magazine, average social media

808

post and average conversation we hear on the streets and in our daily business places. God's children were never meant to live at sea level. Christ intended for us to have the mountaintop view. We are meant to see the happenings in our society and in our everyday lives in the light of the inspired Word from the high viewpoint of His divine purpose. And with our gaze on the ultimate victory in Christ. But how are we going to keep that mountaintop view as we enter the New Year? First, we must hide God's Word in our hearts by studying and prayerfully reading the scriptures. We must find a daily place of prayer, and we must guard against the easygoing toleration of things in our lives that rob us of the closeness that we can enjoy with our Heavenly Father. Many of us have been taught against making New Year's resolutions, but resolving to do better, when made as a new covenant with God, can prove to enrich and bountifully bless our lives if made sincerely and made with the dependence upon the Holy Spirit instead of ourselves. I sincerely hope that this article does not come across as sounding like a sermon but instead will prove to be a blessing to someone who may have been searching for something to sustain and to carry them into the new year with an act of newfound courage and hope. Because we can have courage and there is hope in Jesus Christ if we are only willing to climb high.

Dear Heavenly Father, as we enter a brand-new year. Please help us to dig deep into the Word and to climb high in your promises. We love you, Lord, and sincerely need your spiritual strength. Amen.

DECEMBER 31
I NEED THEM

And I sought for a man among them that should make up the hedge and stand in the gap before me for the land, that I should not destroy it, But I found none. Ezekiel 22:30 KJV.

God is searching for people He can trust. He needs people like you and me. He needs our eyes, our hands, our arms, our hearts, our feet, and our love to evangelize the world. He is looking for somebody to help him reach out to the lost with the gospel of the Lord Jesus Christ. People need faith in God. If there was no hell to shun, real life that we all face sooner or later demands real faith to carry us through. As you reflect on the past year and plan for the new one, think about what you can do in response to God's need. He said he would do what you cannot do. If you do the possible, he will do the impossible. If you work in the natural, he will work in the supernatural. Do your part. Cooperate with God. He needs you.

Dear Lord, please use me this coming year. I want to be your mouth, your hands, and your feet to bring the good news of salvation and hope to this world. Use my hands to heal and my mouth as a witness of your goodness and love toward all men. Show me where you want me to stand in the gap this year to be a blessing to the world. Amen.

www.ingramcontent.com/pod-product-compliance
Lightning Source LLC
Chambersburg PA
CBHW041623140626
46547CB00030B/705